The Self-Driven Child

The
Self-Driven
Child

The SCIENCE *and* SENSE *of*
GIVING YOUR KIDS MORE
CONTROL OVER THEIR LIVES

WILLIAM STIXRUD, PhD,
and NED JOHNSON

Viking

VIKING
An imprint of Penguin Random House LLC
375 Hudson Street
New York, New York 10014
penguin.com

Illustrations by John D. Fair

ISBN: 9780735222519 (hardcover)
ISBN: 9780735222533 (e-book)

Printed in the United States of America
1   3   5   7   9   10   8   6   4   2

Set in Baskerville MT Pro
Designed by Amy Hill

To my parents, who adopted me, were crazy about me, and let me learn to run my own life.

—W. S.

. . .

To my beloved Vanessa, who kindled in me a passion for helping children.

To Katie and Matthew: I am endlessly grateful for having the greatest kids in the world.

–N. J.

CONTENTS

Contents

AUTHORS' NOTE

The stories in this book are all real. They are the stories of the children, parents, and educators we have worked with over the years. Helping and being helped, teaching and learning, requires trust and often invites great vulnerability. We are deeply grateful for the trust and faith so many children and their families have shown us, and we have, in some cases, altered names or certain identifying details to protect their privacy.

The Self-Driven Child

Why a Sense of Control
Is Such a Big Deal

A T FIRST BLUSH, we are not obvious partners. Bill is a nationally recognized clinical neuropsychologist who has been helping kids cope with anxiety, learning disabilities, and behavioral problems for thirty years. People often remark on his calm temperament, most likely a result of the decades he has spent practicing Transcendental Meditation. Ned founded PrepMatters, one of the most successful tutoring companies in the country. He's an energetic Gen Xer, raising young teens, whose students often say he has the enthusiasm of three people.

We met a few years ago as guest speakers at the same event. When we started talking, we discovered something interesting. Despite our differing backgrounds, disciplines, and client bases, we were trying to help kids overcome similar problems in surprisingly complementary ways. Bill approaches them from the perspective of brain development; Ned through the art and science of performance. As we talked, we found our knowledge and experiences fit together like a jigsaw puzzle. And while Ned's client might struggle with the panic that she might not get into Stanford, and Bill's might struggle to get to school at all, we each begin with the same baseline questions: How can we help this kid gain a sense of control over his life? How can we help him find his own inner drive and make the most of his potential?

We came to a sense of control through research on stress and studies of motivation, which we follow because so much of our work involves helping kids minimize the extent to which stress undermines their performance and mental health. We try to steer them to a healthy level of self-motivation, somewhere between perfectionist overdrive and "let me get back to my video game." When we discovered that a low sense of control is enormously stressful and that autonomy is key to developing motivation,[1] we thought we were onto something important. This impression was confirmed when we started to probe deeper and found that a healthy sense of control is related to virtually everything we want for our children, including physical and mental health, academic success, and happiness.

From 1960 until 2002, high school and college students have steadily reported lower and lower levels of internal locus of control (the belief that they can control their own destiny) and higher levels of external locus of control (the belief that their destiny is determined by external forces). This change has been associated with an increased vulnerability to anxiety and depression. In fact, adolescents and young adults today are five to eight times more likely to experience the symptoms of an anxiety disorder than young people were at earlier times, including during the Great Depression, World War II, and the cold war.[2] Are things really harder now than they were during the Depression? Or are we doing something that is dampening their natural coping mechanisms?

Without a healthy sense of control, kids feel powerless and overwhelmed and will often become passive or resigned. When they are denied the ability to make meaningful choices, they are at high risk of becoming anxious, struggling to manage anger, becoming self-destructive, or self-medicating. Despite the many resources and opportunities their parents offer them, they will often fail to thrive. Without a sense of control, regardless of their background, inner turmoil will take its toll.

We all do better when we feel like we can impact the world around us. That's why we continue to push the button to close the elevator door even though most of them don't work.[3] It's why, in a landmark study conducted in the 1970s, nursing home residents who were told and shown that they had responsibility over their lives lived longer than those who were told that the nursing staff was in charge.[4] It is also why the kid who decides on his own to do his homework (or not) will be happier, less stressed, and ultimately more capable of navigating life.

We want our kids to be able to participate in a competitive global economy, to be relevant, to feel they can hack it. We love them and want them to be happy and to thrive long after we're gone. All worthy goals. But to achieve them, many of us have bought into some false assumptions:

False Assumption 1: There is a narrow path to success and God forbid our child should fall off it. The stakes are thus too high to let them make decisions for themselves. This argument hinges on an assumption of scarcity, one that says that for young people to be successful, they must be competitive at all times—whatever the price.

False Assumption 2: It is critical to do well in school if you want to do well in life. There will be some winners and many losers. It is Yale or McDonald's. As a result, too many kids are either driven manically or have given up trying.

False Assumption 3: Pushing more will lead our children to becoming more accomplished and more successful adults. Our sixth graders aren't scoring as well as sixth graders in China? Okay, let's teach them ninth grade math. College admission is getting tougher than ever? Yikes, let's pack our kids' schedules so they'll learn and do more.

False Assumption 4: The world is more dangerous than ever before. We have to supervise our kids constantly to make sure they don't get hurt or make bad decisions.

Now many parents instinctively understand that these assumptions are untrue (and we will spend some time in this book debunking them). But that perspective dissipates when they feel pressured—by peers, by schools, or by other parents—to ensure their child isn't falling behind. The pressure is rooted deeply in fear, and fear almost always leads to bad decisions.

We really can't control our kids—and doing so shouldn't be our goal. Our role is to teach them to think and act independently, so that they will have the judgment to succeed in school and, most important, in *life*. Rather than pushing them to do things they resist, we should seek to help them find things they love and develop their inner motivation. Our aim is to move away from a model that depends on parental pressure to one that nurtures a child's own drive. That is what we mean by the self-driven child.

We start with the assumption that kids have brains in their heads and want their lives to work and that, with some support, they'll figure out what to do. They know it's important to get up in the morning and get dressed. They know it's important to do their homework. They feel the pressure even if they don't show it, and if they are struggling, nagging them about it will only reinforce their resistance. The trick is to give them enough freedom and respect to let them figure things out for themselves. Even if it were possible to control our kids and mold them into who or what we want them to be, we might be less stressed, but they would be more *controlled* than *self-controlled*.

We will talk in this book about important research in neuroscience and developmental psychology and will share our experiences from our combined sixty years working with kids. We hope to convince you that you should think of yourself as a consultant to your kids rather than their boss or manager. We will try to persuade you of the wisdom of saying "It's your call" as often as possible. We'll offer ideas to help you help your kids find their own internal motivation, and we'll coach you in navigating an educational system that is often at odds with giving kids autonomy. We will help you move in the direction of being a nonanxious presence, which is one of the best things you can do for your kids, your family, and yourself. At the end of each chapter, we will give you actionable steps to put into effect immediately.

Some of what we suggest is likely to make you uncomfortable. But much of it should give you a sense of relief. However skeptical you may be, please remember that when we've shared our techniques and the science behind them with the families we serve, we've seen great results. We've seen perpetual defiance transformed into thoughtful decision making. We've seen grades and test scores dramatically improve. We've seen kids who felt overwhelmed, helpless, or hopeless take charge of their own lives. We've seen kids who floundered for a bit but ended up successful and happy—and much closer to their parents than anyone thought possible. It is possible to provide your children with a healthy sense of autonomy and to foster that healthy sense of autonomy in yourself as well. It's easier than you might think. Let us show you how.

CHAPTER ONE

The Most Stressful Thing in the Universe

ADAM, A FIFTEEN-YEAR-OLD SOPHOMORE, walks from his family's cramped apartment in the projects on the South Side of Chicago to his underfunded public school every day. Last summer, his older brother was killed in a drive-by shooting while the two boys were hanging out on a street corner together. Now he finds it difficult to concentrate in school, has trouble retaining lessons, and is often sent to the principal's office for explosive behavior. He's not sleeping well and his grades, never very good, are slipping to the point where he may have to repeat a year.

Fifteen-year-old Zara lives in a multimillion-dollar house and attends a posh private school in the Washington, DC, area. Her parents hope she will make the cutoff for a National Merit Scholarship when she takes the PSAT this fall, so she fits in test prep between field hockey practice, volunteering for Habitat for Humanity, and three to four hours of homework per night. Zara is getting good grades, but she's not sleeping well. She finds herself talking back to her parents and snapping at her friends, and she complains of frequent headaches.

We all know to worry about Adam: statistics suggest he has a tough road ahead. What we don't know is that we should worry about Zara, too. Chronic sleep deprivation and toxic stress during a critical phase of brain development are endangering her long-term mental and physical health. If you put a scan of Zara's brain next to one of Adam's, you'd see striking similarities, particularly in the parts of the brain involved in the stress response system.

In recent years, we've learned a lot about the damage athletes suffer from hitting their heads too much—either on soccer balls or on the 260-pound linebacker in their way. Today, we think about the long-term consequences of concussions: "Yeah, he looks okay now, but too many more of those and he's not going to remember his kids' names."

We think stress should be talked about in this way, too. Chronic stress wreaks havoc on the brain, especially on young brains. It's like trying to grow a plant in a too-small pot. As any casual gardener knows, doing so weakens the plant, with long-term consequences. Rates of stress-induced illnesses are extremely high in every demographic, and researchers are working furiously to uncover the reasons behind the rise in anxiety disorders, eating disorders, depression, binge drinking, and worrisome patterns of self-harm in young people.[1] As Madeline Levine has made us aware, affluent children and teens are at particularly high risk for developing mental health problems such as anxiety, mood, and chemical use disorders.[2] In fact, a recent survey showed that 80 percent of students in an affluent and competitive Silicon Valley high school reported moderate to severe levels of anxiety and 54 percent reported moderate to severe levels of depression.[3] Depression is now the number one cause of disability worldwide.[4] We think of chronic stress in children and teenagers as the societal equivalent of climate change—a problem that has been building over generations and will take considerable effort and a change of habits to overcome.

So what does a sense of control have to do with all of this? The answer is: *everything*. Quite simply, it is the antidote to stress. Stress is the unknown, the unwanted, and the feared. It's as minor as feeling unbalanced and as major as fighting for your life. Sonia Lupien at the Centre for Studies on Human Stress has a handy acronym for what makes life stressful—N.U.T.S.

NOVELTY
Something you have not experienced before

UNPREDICTABILITY
Something you had no way of knowing would occur

THREAT TO THE EGO
Your safety or competence as a person is called into question

SENSE OF CONTROL
You feel you have little or no control over the situation[5]

An early study that looked at stress in rats found that when a rat is given a wheel to turn that will stop it from receiving an electric shock, it happily turns the wheel and isn't very stressed. If the wheel is taken away, the rat experiences massive stress. If the wheel is then returned to the cage, the rat's stress levels are much lower, even if the wheel *isn't actually attached* to the shocking apparatus anymore.[6] In humans, too, being able to push a button to reduce the likelihood of hearing a noxious sound will reduce their stress levels, even if the button has no real effect on the sound—and even if you don't push the button![7] It turns out that it's the *sense* of control that matters, even more so than what you actually do. If you have confidence that you can impact a situation, it will be less stressful. In contrast, a low sense of control may very well be the most stressful thing in the universe.

On some level, you probably know this. You may use it as a justification for cleaning up your desk before starting on a difficult task. Most people feel safer when they are driving than flying (when it should be the opposite) because they believe they are more in control. One of the reasons why traffic jams are so stressful is that there's nothing you can do about it.

You may also have experienced the power of control in relation to your kids. If your child is very sick or struggling and you feel there's nothing you can do about it, your stress level is likely to rise. Even less distressing events, like watching your teenager take the car out alone for the first time, or watching them perform at an athletic event or in a play, also cause stress. You're in the role of spectator, and there's little you can do beyond hope everything turns out okay.

Agency may be the one most important factor in human happiness and well-being. We all like to feel that we are in charge of our own destiny. The same thing goes for our kids. That's why two-year-olds will say things like "I do it myself!" and four-year-olds will insist "You are not the boss of me!" It's why we should let them do what they can for themselves, even if we're running late and it will take them twice as long. It's also why the surest way to get a picky five-year-old to eat his vegetables is to divide the plate in half and let him choose which half to eat. One of Ned's clients, Kara, was incredibly insightful about this: "When I was a kid, when my parents would say, 'You *have* to eat this or that food,' I hated it," she said. "So if they told me I had to eat something that I didn't want to, I'd throw it right back up on the table." Kara remarked that sleepaway camp was a highlight of her childhood because campers got to decide from a range of choices what to do all day, and what to eat. And given the freedom to act on her own, she ate responsibly.

Alas, sleepaway camp is not the world we live in. When she was around twelve or thirteen, Kara began to experience anxiety. "I think I first started having anxiety when people started telling me what to do," she said, "when I didn't feel like I was in control. And then when I switched schools and had to worry about fitting in and about what other people thought, I think that made it even worse. For me, feeling like I have a sense of control, that I am in charge of my own life, is so important. Even now, I like it when my parents give me choices. My friend's mom will say, 'Let's play this game for a while and then let's bake cookies.' And that's great and all, but it would make me nuts to always be told 'Here's the plan' instead of asking me what I want."

These are exactly the circumstances most kids experience every day. Lest you doubt how little control children and adolescents like Kara actually have, think of what their days are like: they have to sit still in classes they didn't choose, taught by teachers randomly assigned to them, alongside whatever child happens to be assigned to their class. They have to stand in neat lines, eat on a schedule, and rely on the whims of their teachers for permission to go to the bathroom. And think of how we measure them: not by the effort they put into practicing or how much they improve, but by whether another kid at the meet happened to swim or run faster last Saturday. We don't measure their understanding of the periodic table, but how they score on a random selection of associated facts.

It is frustrating and stressful to feel powerless, and many kids feel that way all the time. As grown-ups, we sometimes tell our kids that they're in charge of their own lives, but then we proceed to micromanage their homework, their afterschool activities, and their friendships. Or perhaps we tell them that actually they're not in charge—we are. Either way, we make them feel powerless, and by doing so, we undermine our relationship with them.

There is another way. Over the last sixty years, study after study has found that a healthy sense of control goes hand in hand with virtually all the positive outcomes we want for our children. Perceived control—the confidence that we can direct the course of our life through our own efforts—is associated with better physical health, less use of drugs and alcohol, and greater longevity, as well as with lower stress, positive emotional well-being, greater internal motivation and ability to control one's behavior, improved academic performance, and enhanced career success.[8] Like exercise and sleep, it appears to be good for virtually everything, presumably because it represents a deep human need.

Our kids are "wired" for control, whether they're growing up in the South Bronx, Silicon Valley, Birmingham, or South Korea. Our role as adults is not to force them to follow the track we've laid out for them; it's to help them develop the skills to figure out the track that's right for them. They will need to find their own way— and to make independent course corrections—for the rest of their lives.

Hitting the Sweet Spot: A Better Understanding of Stress

Let us make one thing clear: we don't think it's possible to protect kids from all stressful experiences, nor would we want to. In fact, when kids are constantly shielded from circumstances that make them anxious, it tends to make their anxiety worse. We want them to learn how to deal *successfully* with stressful situations—to have a high stress tolerance. That's how they develop resilience. If a child feels like he's in control in a stressful situation, then in later situations when he might actually *not* be in control, his brain will be equipped to handle that stress better.[9] He is, in effect, immunized.

Bill cried every day for the first week of first grade because he didn't know any of his classmates. His teacher was quietly supportive, and when other kids would whisper, "Mrs. Rowe, he's crying," Bill would hear her say, "He's going to be fine. He'll like it here, don't worry." He did, in fact, figure out how to manage the stress of an unfamiliar situation and the coping skills he learned appear to have generalized, as he never cried again in an unfamiliar environment. (So far, anyway.) The teacher was right to let him work it out, instead of swooping in and giving him the sense he couldn't handle it on his own.

The National Scientific Council on the Developing Child has identified three kinds of stress: [10]

1. Positive stress motivates children (and adults) to grow, take risks, and perform at a high level. Think of kids preparing for a play, nervous and a little stressed beforehand, but then filled with a sense of accomplishment and pride afterward. We could call this the jitters, excitement, or anticipation. Unless the jitters are excessive, they make it more likely that a child will perform well. Kids experiencing positive stress know that they ultimately have control over whether or not they perform at all. As it happens, kids are more likely to persevere and to reach their full potential if they know they don't *have* to do something.

2. Tolerable stress, which occurs for relatively brief periods, can also build resilience. Critically, there must be supportive adults present, and kids must have time to cope and recover. Let's say a child witnesses her parents arguing a lot as they're going through a divorce. But the parents are talking to her, and they're not having blowouts *every* night. She has time to recover. This is tolerable stress. Another example of tolerable stress might be an episode of being bullied, so long as it doesn't last too long, it isn't repeated too often, and the child is supported by caring adults. A tolerable stress might even be a death in the family. In an influential study, graduate students took baby rats away from their mothers and handled them for fifteen minutes per day (which was stressful to the rats) and then returned them to

their mothers, who licked and groomed them. The graduate students repeated this for the first two weeks of the rats' lives. The baby rats who were removed and handled for a brief period showed much more resilience as adults than the pups who stayed in the cage with their mother.[11] The researchers referred to them as "California laid-back rats," as they were difficult to stress as adults. This is probably because in situations like these the brain becomes *conditioned* to cope, and this conditioning lays the foundation for resilience.[12]

3. Toxic stress is defined as frequent or prolonged activation of the stress system in the absence of support. Toxic stress is either severe, such as witnessing an assault, or recurs day in and day out, in which case it is chronic. Supportive adults— who minimize exposure to things that a child isn't developmentally ready to handle—aren't readily available. The child perceives that he or she has little control over what happens. There seems to be no reprieve, no cavalry coming, no end in sight. This is the space many kids live in today, whether they are obviously at-risk students like Adam, or seemingly high-functioning kids like Zara. Toxic stress does not prepare kids for the real world. It damages their ability to thrive.[13] To return to rat studies for a moment, when rat pups were taken from their mothers not for fifteen minutes but for three hours a day, the experience was so stressful that when they were returned to their mothers, the rat pups didn't interact with them. They remained easily stressed for the rest of their lives.[14]

So how do you capitalize on positive or tolerable stress while avoiding the bad kind? It is simple in theory, but tricky in execution: kids need a supportive adult around, they need time to recover from the stressful event, and they need to have a sense of control over their lives.

It's All in Your Head

To understand how this works, it's useful to know a few things about how the brain works. In moments of great self-doubt, understanding the brain will help kids grasp that much of their behavior is *chemical*, not *character*. Kids today are tech savvy, but they tend to know almost nothing about the hardware in their heads or the software that runs it. Our hope is that you will find a little brain science explains a lot about the thoughts and emotions that we all have a hard time controlling. Those of you who already know how the brain works will have to bear with us as we outline the nuts and bolts.

Four major brain systems are involved in developing and maintaining a healthy sense of control: the executive control system, the

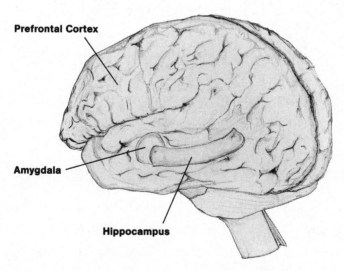

1. Three of the most important brain structures regulating stress and impulse control are the prefrontal cortex, amygdala, and hippocampus.

stress response system, the motivation system, and the resting state system. Let us briefly explain what each of these does.

The Pilot (The Executive Control System)

The executive control system is largely governed by the prefrontal cortex, the seat of planning, organization, impulse control, and judgment. When we are calm, fully rested, and in control—when we are in our right minds—our prefrontal cortex is monitoring, organizing, and regulating much of the brain. In fact, the key variable in determining the extent to which we become stressed by life experiences is how much the prefrontal cortex perceives itself to be in control.

The prefrontal cortex has been called "the Goldilocks of the brain," as it needs a "just right" combination of chemicals—the neurotransmitters dopamine and norepinephrine—to operate effectively.[15] It is easily taken off-line by stress. Arousal, mild stress, excitement, or minor pretest jitters can raise the levels of these neurotransmitters, resulting in sharper focus, clearer thinking, and stronger performance. With sleep deprivation or too much stress, however, the prefrontal cortex becomes flooded with dopamine and norepinephrine and is essentially taken off-line. At such times, the brain is simply unable to learn or to think clearly, a point we'll return to in Chapter Seven. When the prefrontal cortex is off-line, you are more likely to act impulsively and to make dumb decisions.

The Lion Fighter (The Stress Response System)

The stress response system takes over when you are confronting a severe threat like a predator, or even imagining a threat. It is designed to keep you safe from impending harm. It is made up of the amygdala, the hypothalamus, the hippocampus, and the pituitary and adrenal glands.

The amygdala, a primitive emotional processing center that is acutely sensitive to fear, anger, and anxiety, is a key part of the brain's threat detection system. It doesn't think consciously; it senses and reacts. Under high stress, the amygdala is the one in charge. Under the amgydala's reign, our behavior tends to be defensive, reactive, inflexible, and at times aggressive.[16] We're inclined to fall back on habitual patterns or instinct, as our animal nature prepares us to fight, flee, or freeze like a deer in the headlights.

When the amygdala senses a threat, it sends a signal to the hypothalamus and the pituitary gland. Then it's an agitated game of telephone to wake up the adrenal gland, which secretes adrenaline. Adrenaline is the hormone that allows us to lift a car when our child is trapped underneath it. This complex sequence of alarm notifications occurs faster than conscious thought. When we are under threat, we need a vigorous stress response. Our survival may depend on the speed of our instinctive reaction, and evolution shaped us so that we *cannot* think clearly under stress.

A healthy stress response is defined by a very quick spike in stress hormones followed by a quick recovery. The problems come when that recovery doesn't happen quickly. If stress is prolonged, the adrenal gland secretes cortisol, which is slower to come on board and has been likened to bringing in the troops for a long-term battle. If a zebra is attacked by a lion and survives, its cortisol levels will normalize in forty-five minutes. By contrast, humans can retain elevated cortisol levels for days, weeks, or even months at a time. That can be a problem, in part, because chronically elevated levels of cortisol will impair and eventually kill cells in the hippocampus, the place where memories are created and stored. This is why students have trouble learning when they are under acute stress.

The hippocampus has another role to play. It helps turn off the stress response. It says, "Hey, remember last time you freaked out about being late and it was no big deal? Chill." It's like the calm, loyal friend who shows up to talk you off the ledge. It's *perspective*—which is invaluable in all aspects of life. People suffering from PTSD, whose hippocampus has been compromised, don't have this perspective. When they're in a situation that's even remotely similar to one in the past—say they're in a crowded mall instead of a crowded market in Baghdad where an IED went off—their hippocampus can't put those past memories in context, and they panic.

Stress disorganizes the brain. It reduces brain wave coherence, the desire to explore new ideas and to solve problems creatively. It kicks our prefrontal cortex out of the driver's seat and limits the flexibility with which we can pull ourselves together or learn. When the Lion Fighter is in charge, you might have sharper instincts on a lion-infested savannah, but less so in sophomore English. How could you possibly focus on Shakespeare or process math when your body is telling you you're in a fight for survival?

It's not that the stress response system is bad exactly, but it is a bit like the "heavy" you bring in under duress. You want him there for tough times, but you don't want him there all the time. Chronic stress *enlarges* the amygdala, increasing the Lion Fighter's presence and thus your vulnerability to fear, anxiety, and anger.

The next two systems we'll only touch on here and will return to in more detail in later chapters.

The Cheerleader (The Motivational System)

The motivational system is the "reward center" part of the brain that releases the neurotransmitter dopamine. Anything you experience as rewarding—winning a sports match, earning money, having a good sexual experience, receiving recognition—leads to a higher level of dopamine. In contrast, low dopamine levels are associated with low drive, low effort, and boredom. An optimal level of dopamine allows for the experience of *flow*, which we come back to in Chapter Five when we turn to the all-important question of motivation. In acclaimed stress researcher Robert Sapolsky's words, "Dopamine's more about the wanting than the getting."[17] It is the key to drive. When you are under chronic stress, dopamine levels go down the tubes over time. It's harder to want to do something, and as a result, you lose your motivation.

The Buddha (The Resting State)

For years when scientists used MRIs to assess the brain's activity, they studied what *activates* the brain when it's given a specific task (like counting backward from one thousand). But around the turn of the twenty-first century, scientists started looking at what happens when we're just sitting with our own thoughts. What they discovered was that there is a complex and highly integrated network in the brain that only activates when we are "doing nothing." This is known as the default mode network. Our understanding of

Default Mode Network

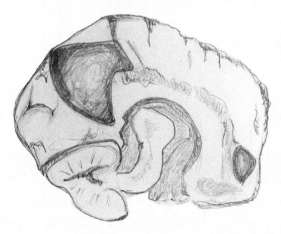

2. The default mode network is concentrated in the shaded areas in the front and back of the brain that activate when we think about the past or the future; think about ourselves and others; and simply let our minds wander.

its functioning is still new, but we know it must be very important, as it uses 60 to 80 percent of the brain's energy.[18]

When you're sitting in a waiting room or unwinding after dinner, if you're not reading, watching television, or on your phone, your default mode network is projecting the future and sorting out the past. It's *processing* your life. It activates when we daydream, during certain kinds of meditation, and when we lie in bed before going to sleep. This is the system for self-reflection, and reflection about others, the area of the brain that is highly active when we are *not* focused on a task. It is the part of us that goes "off-line." A healthy default mode network is necessary for the human brain to rejuvenate, store information in more permanent locations, gain perspective, process complicated ideas, and be truly creative. It has also been linked in young people to the development of a strong sense of identity and a capacity for empathy.[19] Not surprisingly, stress impairs the default mode network's ability to work its magic. Scientists are concerned that because of technology's ubiquity, young people have too few opportunities to activate their default mode network and, as a result, too few opportunities for self-reflection.

That is a lot of brain science to take in all at once. The main thing to remember for now is that chronically stressed kids routinely have their brains flooded with hormones that dull higher brain functions and stunt their emotional responses. Parts of the brain that are responsible for memory, reasoning, attention, judgment, and emotional control are dampened and eventually damaged. Over time these areas can shrink, while the parts of the brain that detect threats grow larger. Ultimately, an overactive stress system makes a child far more likely to develop anxiety disorders, depression, and a host of other mental and physical problems.

One of my students came in after a test one day and reported that he'd blown it. "I had a panic attack and left the testing room again," he said. "Every time, I dwell on one question and waste time. Then when the proctor comes in and says 'You have five minutes,' it's like a trigger and I lose it.

"It was going so well," he said, "and then I just took so long on one thing and it killed me."

"So what was going through your head when that problem got to you?" I asked.

"When I tried doing the next problem, it was almost like I couldn't think logically. Like I couldn't understand what I was reading. Or how to go about the problem."

His Lion Fighter had taken over and the Pilot, who really knew all the answers, was nowhere to be seen.

—Ned

Stress, Anxiety, and Depression

Affluent, high-achieving communities from Washington, DC, to Palo Alto have become all too familiar with suicide clusters impacting their high schools. When they occur, media coverage features a blend of grief, hand-wringing, and disbelief. Comments go along the lines of: "I just can't understand it. He was one of the top students in his grade, taking four AP classes and getting perfect grades. He was a leader in our community, a standout on the varsity soccer team. Why would he take his own life?"

Implicit in such a statement is the belief that it's only people who are somehow losing the game who would want to kill themselves.

A brain that is stretching itself and utterly engaged looks very different from a brain that is high performing but under the influence of toxic stress. Chronic stress can transform into anxiety when you don't give your brain and body a chance to recover. Instead of seeing lions only when you're on the savannah, you see them everywhere, even when they're nowhere near and really you'd do much better to chill out and graze. The amygdala becomes bigger and more reactive than it should be, and with the prefrontal cortex cut off, you have a hard time distinguishing between things that are threatening and things that aren't.[20] Welcome to anxiety.

Chronic stress can create a feeling of helplessness. If nothing you do makes things better, why try to do anything at all? This sense of helplessness will leave you feeling that you just can't accomplish a task, when in reality you could do it very capably.[21] Chronic stress leads to behaviors like problems sleeping, binge eating, procrastination, and a lowered willingness to take care of yourself. Dopamine levels fall, as do levels of norepinephrine and serotonin.[22] This is how stress can spiral into depression.

The kicker here is that a significant amount of this mental and emotional suffering can be prevented. Unlike juvenile diabetes or autism (which are highly heritable), experience plays a major role in anxiety, depression, and addiction. This means that if we change what we're doing, it should be possible to bring the numbers down.

Why This Matters So Much

Toxic stress isn't good for you at any age, but there are certain times in your life when it's worse than others. Just as eating disorders can have a profound effect on young, growing bodies, chronic stress can have devastating effects on young, developing brains.

The times when our brains seem to be the most sensitive to stress are: 1) prenatally (highly stressed pregnant women tend to have children who are more responsive to stress), 2) in early childhood, when neural circuits are particularly malleable, and 3) during adolescence, that powerful but vulnerable period between child-hood and adulthood.[23]

Let's look more closely at the adolescent brain, for it is a very active place. Children between the ages of twelve and eighteen show more brain development than at any time in life other than the first few years. The adolescent brain makes important new pathways and connections, but the cognitive functions of the pre-frontal cortex, the seat of judgment, don't mature until around age twenty-five. (The emotional control functions follow at around thirty-two!) When the stress response system is turned on for ex-tended periods of time, the prefrontal cortex can't develop as it should. This is problematic because teens are more vulnerable to stress than children or adults.

Normal adolescents, even those who aren't experiencing any particular stressor, have exaggerated stress responses. In a study at Cornell led by B. J. Casey in which adolescents were shown images of frightened faces, their amygdalas were far more reactive than those of children or adults. Adolescents also demonstrate a higher stress response than other groups when speaking publicly. Animal studies have found that after a prolonged period of stress, the adult brain will tend to bounce back within ten days, while the adoles-cent brain takes about three weeks. Adolescents also have less stress *tolerance* than adults. They are much more likely to develop stress-related illnesses such as colds, headaches, and upset stomachs.[24]

Anxiety begets anxiety, regardless of your age, but a 2007 study suggests that this may be even more true for teens.[25] A steroid called THP is usually released in response to stress, to help calm nerve cells and lower anxiety. But while THP worked in a study of adult mice, acting like a tranquilizer in the brain, in adolescent mice it had very little effect. What this means is that adolescents have it rough: more vulnerability to stress and fewer tools to deal with it. Anxiety builds on itself, with little hope of relief.

This is also true of depression, which appears to leave "scars" in the brain, so that less and less stress is required to trigger a subsequent episode. Eventually, depression can develop with no environmental stressor. Adults who experienced even a single bout of major depression in adolescence are likely to display long-term problems in their work, their relationships, and the pleasure they take in life.[26] Even after teens appear to have fully recovered, they are more likely to have mild but persistent symptoms like pessimism or sleep or appetite issues that will make them more vulnerable to depression later in life.[27]

Bill first tested Jared when he was ten in order to rule out ADHD (which he had). Jared was funny, good-humored, and very enjoyable to be around. His parents and teachers raved about his positive disposition, which endeared him to others. Everyone called him the Teflon Kid, because problems just seemed to bounce off him. Bill next evaluated Jared as a sixteen-year-old sophomore. He'd done very well in school and was highly motivated to get into Duke University. Bill was troubled to learn, however, that after starting high school Jared had become depressed and had been taking an antidepressant since then. He told Bill that the combination of high stress about school and being tired all the time had eventually "pushed him over the edge" and caused him to become discouraged and pessimistic. While his medication helped, Jared explained that he still felt highly stressed and exhausted, in part because he commonly stayed up to do his homework until 12:30 or 1:00 A.M. He felt he had to stay up this late: "I'm afraid that if I went to bed earlier, a kid in Idaho would be staying up until one and would get my spot at Duke."

Jared isn't doomed to a life of severe depression, but he will forever be more vulnerable to depressive episodes. His story is a powerful reminder of the dramatic changes that can ensue when kids are tired and stressed for long periods and how a disposition that is by nature easygoing can be scarred by stress. In fact, it is through working with kids like Jared that Bill concluded that being too tired and too stressed for too long is a formula for anxiety and depression.

A Caveat about Control

We have a tendency in our society to think that "with enough hard work, anything is possible." *Well if you didn't make it,* the dangerous corollary goes, *you must not have worked hard enough.* There are enormous differences in people's natural aptitudes and in how their brains work. (Different people will have different processing speeds, memory, and tolerance for stress.) And you can work hard and still not get what you want. The real question is, what do you make of that setback? Do you take it as a verdict on your worth? Do you decide to come up with a different strategy? Or do you take the hit and try for a different goal?

Ned sees this dynamic play out vividly in the realm of college admissions. The idea that the admissions process is a pure meritocracy is stressful—and untrue. Colleges value academic rigor, sure, but most also give preferential treatment to recruited athletes, legacies, and diversity of every type (socioeconomic, geographic, ethnic, first generation to college). Harvard could likely fill its entire incoming class with affluent white students from Massachusetts with GPAs of 4.0 and SAT scores over 1400. But they don't. If someone isn't admitted to their first-choice college, does it mean they didn't work hard enough? Of course not. There are so many factors you have no control over, like what the applicant pool looks like that year, or whether the admissions rep was having a bad day or was tired of seeing applications from private school kids in Iowa who were black belts and spoke Russian. We get into dangerous territory when we take all that on ourselves and believe we can control the uncontrollable.

———

A major goal of this book is to help parents help their kids increase their stress tolerance—their ability to perform well in stressful situations—and to "throw off" stress rather than accumulate it. Stress tolerance is highly correlated to success in all aspects of life. We want to challenge our kids without overwhelming them, to stretch them without breaking them. We want them to experience some positive stress and some tolerable stress, but in the right ways, and with the right bolstering. We want to give their brains all the support and room they need to grow strong. The *how* of all of this comes back again and again to a sense of control. What this means for you as a parent will become clearer in the next chapter, where we encourage you to be a consultant for your child, not his boss or manager.

What to Do Tonight

- Make a list of the things your child has control over. Is there anything you can add to that list?

- Ask your child if there are things he feels he'd like to be in charge of that he currently isn't.

- Consider your language around making plans. Do you say, "Today we're going to do this and then this," or do you offer choices?

- Tell your kids (if they're ten or older) something like this: "I just read something really interesting—that there are four things about life that make it stressful: new situations, situations that are unpredictable, situations where you feel you could be hurt, criticized, or embarrassed, and situations where you don't feel you can control what's happening. It's interesting, because in my job I get most stressed when I feel I'm expected to make something happen but I can't control everything that is necessary to make it happen. Are there things that make you stressed?" By identifying stress in your own life and talking about it, you are modeling stress awareness—a critical step in curbing the effects of stress. As the saying goes, "You've got to name it to tame it."

- If your kid seems to be really anxious, talk to your pediatrician about it. Determine whether some kind of professional intervention is necessary. Research suggests that treating anxiety early significantly lowers the risk of recurring problems.

- You can let your worried child know that she's safe, that you're there for her, but don't reassure her excessively. Let her know that you have confidence in her ability to handle the stressors in her life. But don't minimize what she is feeling or try to fix it for her.

- Think about ways in which you may, intentionally or inadvertently, be trying to protect your kids from experiencing mildly stressful situations that they could grow from. Are you too focused on safety? Are there situations in which you could give your child more independence or more choices?

- Dozens of scales have been developed over the years to measure a person's sense of control. The granddaddy of them all is the Rotter Scale, developed by J. B. Rotter in 1966. We highly encourage you to take it so that you can assess your own strengths and struggles when it comes to autonomy. For kids, we like a scale developed by Steven Nowicki and Bonnie Strickland, which asks questions such as "Do you believe that you can stop yourself from catching a cold?" and "When a person doesn't like you, is there anything you can do about it?" You may be surprised by where your child lands.

CHAPTER TWO

"I Love You Too Much to Fight with You About Your Homework"

The Parent as Consultant

BILL ONCE WORKED with a fifteen-year-old named Jonah who hated homework. What Jonah hated even more than the homework itself was his parents' hectoring and constant oversight. When Bill asked Jonah to walk him through a typical evening at home, he said, "We usually eat dinner between six and six thirty. And then I can watch TV from six thirty to seven. Then from seven to eight thirty, I pretend to do my homework."

An hour and a half *pretending* to do his homework? That's a whole lot of effort put into *not* doing something. Imagine Jonah sitting there, his homework in front of him, devising excuses for why he isn't doing it. Why didn't he just do the damn thing? In part, he was tired of hearing these common refrains from his parents:

"You only get one shot at getting into a good college, and you're blowing it."

"You'll thank us when you're older."

"You're gonna have to learn to do things you don't want to do."

"If you don't learn to be successful in school, how will you be successful in life?"

Jonah's parents meant well, but out of the cacophony of voices around him, one message was coming across loud and clear: *We know what's right for you, and you don't.* Imagine if you had a conversation with your spouse in which he or she said something like:

> *"How was work today? Did you get a good report on your project? You understand how important it is for you to take your work seriously, right? I mean, I know it isn't always easy or fun, but you really should see if you can get a promotion so you'll have more options in the future. It just seems like maybe you aren't doing your best all the time. Like maybe you could work a little harder."*

You get the point—it would drive you nuts. It drove Jonah nuts, too. The only way he felt he could assert his own identity was by not doing his homework.

We understand where Jonah's parents were coming from. They loved him more than anything, and it pained them to see him failing to apply himself. They knew how capable he was, and they felt he was shooting himself in the foot, limiting how far he could go in life because he was too stubborn and undisciplined and too—well, fifteen to do the work. They could see the big picture, but he couldn't. And if they could just ride him hard now, if they could just make him push through and do the work, they could keep him from getting stuck in a rut and from suffering consequences he couldn't foresee. They were doing this not just because they wanted him to be successful, but because it was their responsibility as parents.

This is the way a lot of loving parents think. But we're going to ask you to let go of that way of thinking. To begin with, it doesn't work. Despite extreme efforts on the part of adults to protect Jonah from himself, he continued to waste his time and theirs because he was not getting the message from his environment that "this is your work, this is your life, and you're going to get out of it what you put into it." He needed his parents to offer help, but also to let him know they understood that no one could make him work. Over the years, Bill has seen many kids like Jonah go on to be very successful, but this has only happened when their parents and teachers gave up trying to make them be successful and the kids were given a chance to figure it out on their own.

In this chapter, we're going to explain why trying to control your child will not give you the results you want, and why it risks creating kids who must then constantly be pushed because their own internal motivation has either not developed or has been eroded by external pressure. We're also going to ask you to consider a different philosophy than that of parent as enforcer: that of parent as consultant.

Think about what good consultants do in the business world: They ask what the problems are and which ones are most important. They ask what their clients are willing to commit to or sacrifice in order to reach a desired goal. They give advice, but they do not try to force their client to change, because they recognize that ultimately it's the client's responsibility.

"This is my child, not a client," you might be thinking. True. But what's also true is that it is your child's life, not yours.

Our instinct as parents is to protect and lead our kids, usually with the assumption that we know what's best for them. With infants, this is generally true. We have to take responsibility for managing all aspects of their lives. Yet even newborns assert their individuality in ways that can be completely humbling—and terrifying. Consider infants who won't sleep or won't eat. Experts in neonatology and infant development emphasize the importance of adapting to your baby's personality and needs.

When parents come to us concerned about a lack of motivation, difficulty with peers, or poor academic performance, we begin by asking them a simple question: "Whose problem is it?" The question is meant to be rhetorical, but parents often look at us quiz-zically. When your child is crying because she was excluded by two of her friends or was criticized in front of the class by her teacher, it's easy to feel that it's your problem, too. It hurts you to see her hurt—few things inspire the ire of parents more than seeing some-one mistreat their child. That hurt may even stay with you long after she's forgotten it. But ultimately, it is your kid's problem, not yours.

This is a reframing that is difficult for many parents, who want the best for their kids and want as much as possible to protect them from suffering. But the reality is that if you want to give your chil-dren more of a sense of control, you will have to let go of some yourself. A consultant who loses his wits when the company doesn't hit its targets or fails to reach its full potential becomes part of the problem. Remember that your job is not to solve your children's problems but to help them learn to run their own lives. This re-framing means that while we should guide, support, teach, help, and set limits for our kids, we should be clear—with them and with ourselves—that their lives are their own. As Eckhart Tolle wrote, "They come into this world through you, but they are not 'yours.'"[1]

We're not saying this is easy. After all, we invest a lot in our children, and it can be terrifying to realize how little control we really have. But our years of experience have taught us that trying to force kids to do things you think are in their own best interest will compromise your relationship and waste energy that could be spent building them up in other ways.

The Homework Wars

"I dread the time between dinner and bedtime because all we do is fight," said one parent.

"It's like a war zone," said another.

"It's World War Three in our house every night."

It startles us how often war metaphors are invoked when parents talk about their kids' nightly homework. To give you some idea of the scale of the Homework Wars, all three of the parents quoted above said those things to Bill *in the same week*. That's why we've found that there's no better forum to explore parents' doubts and questions about the parent-as-consultant model than the fraught space of homework. And so while this chapter is about homework, it's really about much more.

There are three main reasons why fighting about homework doesn't make sense.

First, you may find yourself enforcing rules and attitudes you don't really believe in. One dad was horrified to find himself telling his ten-year-old daughter how very important it was to memorize all the state capitals—even though, as he put it, "I made it through college and law school, but gun to my head, I have no idea what the capital of Wyoming is." (It's Cheyenne. But please don't test us on the other forty-nine.) Parents commonly feel responsible for policing homework without thinking about the underlying goal: to raise curious, self-directed learners.

Second, when parents work harder than their kids to solve their problems, their kids get weaker, not stronger. If you spend ninety-five units of energy trying to help your child be successful, he or she will spend five units of energy. If you become frustrated or anxious and raise the ante, spending ninety-eight units of energy in clamping down even harder, your child will respond accordingly, and spend just two units. In Jonah's case, he had a tutor, a therapist, and a school counselor who communicated regularly with his parents about his missed assignments. Jonah took no steps himself. This counterproductive dynamic will not change until the energy changes, which often happens when a parent, fully exasperated, says, "I can't take this anymore. You're on your own."

If you act as if it's your job to see that your child does his homework, practices the piano, or plays a sport, you reinforce the mistaken belief that somebody other than he is responsible for getting his work done. He doesn't have to think about it because, on some level, he knows that eventually someone will "make" him do it.

Third, and this is perhaps the most critical point, you can't force a kid to do something he's dead set against. Buying into the idea that you should and must try will just end up frustrating you when it doesn't work.

You've probably heard of the Serenity Prayer, the one that goes like this: "God, grant me the serenity to accept the things I cannot change, the courage to change the things I can, and the wisdom to know the difference." It's a good thing to keep in mind as a parent. We have a coda that spells things out even more clearly:

1. You can't make your kids do something against their will.
2. You can't make your kids want something they don't want.
3. You can't make your kids not want what they want.
4. It's okay, at least right now, for them to want what they want and not want what they don't want.

When we make the point in lectures that you can't make someone do something against his will, many people will nod their heads in agreement, as if this were completely obvious. But others will vehemently disagree. (A psychologist in Bill's practice said, "Don't tell that to my kids!") This question of enforcement can evoke an intensely emotional reaction. When Bill said this to a group of teachers and tutors, one teacher angrily argued, "Of course you can. I make my kids do things all the time." But this isn't really true. Suppose your child doesn't want to eat what he is served and you set about to "make him." What do you do? Do you force the child's mouth open, put food in it, and move his jaws up and down? If you do, who's really eating? The child isn't eating—he's being force-fed. With homework, if a child truly resists your attempts to get him to work, what are you going to do? Prop his eyes open, move the book in front of his face? Even if this were possible and actually worked, would it be good for him? Would he actually learn?

Ned had a student whose mom insisted that she apply to the University of Chicago if she didn't get into her first choice school. "But Mom," she said, "I don't even like Chicago."

"It doesn't matter," said the mom. "It's a very good school."

"I won't apply," said the daughter.

"I'll send in an application for you. I'll have your older sister write the essays," said the mom.

Thankfully, the girl got into her first choice before anyone's resolve was put to the test, but we worry about the ongoing dynamic in that family.

At times, we can stop children and teenagers from doing things we don't want them to do by physically restraining them or coming up with onerous consequences. We can physically do things to them, like carry them to the dentist's office kicking and screaming. We can try to reframe the proposition in an effort to get their cooperation or buy in. And we can try to motivate them by offering incentives or making threats. But the reality is that you can't really make them do anything. We do not live in the totalitarian world of *A Clockwork Orange,* where people's behavior can be controlled by hooking them up to machines. The best we can do is make it unpleasant enough so that they will comply. Even if this method sometimes seems to work in the short term, it doesn't work at all in the long term. It's like fear—a short-term motivator that will get you to run fast, but with negative long-term implications, because who can really live that way?

Coming to peace with the reality that you can't make your kid do things is liberating. You can take the pressure off. The next time you find yourself trying to force your child to do something, you might stop and remind yourself, "Something's wrong with this picture. I'm acting like I can make my child do this, and I actually can't."

This is the message Bill conveyed to Jonah's parents. He explained that their attempts to assert control triggered Jonah's determination to reassert his own control, even if it meant doing the opposite of what was in his own best interest. By communicating to Jonah that he was ultimately responsible for his homework, his parents would release him from the reflex to fight tooth and nail against any display of dominance. Bill also wanted Jonah's parents to understand that just because they were worried about some of his choices didn't mean they had to constantly project a tone of disapproval. They could—and should—have fun and relax with him without thinking that every minute of their time together needed to signal the gravity of the situation.

"So what are you saying?" his parents asked. "That we should just let him fail?"

Their question reflects a common misconception. Parents tend to think there are two ways to be: autocratic or permissive. Autocratic parenting places a premium on obedience, and permissive parents emphasize the importance of their child's happiness and attempt to fulfill their child's desires to make them happy.

But virtually all child development experts, including influential psychologists and authors like Madeline Levine and Laurence Steinberg, have advocated a third option: authoritative parenting. This entails being supportive, but not controlling. Authoritative parents want their kids to cooperate because they like and respect them, and want kids to learn from their own experiences. At least sixty years of research has validated the fact that authoritative parenting is the most effective approach.[2] It emphasizes self-direction and values maturity over obedience. It's a style that sends the message, "I am going to do everything I can to help you be successful, but I'm not going to try to force you to do things because I say so." Authoritative parents don't give their children free rein. They enforce limits, and say when they don't feel right about something, but they are not controlling. With authoritative parenting, the child's developing brain doesn't spend enormous amounts of energy resisting what's often in their own best interest.

Jonah's parents took Bill's advice, though it was not easy. Instead of asking, "Do you have homework tonight?" his mom started saying, "Is there anything you'd like help with tonight? I'd like to know, so I can plan my evening." She made it clear that she was willing to do what she could to help, and that she'd set aside time to help him if he wanted help. She made sure there was a quiet room for him to study without distractions. She offered to hire a tutor or an older high school kid to come over and help. (Many children who fight their parents during homework time will work eagerly for a tutor or a high school student, who can be employed at relatively low cost as a homework tutor.) But Jonah's parents also said, "What we're not willing to do is to act like it's our job to make you work—because we'll weaken you if we do." And as you'll see when we pick Jonah's story back up, it worked.

Why the Brain Likes the Consultant Model

Some parents who are familiar with research on brain development say, "How could I possibly trust my kid to be responsible for his education? His brain isn't mature yet." This is true at some level—his sense of judgment is still developing. But that's just it: he needs room to develop. Kids need responsibility more than they deserve it. For most adolescents, and even for younger kids, waiting until they are mature enough to get all their homework done and to turn it in on time before giving up the enforcer role means you've waited too long. As we mentioned, the parts of the prefrontal cortex that regulate emotions don't mature until you reach your early thirties, but we'd be hard pressed to find a parent who would want to wait that long to let their "kids" make their own decisions.

The brain develops according to how it's used. By giving your child the opportunity to make decisions for herself while still young, you will help her brain build the circuits that are necessary for resilience in the face of stress. A small experience of control over her circumstances, such as choosing her own clothing or decorating her own room, will activate her prefrontal cortex and condition it to respond effectively.[3] Strengthened by this sense of control, the brain's Pilot grows stronger, rather than ceding power to the Lion Fighter at the first hint of stress. By giving your five-year-old the ability to wear clashing clothes if she chooses, you will be helping her to cope better in every situation, including those she can't control, such as where she's seated in a testing room, or when someone breaks up with her.

Granted, the path to an activated prefrontal cortex is sometimes painful (and not just visually). Remember the motivational saying "Anything worth doing well is worth doing badly first"? Well, there's a famous model that says there are four stages of competency,[4] which is another (albeit more long-winded) way of saying the same thing:

Stage 1: Unconsciously incompetent. This is the kid who thinks, "I'm fine. I don't need to study math, I've got this." In reality, he hasn't a clue. This is when it's easiest to get off track as a consultant. You can see the doomed test ahead, and you want to help him avoid the failure. But once you have offered help and he has made it clear that he doesn't want it, you really can't enlighten him as to his incompetence, nor should you. To be clear, this kid will *bomb.* . . . But then he'll move on, and if you can help him get the message that a failure is nothing more than a temporary stumble to learn from, he will have learned a valuable lesson.

Stage 2: Consciously incompetent. The kid now thinks, "Okay, wow. That was harder than I thought. I guess I need to study math." He still doesn't have a handle on the material, but he knows that. He'll usually take the next step and, you know, *study.*

Stage 3: Consciously competent. The kid thinks, "I've studied really hard, I know my math, this test will be fine." He's right. We're delighted when our kids get here. This is the dream, people.

Stage 4: Unconsciously competent. Fast-forward twenty years, and that kid is now a parent. He's been doing math for so long that he doesn't even have to think about it anymore. He can't really understand why his daughter is struggling so much with something that's become like breathing to him. (Incidentally, this is why older kids often make better tutors than parents. They learned their times tables not so long ago themselves, so they remember all the steps it took before it really sunk in.) Kids might become unconsciously competent in some areas—like reading or tying their shoelaces—while they're still living at home, but for the most part, you don't need to worry about Stage 4 except to note when you yourself might be in it.

We want our kids to get to Stage 3, the consciously competent stage, but we can't do that without letting them graduate through the other stages on their own. You shouldn't be absent during this process; you should be standing behind them, offering support and guidance the whole time.

With some kids, taking a step back the way Jonah's parents did is enough. Once the kids have control over their schoolwork, they rise to the occasion. Many will flounder at first, as Jonah did. His day-to-day relationship with his parents improved, but his poor performance continued for several months. Then one day he met with his guidance counselor, who pointed out that he would need to plan for an extra year of high school as he wasn't meeting the requirements for graduation. This got Jonah's attention. It meant he wouldn't be graduating with his friends. He started paying more attention to schoolwork, and asked his parents for help. He actually went to night school on top of his regular school day for two years in order to graduate on time. He went on to be successful in college as a psychology major, something his parents would at one time have hardly believed possible.

There's another moral to Jonah's story. Teachers can teach, coaches can coach, guidance counselors can outline graduation requirements, but there's one thing only parents can do: love their kids unconditionally and provide them with a safe base at home. For children who are stressed at school or in other parts of their lives, home should be a safe haven, a place to rest and recover. When kids feel that they are deeply loved even when they're struggling, it builds resilience. Battling your child about due dates and lost work sheets invites school stress to take root at home. So instead of nagging, arguing, and constant reminding, we recommend repeating the mantra, "I love you too much to fight with you about your homework."

Think of kids yelling out "I'm on base" during games of tag to prove they are safe to rest and regroup. When home is a safe base, kids and teens feel freer to explore the possibilities away from home in healthy ways. They'll return periodically, checking back in for reassurance and security. Without that sense of security, teens will tend to swing in two different directions: folding in on themselves, or leaving home every chance they get, desperate to create a safe base somewhere else. The dots connect themselves: if there's a lot of stress at home, kids are much more susceptible to risky behavior.

One parent said recently that deciding not to fight "lowered the temperature in our house by twenty degrees." Because it takes two to fight, fights don't usually last very long if you decide you won't give in to it. As a famed psychiatrist put it, "Choosing not to fight takes the sail out of a child's wind."[5]

Over the years, dozens of parents have told us that the safe base idea and the message "I love you too much to fight with you about your homework" have radically transformed their family lives.

In my first few months working as a neuropsychologist, I saw two kids with ADHD in the same week. One was a bright second-grade girl who would not go outside to play on school days until she had finished her homework. The other was a bright second-semester college freshman who had flunked three of his four first-semester courses, largely because he did very little work and eventually stopped going to class (which his parents only learned after he was placed on academic probation). When I saw him in late March, his parents said that, by their son's report, he was doing much better, attending all his classes, going to the library every night, and seeking out his professors for extra help. When I spoke to him one-on-one, I found out that in fact he hadn't been to a class in three weeks and would probably fail all his courses.

As I talked more with this boy and his parents, I learned that like many kids with ADHD, he had needed extensive tutoring and extra supervision through much of his school career and that he generally resisted doing schoolwork until someone—parent, teacher, tutor, or coach—got on him. He had spent much of the incredible energy with which adolescents are blessed resisting others' attempts to get him to do what he did not want to do—or, to put it another way, resisting what was probably in his own best interest.

The difference in attitude and performance of these two kids was not a matter of brain maturation or emotional maturity (she was eight and he was nineteen), and while ADHD is what brought them to my office, that diagnosis is beside the point here. The real issue was the internalized sense of who's responsible for what. The girl accurately saw her homework as her responsibility and willingly did it, further strengthening her sense of mastery and autonomy. Throughout his life the boy saw homework as something that was being forced on him and that he didn't need to think about because someone eventually would get on him about it. This mindset didn't translate into college success. He had a very low sense of control regarding his own academic life, accompanied by a lot of anxiety, difficulty sleeping, and emerging depression. He did get back on track eventually. But it took time and a break from school until he determined that he was ready to try again.

—Bill

"But . . .": The Challenge of Parent as Consultant

We recognize the parent-as-consultant model is easier said than done. We hear *plenty* from parents who, even though they're philosophically on board, experience situations in which they find themselves inching from consultant to policeman. Here are some of the most common concerns and how we respond:

"I tried to let him do his homework on his own for a week, but he didn't do any of it. It clearly didn't work."

On the contrary, it worked perfectly. He didn't do his homework without your being on him, and now he gets to figure out how to solve the problem. The idea that once you hand over responsibility, your child will take it up with aplomb is mistaken. As the dynamic changes, it takes time for him—and you—to adjust and develop the skills needed to do things differently. You need to take a long view. And that long view is that he can't do it perfectly the first time out, or do it as well as you would with decades more experience. Remember that he needs to build competency. He needs to learn firsthand what he doesn't know before he can become consciously competent.

"It sounds to me like what you're suggesting is laissez-faire parenting. Like I should just let my kid do whatever he wants."

Definitely not. You should set limits, and you should be involved in problem solving, both of which we cover in the next chapter. Kids feel safer and will be more self-motivated when they know that adults will take care of the things they're not yet ready to take care of themselves. In no way do we think you should shrug your shoulders and say, "Sink or swim, buddy." Offer a life raft every step of the way, in the form of your counsel. Tell your child what you're worried about, and talk those points through. In this way, you are supportive and engaged, but you're not steering the boat. So many parents have swung so far the other way that anything less than total control seems irresponsible.

"What about things like practicing a musical instrument? My kid won't practice on his own, but it's important to me that he learn to appreciate and understand music."

We strongly support music training for kids, in part because there are few things that are better for the developing brain. At the same time, Bill has always been grateful to his own parents for letting him quit piano lessons in third grade—and not ruining music for him. Bill's parents could tell that he had some musical ability and were willing to get him the instrument he wanted to play (the accordion—don't ask), but they insisted that he first demonstrate that he could practice regularly on the piano that the family already had. Because Bill was pretty good at picking out tunes by ear, he chafed at being required to read music, and asked to quit after about four months of lessons, to which his parents agreed. Six years later, when the Beatles came to America, Bill took electric bass lessons and organ lessons and taught himself to play guitar—all in order to play the music he wanted to play. Today Bill still plays in a rock band and spends a fair amount of time every week playing and singing—much more so than most of his friends who were "made" to practice as children. He has also followed many kids who quit their lessons with their parents' blessing and later passionately took up the same instrument or another one when they didn't feel forced.

The fact is that many kids love to play an instrument, practice independently, and experience playing in the school band or orchestra as the most enjoyable thing in their life. Many other kids are willing to go along with practicing, even if they don't love it. They know that their parents want them to play, and they sometimes like a particular piece of music or feel proud that they can play. The challenge is what to do with kids who don't go along—and *really* don't want to go to their lessons or practice their instrument. Because it's impossible to make a truly resistant kid practice, and because chronically fighting about anything is not healthy for families, we recommend taking the same approach that we recommend for homework: consult, but don't force.

Explain to your child how important music is to you and your family. Let him know that for many people, it brings great happiness and satisfaction. Tell him that although it's a lot of work, it's worth it if you learn to play. Tell him you want him to be able to play, that you're willing to pay for lessons as long as his teacher says he's practicing enough, and that you're willing to help in any way you can to make practicing an enjoyable experience. But as with homework, also tell him that you're not willing to fight with him about practicing because you love him and don't want a constant hassle at home—and you don't want to ruin music for him by making it nothing but a chore. If the child starts lessons, offer to help him develop a practice schedule. Tell him that you're willing to sit with him during practice time and that if he wants to practice but just can't make himself do it, you'll offer a little incentive.

If your child strongly resists going to lessons and/or practicing, suggest that he take a break from lessons for three months and see if he misses playing. If he does, he can always start again. If he doesn't, he may want to play at another time when something makes it more appealing (e.g., The Beatles). If that doesn't help either, remember that most adults don't play an instrument and that playing an instrument isn't necessary for music to be an enriching part of one's life.

"What about playing a sport? Exercise is critical, and there's so much social currency in playing on a team, particularly for boys. But my kid wouldn't do it if he weren't forced."

Many kids love sports and would play all day if they were allowed to. Many others, though, hate team sports, which puts their parents in a bind because they know that exercise is important for kids, as is the social dimension of being part of a team. But trying to force a kid to play a sport is painful for everyone.

We encourage parents to teach their children that movement is crucial for good health, and we want parents to help kids find ways of moving that they really enjoy. We suggest parents say something like, "In our family, everybody does something active. Let's try different things and find out what works for you." We support parents in signing kids up for soccer, T-ball, gymnastics, or swimming lessons when they're young, so long as their kids have some interest in doing so.

Many kids, especially those who aren't very athletic, don't like organized sports. For some, it's the social challenges inherent in being on a team. For others, it's the drudgery of practice or the stress of constantly being told what to do, or the embarrassment of not being very good in front of their friends. Trying to force these kids to play a team sport is not a good idea. For these kids, we recommend enforcing the family rule that everybody does something active—and encouraging them to explore individual sports that most other kids don't participate in, like fencing, which can allow a child to excel at something in relation to most of his peers. We also recommend swimming, rock climbing, horseback riding, and martial arts—all things that kids can get better and better at through practice, and where most of the competition is with one's own previous personal best.

"I tried giving my daughter control of her homework, offering my help if she needs it. But she turned me down and now her teacher is pressuring me to become more involved."

This scenario can be extremely stressful, especially if you feel you're the only parent who isn't 100 percent on top of your kid's homework. Start by thinking about why you're hearing from the teacher at all. In today's world, accountability has shifted away from kids and onto teachers. If a child doesn't perform well, parents (and often schools) blame the teacher. Teachers are conditioned to think that somebody needs to make the kids do the work. They may well be scarred by parents blasting them for poor report cards, or fearful that if their students perform poorly on tests, it will jeopardize their job security. So we suggest you start by explaining that 1) you do not want to weaken your child by taking responsibility for her work, and 2) you have not found it useful to try to monitor her assignments against her will or try to force her to do her homework. Teachers may be shocked or delighted by parents who take the consultant approach. In our experience, making homework an issue between the child and her school is usually effective. Be clear with the school that you're willing to help, but that you're reminding your child it's her responsibility.

Ned found himself in a situation much like this when he and his wife decided to give their son more responsibility for his work. He stumbled, and the teacher wrote the following e-mail:

> I've noticed that over the last few months Matthew has been scrambling to finish homework during the advisory time before the day begins and seems really stressed about it. Do you get the sense that he has not finished his homework when he leaves for school in the morning, or is it more that he has forgotten about assignments and is rushing to finish them before class?
>
> I'm just wondering if perhaps he needs some more coaching about managing homework completion at home. I also know he is busy outside of school with many commitments, so I'm not sure if he simply doesn't have enough time at night or over the weekend to finish his homework given all that he has going on.
>
> Let me know any insights as to how I might help him so he doesn't get so crunched time-wise. I want this last month of middle school to be as enjoyable as possible for him.

Here's Ned's response:

> Many thanks for writing. Matthew is doing work last minute because he hasn't finished his assignments. We have worked hard this year to avoid asking, "Have you done it? Are you finished?" and

instead asking, "Do you need help with any of your work? Do you have a plan? Have you got it?" My belief is that he, like many boys, only works under pressure. So he dawdles in the evenings and rushes in the morning, in part because that's the final deadline.

If you think it seems reasonable, might you ask, "Hey, Matthew, you seem stressed about getting your work done last minute. Would you like to talk about how to make that better?"

I love that you want to have the end of eighth grade be fun and less stressed. We want that too for him. If you have specific advice for us, we are learning too.

"I used to let my kids do their homework on their own, but once they hit high school, the stakes became too high."

You're right. The stakes are high, particularly in eleventh grade. But not just because of college admission. Your real challenge is to raise a child who is capable of acting in his or her own best interest. And think of the message you're sending when you take hold of the reins: "We've trusted you in the past, but when things really matter, it would be a mistake to let you be in control." If you give them that message, they are much more likely to flounder in college when they suddenly find themselves in charge of their own time and without supervision.

"I set my consulting hours from seven to eight, but my daughter wastes a lot of that time by not focusing, and then gets upset when it's eight and I need to move on to other things. Should I stay to help her longer?"

You can work overtime, but only as a reward to your child for good effort. If she's worked hard the whole time you've allotted, but the material is particularly challenging, by all means, help her until she's done. But if not, we'd suggest you tell her that you'd be happy to help her again the next evening from 7:00 until 8:00, and hopefully she'll focus more. Similarly, if your kid passes on your offer to help with homework at the appointed hour, but then comes to you for help at 9:00 or 10:00, say, "The time for homework has passed. It's time for bed. You need your rest so you can think clearly tomorrow, and so do I." If she wants to get up early to complete it, that's fine, but you shouldn't help her. Your consulting hours are clear, and she can either take advantage of them or not. That said, if she procrastinates only occasionally, you should feel free to make exceptions and help her out.

"My son's basketball coach is more like the autocratic model you talk about, and it works—he gets great results from my kid! Why wouldn't it work with me?"

That's great, but don't forget, your roles are different. Your child can elect to sign up for basketball, and is thereby choosing to be bossed around by this coach. Playing on a sports team is a controllable stressor. That coach has many kids to keep an eye on and a mutual (relatively short-term) goal that he's trying to help everyone achieve. It's totally different with you. Remember, while teachers can teach and coaches can coach (and cut your kid from the team), only you can be the safe base.

"If our son's not successful, we're worried that he'll feel bad about himself and could get depressed."

The implication here is that you feel you have to protect your son from himself. In actuality, he is much more likely to get depressed from a low sense of control than from experiencing a failure, especially if you are supportive in the aftermath and help him see it as a learning opportunity and not The End.

"Doing well in school is the most important thing for a successful future."

We disagree. We think that developing a clear sense of who's responsible for what is more important than always doing well. That is the key to raising a self-driven child.

"My daughter is in second grade, and the expectation for all the parents in her class is that we log on to the school's system and help our kids track their homework. Is this wrong?"

If your child values your help and support, and if she's too young to log on and keep track of her assignments herself—which second graders are—then there's no harm in helping her manage it. But don't monitor it. In other words, you might help her log on, and you might say, "Oh, it looks like you have a math work sheet due tomorrow. Would you like help with that?" but don't then make her sit down to do it, or follow up to make sure she's done it. You've informed her, and you've offered to be there for her. That's all that's needed. Also, be careful that as she gets older and more capable, you don't retain the role out of habit. We recognize that there comes a point when a child no longer needs help getting dressed or putting on her shoes, and we also need to recognize the point when that child no longer needs our help managing her homework.

"I don't want my child to make the same mistakes I made."

Bill hears this a lot. He usually responds by asking the parent whether she felt she learned from her mistakes and, if she had to do it over again, whether she would choose not to make these mistakes—and thus not have learned from them. Sometimes this leads to the parent suggesting that she is worried that the child will turn out like her. Bill then asks, "Would it be okay if your child turned out like you?" If the answer is no, Bill knows his real work is to help that parent be more accepting of himself or herself.

"If I'm not on him all the time, I'm worried that he won't reach his potential."

Kids won't reach their potential by constantly being driven. In fact, the opposite is true; they will do what is necessary to get you off their back, but they won't do more. People go the extra mile when it matters to them, not when it matters to you.

The Big Picture

The parent-as-consultant model takes some getting used to. In the next chapter, we will dig in deeper to consider what it looks like when you step back and let kids make decisions. But there are a few big-picture thoughts we want to leave you with before moving on.

Your lack of control as a parent is good news, even if it may not seem so at first glance. When Ned's son was in the fifth grade, he tried to blame his mom, Vanessa, when he failed to complete an assignment. "Well, you didn't remind me to do it," he said. In his defense, he had every expectation that his mom would check his assignments, because she usually did. So as a family, they talked about how, from that moment forward, it wasn't Vanessa's responsibility and she should no longer act as if it were. Ned and Vanessa made it clear they would be happy to remind Matthew to do his homework if he wanted this reminding, or to help if he really needed help, but that ultimately Matthew's homework was Matthew's responsibility.

When we strip away all the angst and fighting over homework, it's amazing what will sometimes happen. When Matthew was left in charge of his homework, he messed up at first. On one occasion, he did poorly on a science test (his favorite subject) because he studied the entirely wrong sheet. Whoops! There was no fighting afterward, no "I told you so," no determination on Ned or Vanessa's part to swoop back in for the next test (though it took some self-discipline). Instead, there was a non-loaded discussion about what went wrong from Matthew's point of view, and what his thinking was about how to fix it.

As it turned out, though Matthew had botched the test, he was fascinated by the material it covered (the biological principles of life). The whole family went hiking the weekend after the test, and as they walked, Ned asked Matthew more about what he'd learned. Matthew went on and on enthusiastically about the subject of the test. He revealed that he'd spent quite a bit of time independently researching the topic since the test. Top grade? No. Real curiosity and learning? Yes!

Botched tests and missed homework aren't what we're going for, of course. But we would all do well to remember the big picture: that we want our kids to be thoughtful learners, and want them to be self-disciplined, not well disciplined. Assuming authority over your kids' responsibilities robs you of quality time and takes away home as a safe base. A mom recently told us she had been bemoaning her latest battle with her teenage son when one of her friends, whose son was in his twenties, told her, "It's not worth the fight. One of my greatest regrets is that the last few years my son lived at home, we spent most of the time fighting about homework. I wish I could have those days back and just enjoy him. Now all that fighting seems so pointless and I feel like I missed out on him."

What to Do Tonight

- Practice asking, "Who is responsible for this?" "Whose problem is it?"

- Determine if your home is a safe base. Do you fight frequently about food or screen time? What's the emotional temperature? If you are feeling frustrated with your kid, chances are he is with you as well. Ask him.

- If a kid hates or resists homework, suggest a homework club at school, find older kids to work with him, or approach your child's teacher about minimizing mandatory homework. If your child's strong negative reactions to homework are out of character, have your child evaluated to rule out a problem like a learning disability.

- Help your child create an effective learning environment and, if necessary, develop her own system of rewards for completing goals. If she does not meet a goal, respond with compassion: "I'm sorry you weren't able to meet your goals tonight." Don't get angry or threaten punishment. Your job is to help her develop ways to motivate herself.

- Express confidence in your child's ability to figure things out.

CHAPTER THREE

"It's Your Call"

Kids as Decision Makers

W HEN MATT WAS IN HIGH SCHOOL, he had an insatiable need for independence. Give him a rule and he'd break it. Set down a curfew and he'd sit in the driveway an extra half hour rather than comply. Matt wasn't a jerk. He was just allergic to complying with other people's imperatives. He suffered from anxiety, and feeling out of control gave him acute stress.

His parents set a high value on their relationship with their son, and a fairly low one on determining the choices he made day by day, even choices that could—and did—affect his future. Here's what happened, in Matt's words:

> *I turned eighteen halfway through my senior year of high school and my mom signed a notarized letter to my school making me my own legal guardian, which meant that for the rest of that year I could sign myself out of school anytime I wanted and my parents couldn't access any of my private information, including grades. I don't really know why she agreed to do this. I think she wanted me to know that she believed in me as an individual, that I had an adult life fast approaching, and that I'd better decide for myself what I wanted to do with it. Anyway, it meant a lot to me. So much so that I never abused the privilege.*

That's not true. I completely abused the privilege, and it was amazing. The lady working in the student services office at school would have a slip already filled out for me every day and I would walk into her office, skip the line of students waiting for her to help them, get my slip, and leave. Maybe somehow my mom knew how awesome that would make me feel. For once in my life, I felt I was in control.

It was tough for Matt's parents to give him this freedom, but they realized at some deeper level that this was what he needed. Matt graduated from high school, and then bounced through a few different colleges before getting his degree. By his midtwenties, he had conquered his anxiety. Now, years later, Matt runs a successful think tank in Washington, DC, and draws on his childhood lessons to parent his own children.

Matt credits his parents' support for his long-term success. "Though I went to several different colleges before getting my degree, I wouldn't have gone to college if they hadn't helped me learn to figure this out myself, without breathing down my neck."

As you can probably sense, if Chapter Two nudged you to the edge of your comfort zone, this chapter is likely to push you over the edge. We've talked about your role as a consultant. Now it's time to delve into the point of view of your child and to consider what it actually looks like when he or she is a decision maker.

Panicked yet? Don't be. Start with the basics, by adopting the following three precepts when it comes to your kids:

1. "You are the expert on you."
2. "You have a brain in your head."
3. "You want your life to work."

When you buy into these three things, it's much easier to tell your kid, "It's your call. I have confidence in your ability to make informed decisions about your own life and to learn from your mistakes." The trick is, you can't *just* tell them this—you have to follow through. Sometimes you won't like their decisions, but unless they're outrageous, we suggest that you let them go with them anyway.

Bill recently sat with Greg, the father of a bright twelve-year-old girl who was unhappy at her new private school and wanted to return to public school. When Bill suggested that he let his daughter decide where it made the most sense for her to go, Greg practically laughed and expressed the common view that important decisions by definition are *too important* for young people to make themselves. "I'm not letting a twelve-year-old make that kind of decision," he said. He assumed that he knew what was right for his daughter, and he didn't want to entrust the decision to her because he was fairly sure she would not do what he wanted. Many other parents come to this conclusion, too, reasoning that young people do not have anywhere near the range of experience or knowledge about life that their parents do, and that they are likely to prioritize emotional concerns like familiarity and friendship.

This is true. But when we say we want children and teens to make their own decisions as much as possible, what we really want is for them to make *informed* decisions. It's our responsibility as parents to give the information and the perspective that we have—and that they lack—in order to enable them to make the best possible choices. Once properly informed, kids usually do make good decisions for themselves—and their decisions are almost always as good as or better than our own.

In this chapter, we'll first clarify what kids as decision makers *does not* look like, and outline the exceptional cases—the kids who are just not ready. Then we'll make a compelling argument (irrefutable, really!) for why you should encourage your kids to make informed decisions, and be willing to go with these decisions unless doing so would be nuts. We'll also explain what kids as decision makers looks like as children grow, so that you are equipped to implement this strategy whether your child is two or twenty-two. Finally, as in the previous chapter, we'll cover why giving up control is so hard to do, and will recount the most common questions and concerns we get from parents on the subject. We'd bet money that some will sound familiar.

What "It's Your Call" *Doesn't* Mean

"It's your call" does not mean kids get to call all the shots at home so that the family is ruled by its youngest members. ("Chocolate cake for dinner every night!") You have rights and feelings as a parent, and you shouldn't bury them. If your five-year-old is dead set on going to the zoo but you're tired, we're not suggesting that you take her. And if your sixteen-year-old wants to drive at night to a concert in another city but you have safety concerns, trust your instincts. As a parent, you have to do what feels right to you, and you should help your child understand that. "I can't in good conscience let you make that decision. It doesn't feel right" is a perfectly reasonable thing to say. So is "It's your sister's turn to pick a movie tonight. You get to choose next week."

"It's your call" does not conflict with limit setting, which will always be an essential part of parenting. If a young child refuses to stop doing something he's enjoying, like playing in the park, you want to stay calm, practice empathy, and offer choices. ("Would you like to finish up your game? We need to move on now, but would you like five more minutes?") If after that he still won't comply, it's entirely appropriate to say, "Do you want to hold my hand or should I carry you?" If the child will not agree to hold your hand, pick him up and carry him to the car—even if he's kicking and screaming. Before the next outing to the park, you might say,

"I'm willing to go to the park if you will follow a five-minute warning when it's time to leave. I'm not willing to chase you around or fight with you, and if leaving is a big hassle again, we'll wait for a couple of days (or a week) before we go back to the park."

Though we can't carry a kicking adolescent around, there are still ways to set limits with teens when it's necessary, and that's by limiting what we are willing to do for him. We can say to a teen who spends too much time texting that we cannot in good conscience pay for their phone. We need to set clear ground rules, while keeping in mind that our ultimate goal is not to produce compliant children as much as children who understand how to act and interact successfully in this world.

"It's your call" isn't about giving kids unlimited choices. That, in fact, is a sure way to stress them out. As we mentioned in Chapter One, kids feel most secure when they know that adults are there to make the decisions they're not yet ready to make themselves. Part of the reason why laissez-faire parenting doesn't work very well is that kids find it stressful if they have to do something they're not prepared to do. We know kids feel most comfortable when the world feels safe, and the world will feel safest to them when we create an environment that's predictable and structured.

Finally, "It's your call" isn't about manipulation, or sneakily getting kids to think a decision is theirs when it's really yours. You want to parent with honesty—that's what builds trust. You want to show your kids that you have respect for them. And if you're going to foster autonomy, you *have* to genuinely let them have more control, bit by bit.

So what does "It's your call" mean? Most simply: When it comes to making decisions about your kids' lives, you should not be deciding things that they are capable of deciding for themselves. First, set boundaries within which you feel comfortable letting them maneuver. Then cede ground outside those boundaries. Help your kids learn what information they need to make an informed decision. If there's conflict surrounding an issue, use collaborative problem solving, a technique developed by Ross Greene and J. Stuart Albon that begins with an expression of empathy followed by a reassurance that you're not going to try to use the force of your will to get your child to do something he doesn't want to do. Together, you identify possible solutions you're both comfortable with and figure out how to get there. If your child settles on a choice that isn't crazy go with it, even if it is not what you would like him to do.[1]

"Crazy" will be defined differently by different people, of course. A helpful yardstick is to ask if most reasonable people (like an aunt or uncle, a teacher or coach) would consider the choice to be a terrible one. We wouldn't consider it crazy for Greg's bright twelve-year-old to decide to go back to her local public school. The school may have had fewer resources than the private school her parents decided to switch her to, and some of the classes may have been less well taught, but if she felt at ease and surrounded by supportive friends, it is possible that she would perform better and be happier. If she decided she wanted to leave home and join the circus, that would be another matter.

There are a number of situations in which a child can't be trusted to make a good decision. If Greg's daughter were not willing to listen to pros and cons and solicit advice, it may not be her call after all. Your kids have to be willing to listen and to think the options through, period.

Beyond this, if a child is seriously depressed or suicidal, all bets are off. Her logic is impaired and you cannot start with the baseline belief that she wants her life to work out. People who are depressed can't think clearly, as depression is defined, in part, by disordered thinking. Likewise, if a kid is dependent on alcohol or drugs or engaging in self-harm, he or she cannot adequately weigh the pros and cons and come to a good decision. We at times need to make decisions for kids who are temporarily not capable of making reasonable informed decisions for themselves, but the general principle still holds.

6 Reasons Why We're Right

1. Science is on our side.

When you are given room to make your own decisions, it allows you to feel in charge in other contexts. The brain is learning to make hard choices and protecting itself from the stress of feeling helpless. It is also benefitting from the internal motivation that comes from autonomy. The more experience kids have of managing their own stress and overcoming their own challenges, the more their prefrontal cortex will be able to regulate their amygdala.

Many of our clients are familiar with research on adolescent brain development. They know that teenagers have a tendency to take seemingly stupid risks, especially when they're around friends. These parents know that the prefrontal cortex hasn't fully matured. But as we pointed out in Chapter Two, it doesn't make sense to wait until your children's brains have fully matured before entrusting them with decisions, or you would be waiting until their late twenties or early thirties. The brain develops according to how it's used. This means that by encouraging our kids—and requiring our adolescents—to make their own decisions, we are giving them invaluable experience in assessing their own needs honestly, paying attention to their feelings and motivations, weighing pros and cons, and trying to make the best possible decision for themselves. We help them develop a brain that's used to making hard choices and owning them. This is huge and will pay big future dividends.

2. Kids shouldn't feel like an empty extension of their parents.

When we try to direct our kids' lives, we might see short-term gains, but there will be long-term losses. Kids often resist doing what is good for them if they feel pressured to do so (remember Matt, sitting in the driveway so as not to be on time for curfew). If they happen to be the type of child who will comply rather than rebel, there's still a problem: if they succeed later in life, they'll feel like impostors, like the success isn't really theirs. Therapist and writer Lori Gottlieb wrote an article for the *Atlantic* questioning why so many of her twentysomething patients were unaccountably depressed, even though they had great parents and on the surface great lives. This category of patients stumped her until she discovered the right questions to ask. "Back in graduate school," she wrote, "the clinical focus had always been on how the lack of parental attunement affects the child. It never occurred to any of us to ask, what if the parents are too attuned? What happens to those kids?"[2]

She explores this question through the example of a toddler who falls and whose parent swoops in to pick her up before she even has a chance to register what's happened. The parent is working like mad to make sure the child doesn't suffer—but why? Suffering, though painful to watch, is essential for the development of resilience. Does it hurt them too much to see their child suffer? Or do they need to feel needed?

We see this type of helicopter parenting, and its consequences, all the time. Sarah, a student of Ned's, came to see him with her parents before going abroad for a semester. At the meeting, her mom and dad explained their goals and concerns about the coming semester. They asked questions like, "What should we do about the math she'll miss? How will we handle the SAT?" Her parents did most of the talking, and though ultimately a plan was agreed to by all, Ned couldn't help feeling that Sarah was uncomfortable.

So the next time he met with her alone, he asked her how she really felt about it.

"The plan's fine," she said. "The problem is the *we*."

"What do you mean?"

"It's all 'We have to get a good score on this,' and 'We have to get good grades this year,' and 'We have to write better essays.'" Clearly, Sarah had been holding her frustration in for a while. "My parents aren't writing the essays, I am. There is no 'we' here, and it drives me crazy when they talk that way. It's my life and it's my work, and it's my stupid essay that I have to write."

Remember that magic line: "I have confidence in your ability to make informed decisions about your own life and to learn from your mistakes." Sarah's parents were communicating the exact opposite to her. It's the same, really, as the mother who refuses to let her toddler fall. Sarah was a bright, motivated girl and all she could hear was that her parents didn't trust her decisions, or even consider them hers to make.

3. Giving kids a sense of control is the only way to teach them competency—in decision making, and in whatever skill they're learning.

As the adage goes, "Wisdom comes from experience, and experience comes from bad decisions." Kids need to practice making their own decisions before they can do so legally. Telling our children how to make good decisions (or telling them how to do things for themselves) isn't enough. It's not enough to show them, either. They need to actually do it. They need practice. They need to experience the natural consequences of their choices, ranging from being uncomfortably cold when they decided not to wear a coat, to getting a bad grade on a test because they decided not to study. We commonly see adolescents and young adults go off to college without having had much of an opportunity to make decisions about the things that matter, including how they want to structure their time, what they want to commit their energy to, or whether they want to be in school at all. Not surprisingly, they have difficulty setting and meeting goals and making good decisions when it comes time to pick classes or a major or more generally to manage their day.

This is true for a variety of other life skills, too. One mom who brought her two kids in for tutoring with Ned asked if he accepted checks. Though she knew a credit card was easier all around, she wanted her kids to have the experience of actually writing a check so they'd know how to. It reminded Ned of how he had once stopped to check on a car by the side of the road with its hazard lights on. The car had a flat tire, but none of the kids in the car knew how to change the tire. Presumably, they'd all been shown how to as part of driver's ed. But you can watch a hundred videos on changing a tire and still be helpless if you've never actually done it. Sure, AAA would have been there in an hour. But that is an hour in the dark by the side of the road when you could be taking care of the problem yourself. Agency takes practice.

4. You don't always know what's best.

This may be a hard one to swallow, but it's really hard to know what's in your child's best interest. In part this is because you don't know who your kid wants to be—that's for him to figure out, ideally with your help. Also, what seems like a disaster often turns out to be a blessing in disguise. There are many paths to success, and sometimes we only find the right one by getting a little lost.

As parents, we often make decisions for our children that seem perfectly reasonable, like signing them up for soccer instead of drama, only to kick ourselves later. The same is true in our own lives. Most of us work too much, eat too much, sleep too little, make bad investments, and find ourselves in careers that do not go as planned. Remember to be humble. Sometimes you just don't know what's right.

In the first few months of his freshman year in college, Ned wanted to withdraw for a year. His parents, concerned that he wouldn't return, rejected the idea. He muddled his way through freshman year and when he found himself in the same funk sophomore year, he again tried to withdraw for the year. This time, his parents let him do it. That year off gave Ned a chance to step off the conveyor belt. It gave him a chance to decompress and think about what he really wanted to do. He didn't find all the answers, but he did return to college in a better place. It was during that second attempt at sophomore year that he joined an a cappella group, and he sings with several of its members to this day. Most important, in his junior year Ned started dating Vanessa, who is now his wife, and she is the one who turned him on to tutoring. Without that year off, he wouldn't be writing this book right now, and he wouldn't have the amazing kids he has. It's all very *It's a Wonderful Life,* but that movie is a classic for a reason. Serendipity is the stuff of life. All that parental planning isn't always for the better.

5. Kids are capable. Really.

When Bill first started to work as a neuropsychologist in 1985, it was common for students to repeat kindergarten or first grade. What struck him was how often he'd work with college students who, in response to being asked what year they were in school, replied, "I'm a sophomore in college. I should be a junior but my parents made me repeat first grade." These kids still carried an enormous grudge because a decision had been made about their lives over which they'd had no control—when they were six or seven. Eventually, although he was nervous about it at first, Bill started to advise parents of younger children to bring their child into the decision-making process. He suggested that they say something like, "No one is going to make you repeat first grade. It's going to be your call, but we want to think through the pluses and minuses of going on to second grade so that you have the information you need to make a good decision." What Bill found was that even young kids were consistently able to make a decision that was at least as good as the one adults might make for them. He also saw that when faced with a problem, a kid will often come up with a solution that neither parent had thought of. Several kids eventually said things like, "I'm not ready for second grade, and if kids tease me about repeating I'll just ignore them." Or, "I think I can do it. Can I have a tutor, though, to help me if the work is too hard?"

Over thirty years ago, a fascinating study looked at the decision-making abilities of kids from ages nine to twenty-one.[3] The study asked the participants how they would handle a really sensitive situation: a boy who refused to talk to family members or come out of his room for several weeks. Turns out, fourteen-year-olds made decisions that were very similar to those of eighteen-year-olds and twenty-one-year-olds. And those decisions resembled the recommendation made by most experts (which was that the boy get outpatient psychotherapy). Interestingly, half of the nine-year-olds chose that option, too. Overall, the fourteen-, eighteen-, and twenty-one-year-olds got virtually identical scores on decision making, and the nine-year-olds' scores were only slightly lower. We think this shows not only that nine-year-olds are capable decision makers, but also that when they come up short it's because of lack of knowledge, not necessarily judgment.

Robert Epstein, the former editor of *Psychology Today*, has written extensively about the power and potential of adolescence. Along with his colleague Diane Dumas, he developed a "test of adultness," which asks questions about love, leadership, interpersonal skills, and handling responsibility. He found that teens generally perform as well on this test as adults do.[4] (For the record, we both passed.) Epstein argues that here in America we infantilize adolescents, in part by acting as if they aren't capable of making responsible decisions. While we can't entirely stop teenagers from making impulsive choices, we can entrust them to make informed decisions about things that are important to them. Research has found that by the time kids are fourteen or fifteen, they generally have adult-level ability to make rational decisions. In fact, most cognitive processes reach adult levels by midadolescence.[5]

6. Good decision making requires emotional intelligence. Kids need to learn what matters to them.

Good decisions are informed by knowledge, but not just that. In the Pixar movie *Inside Out,* the characters Joy, Anger, Sadness, Disgust, and Fear share the control panel in a little girl's brain. The movie reflects a basic scientific truth: emotions play a crucial role in guiding our thinking, our decision making, and our behavior. It is impossible to evaluate whether something is good or bad, right or wrong, beneficial or harmful, without the guidance of our emotions. People whose emotional brain centers are damaged can't make simple decisions like whether to go out to dinner, because they don't know what they want.[6]

We want kids to pay attention to their emotions. That is not the same as saying that we want them to act impulsively and emotionally. If you're angry, that's not a good time to make a decision. What we're talking about is informed decision making. They have to be able to access feelings such as envy, guilt, compassion, and admiration in order to consider other people's needs and wants. They also have to know what to make of anger, jealousy, resentment, and hatred when they feel it.

How children *feel* about things and what they *want* are important components in their decision-making process—as important as the hard facts. However much we may want to override our kids' negative emotions, we can't. If a child is afraid after seeing a frightening movie, we can help her see that it is just a movie, but her response is real and will inform her readiness to watch a scary movie again. If a child is angry and feels betrayed, we can help her process her pain and learn to take a step back and consider the person she wants to be before retaliating. We want kids to practice tuning in to their own emotions, and asking, What's right for me?

A Sense of Control in Action

Encouraging your child to make informed decisions hinges on your being behind them and offering guidance. It means saying something like, "I trust you to make a good decision, and this will ultimately be your call, but I want to be sure you make the best decision possible, so I'd like to help you think through the pros and cons of either option. I also want you to talk to people who have more experience and to get their feedback. Finally, I think it's important that we talk together about a possible Plan B if your decision doesn't go the way you want."

There are many messages in this "speech." You are letting your child know, first and foremost, that you trust him. You are making it clear that you are present and that you will support him. You are helping him to think through what kinds of information he needs to make a good decision. And you are helping to gird him against setback, framing a misstep not as a failure but as a signal that it's time to come up with another plan.

Obviously, you can't use this exact speech at every age. But its basic principles can be marshaled even with very young children. Here are some examples of what "It's your call" looks like through the ages:

Toddlers: Offer to let them choose between two outfits. Or, if they are up to the challenge, let them dress themselves, offering your help but not forcing it on them. It may take them ages to put on their pants, and they may grapple with the frustration of not being able to do it correctly or easily. But they are learning to master important skills. You can also offer them agency within a larger framework. "Would you like to play with blocks or to paint?"

Preschoolers: Good preschool teachers have long known that one of the most important things they can offer children is an opportunity to make decisions about how to spend their time and what is important to them. There's a reason that "free choice time" is an important staple of the preschool world.

Parents of preschoolers can encourage dramatic play rather than video games or adult-organized activities such as sports. When children play in unstructured ways, they are making autonomous decisions about how to spend their time. They ask questions like, Should I make this cardboard box into a train or a castle? Should I dress up that doll or this one? Should I build a Lego airplane or a Lego vet clinic? Should I play dress-up or should I color?

When children are young, much of the work is demonstrating to them that they do have control. One wise friend of ours who was a parent educator for twenty years advises giving calendars to preschool-age children and writing down all the important events in their life, in part because it helps children understand the passage of time better, and how their days will unfold. We can't overstate the importance of the calendar tool in helping kids feel in control of their day. Have them cross off days of the week as you come to them. Spend time going over the schedule for the day, giving them choice in that schedule wherever possible. This communication expresses respect—they see that they are not just a tagalong to your day and your plans, and they understand what is going to happen, when, and why. As they get older, children will then start to write in important things for themselves, which further helps them develop their sense of control.

Elementary schoolers: As children get older, you can start to offer them more choices about what activities to participate in, what foods to eat to stay healthy, and what schedule would work for getting enough sleep. "It's your call" starts to make more sense to them. You might say something like, "I understand you really want to go to the movie opening tonight, and so do I. I will let you make the decision, but first let's think through the pros and cons. Because it's opening night, it's likely that the line will be very long, so we'll have to get there early and wait. It's cold outside, so you might be really cold while we wait. But to see the movie on its opening night with everyone else who is really excited about it would be fun." Let's say that the child decides to go to see the movie. Then you might say, "Great. Let's also think about a Plan B in case it doesn't work out the way we want it to. If you get tired in line or if there are no good seats available, how do you think we should handle that?"

A movie outing is a pretty innocuous proposition either way, but elementary-aged kids can also make good decisions when the stakes are higher. Bill recently met with the parents of an eleven-year-old boy with a learning disability. Andy's parents thought it was a good idea for him to work with a tutor through the summer. Andy thought not so much. Bill suggested that they offer to help Andy make an informed decision about whether to do it. They could explain to him that, if he didn't fight the tutoring and committed himself to it, it could change his brain in a way that would make reading and writing easier for him. Andy could remind himself that the tutoring would only take about 2 or 3 hours in a 168-hour week—there would still be plenty of time to have fun and recover from the stress of the school year. Those were the pros. But they should also acknowledge the cons. So Bill suggested they explain to Andy the benefits of downtime, of taking a break from school altogether and letting the brain develop without any stress at all.

Finally, the parents could say, "When I think about the pros and cons, I think it's a tough call. It could go either way. Ultimately, nobody knows what the right thing to do is in this situation better than you do. So I want you to decide, and I'm confident that you'll make a good decision and that you'll learn from whatever decision you make." The parents took Bill's advice, and Andy chose to forgo tutoring. It wasn't what the parents would have chosen, but it also wasn't crazy. They followed through with their promise that it was his call.

Let's look at what it might have looked like if Andy's parents *hadn't* given him the choice and had forced him to get a tutor:

Benefit: It's possible that a great tutor would light a fire under Andy and he'd be grateful later that his parents had insisted on tutoring. Or if Andy got into it and worked hard, we might have seen the pace of his academic development—and his confidence— improve slightly over the six or eight weeks of tutoring. More likely, Andy would do the sessions and maybe get a little bit (but not much) out of them because kids benefit very little from academic help they resist and don't feel they need or want.

Cost: Strain in the parent-child relationship would come from trying to force the child to do something he doesn't want to do. There would be negative consequences from essentially telling Andy, "I know better than you do. Your opinion doesn't matter." Andy would miss out on the empowerment that comes from really having to think about what's best for his future, and the maturation that would come from doing so. His parents would lose out on Andy's turning to them for advice.

Middle schoolers: In the greater Washington, DC, area where we live, one of the most important decisions parents make for their kids is about where to send them to school. Over the years, dozens of parents have come to Bill with the question, "Where is the best place for my child to go to school?" He has always responded by saying, "In my opinion, a better question is, 'How can we help your child figure out the best place for him to go to school?'"

Bill worked with a boy named Max whose struggle with learning disabilities was severe enough that from first through eighth grade he needed a school especially designed for students like him. Like many children who attend small schools during childhood, Max was eager to "bust out" of his small, supportive school and go to a larger high school with a wider range of social options. He also wanted to prove to himself that he no longer needed a school for kids with learning disabilities. Max's parents were understandably anxious about the possibility of his going to a less supportive school, and they asked Bill how they could help Max see that it would be in his best interest to stay put. Bill recommended to Max's parents that they tell him he would ultimately make the decision himself and that they would do everything possible to help him make a good decision, including offering their best advice.

Bill met with Max and reviewed the two or three private school options Bill thought might be within Max's reach. He also shared with him the conversations he'd had with a school psychologist about the kinds of support Max might expect if he were to enter a public high school. Max took this decision-making process very seriously. He asked his parents, the admissions directors at the other private schools, and Bill thoughtful questions about what his experience might be like if he were to change schools. At the end of the process, Max came to the conclusion that he needed the academic support that was offered at his old school and decided to stay there. He then went on to have a successful (and happy) high school career during which his confidence soared. He's now knocking it out of the park in his third year of college and is planning on going to graduate school. In this instance, he came around to his parents' viewpoint—but he did so on his own steam. Had he been forced to go back to his old school against his will, we suspect he would have continued to believe that he didn't need to be there and would have resented his parents for making him stay.

High schoolers: "It's your call" is hard for a lot of parents of high schoolers. Teenagers are known for taking outsize risks and for being particularly vulnerable to peer pressure. For anyone who remembers driving, dating, and the party antics of high school, it's not any different today. But the good news is, current research on adolescent brain development suggests that teenagers *do not* think that they're immortal. They're very aware of the risks entailed by their behavior. It is true that they put stronger emphasis on the possible positive outcomes of an action than the potential risks. Experts call this hyperrationality.[7] When engaging in collaborative problem solving with teenagers, know that they have this bias and put a special focus on helping them to really think through the possible downsides. If they're not having it—if they're seemingly put out by your collaborative problem-solving approach, suggest going back to a more autocratic system of consequences. "Okay," you might say, "we don't need to work through this together. You can just lose the car for three days as a consequence." We bet you anything they'll concede to talk it through instead.

Teenagers are the closest to legal age, and they are the ones who most need to hear this message: "I have confidence in your ability to make informed decisions about your own life and to learn from your mistakes." That doesn't mean they won't make mistakes—they will. But with every mistake, they'll develop better instincts and self-awareness, especially if you help them process what went wrong without blaming or saying, "I told you so."

And beyond: Parenting doesn't stop the moment a child turns eighteen. Watching the choices our kids make in college and during young adulthood can be excruciating. A few years ago Bill was talking with one of his best friends, Kathryn, about her son, Jeremy, who was a college freshman. Jeremy had developed a relationship with a girl who eventually became controlling and abusive. Kathryn shared the various ways she had tried to get Jeremy to leave this girl, and sought Bill's advice about what else she might try. Bill said, "I think it's disrespectful to give Jeremy the message that you think he's incapable of resolving this situation himself and needs his mom to step in." Kathryn is one of the kindest people on the planet, and she was mortified to think that she may have been treating her son disrespectfully by trying to get him to break up with this girl (to whom he clung tighter because no one likes to feel coerced). They talked about ways of communicating confidence in Jeremy's ability to figure this out.

Kathryn then went back to Jeremy and expressed her confidence in him and her sympathy for his situation (he loved the girl in many ways—even though it was an unhealthy relationship). She offered to help in any way he'd like. Within a few weeks, Jeremy decided to take a leave of absence from school and to go work with his father, who lived in another state, to make it easier to end his relationship. He came back a semester later, finished college, and started on a successful career in law enforcement.

Now it doesn't always work out this ideally, but by conveying to Jeremy that she trusted him to make his own decisions and learn from his mistakes, Kathryn opened herself up to being a resource and sounding board.

Here's Why It's Hard: Frequently Asked Questions

As you can imagine, we have many conversations with parents who struggle with relinquishing control. At times as a parent, emotions will flood your thinking and none more so than fear. Fear will cause you to fret, *What if he chooses the wrong thing? What if he gets hurt? What if he's unhappy? What if I lose him?* We're parents and we get it. We've been scared ourselves, too. That's why we've devoted this next section to the areas where parents really get stuck. In our responses, you'll see how "It's your call" plays out in the real world all the time.

"Last week my fifteen-year-old daughter was at a party where the kids were drinking. She drank too much, passed out, and got a concussion from hitting her head on the floor. She clearly doesn't make good decisions. I don't see how I can say to her, 'Honey I want you to decide for yourself' when she used such poor judgment."

Let's consider the options. First, you could conclude that your daughter isn't capable of making good decisions and needs to be more closely supervised and that you need to step in until she shows better judgment. This generally doesn't go well, in part because unless you hire a private investigator, you can't really know if your daughter is doing things she's not supposed to do. It's very difficult to monitor teenagers 24/7. So while we strongly support letting your daughter know that she won't be going to a party for the next month or so, we suggest that you express confidence in her ability to learn from her experience. Share your concerns about her safety and give her an article or ask her to watch a YouTube video about what binge drinking does to a developing brain. Remind her that you can't protect her from the many dangerous things in life. Tell her you will always be willing to pick her up from a party or to send her home in a cab or an Uber if she feels pressured to do things she doesn't want to do, but avoid giving her the message that she can't be trusted because she used poor judgment that night. You want to help her learn from her mistakes.

Now here's the really hard part: What if she does it again? What about kids who seem to continually make poor decisions? Believe it or not, this is rare. We only want kids to make *informed* decisions and will override a child's decision if it seems crazy. But if your child is repeatedly making the same bad decision, then it's even more impor-tant that they practice exercising judgment—with your help—so they can get better. If frequent chemical use is a problem, remember, all bets are off and you need to intervene. For most judgment lapses, though, we suggest asking Dr. Phil's question, "How'd that work for you?" and discussing ways to make better decisions next time.

"I feel like if I don't come down hard on my child for misbehavior, if I don't tighten the reins, I'm letting her get away with it and she'll learn the wrong lesson."

This isn't necessarily true. A child does not have to receive a negative consequence for every misbehavior in order to learn which behaviors work well in this world. Bill will never forget when his daughter was six and participating in a day-care program. When it was time to leave, Bill's daughter passively refused to clean up. Bill encouraged her to do so and tried to explain logically why it was important for her to do her part. Eventually, he told her that they couldn't go home until she did. After a standoff of seven or eight more minutes, one of the parent volunteers at the child-care program said, "Bill, who's winning?" at which point Bill cleaned up the toys and took his daughter home. When it comes to discipline, nothing works every time.

"If my son makes a really bad decision, he could be stunted for life."

If a thirty-year-old came into Bill's office and said that his life had been wasted because he'd made a bad decision in the eighth grade, or in high school, and had closed off all his options, Bill would say, "Buddy, get over it. You still have plenty of opportunities to shape your life." Bill shares this hypothetical with kids who are panicked by a seemingly insurmountable setback, and also with their panicked parents.

This question speaks to one of the assumptions we need to get to the bottom of: that life is a race with one clear route to the finish line. That's simply not true. We understand that children develop at different rates physically and mentally and the same is true of the rest of their development. Molly, for instance, was a bright but fairly sheltered high schooler who went nuts when she found the freedom of college. She performed so poorly her first semester that her parents told her they would stop paying for her tuition unless she improved her grades. Molly worked herself to the bone for her remaining three and a half years of undergrad to undo the GPA damage she'd done in that first semester. It wasn't easy, and it wasn't fun. When she interviewed for medical school admission, she was repeatedly questioned about her poor first-semester grades. She explained that she'd gone off the rails a bit, but emphasized how proud she was that she had clawed her way back from the brink, and said that it was the most character-building experience of her life. She knows now what she's capable of. As you can guess, Molly was admitted to an excellent medical school.

Often what we think of as a cataclysmic setback is really nothing more than a ripple. Parents tend to worry far into the future, thinking, "If he gets stuck now, he'll always be behind." But that's not true. Most development of children's brains happens just by getting older. Letting them get stuck every once in a while, while you're available to help them get out of the ditch, can actually help them grow.

"What about kids who won't do anything or go anywhere unless they're forced? Or teenagers who want to stay home and play video games all summer?"

Stephen Covey famously said (paraphrasing the well-known prayer of St. Francis), "Seek first to understand, then to be understood." Ask your child questions in an effort to understand what's behind her resistance. Is it that she prefers to spend her time doing lower-key things around the house than going out, just as some adults do? Does she resist because she's anxious about "Novel" or "Unpredictable" experiences? (Remember the N and U in N.U.T.S. from the first chapter?) Really hear her concerns. It doesn't mean she will get her way—perhaps it's important to you that the family go on a hike and you want everyone to be together. But understanding where she's coming from, addressing her concerns, and compromising if possible is a healthy approach.

You are also well within your rights to say something like, "If I let you sit around and not do anything all summer, I'll feel like I'm a terrible parent. That's not what good parents do. So I want you to decide. I want you to have at least one extracurricular activity. Let's brainstorm about what that might be."

"Religious faith is very important in our family. How can we ensure that our children will follow in our faith and religious practices and still nurture a strong sense of control?"

In our experience, most kids go along with their parents. Although they may not like it, most children do not put up a major fight against going to church, synagogue, or mosque if it is something that you do regularly together as a family, and most eventually assume the religious faith of their parents. We thus believe that modeling positive religious values and taking the attitude that "our family holds these beliefs and practices" is a perfectly appropriate way to start. If your children question their religious teachings or the basis for faith, we believe in answering as honestly as we can. If your children hate going to church or synagogue, we recommend treating them respectfully and using the collaborative problem-solving approach to find a mutually agreeable solution.

"What if my kid is a good athlete but doesn't want to stick with his sport, which could limit his options for college?"

First, figure out why it is important to you that your child play a sport. Is it because you won't be able to afford college otherwise? If so, use collaborative problem solving. Explain the pros of sticking with the sport and how it could open up the choices of schools he can attend and that you can afford. It might also mean that he won't need to get a job in college. The cons might be that he doesn't enjoy the sport and it takes all his extra time. After weighing the pros and cons with him, let him decide.

If money isn't the issue, ask yourself why it matters to you. If it's not for him, it's not for him. So often, parents want to play Edward Scissorhands and start pruning their child like a tree, but the reality is that your tree has just begun to grow, and you don't even know what kind of tree it is. Maybe it's not a sports tree.

"What about anxious, perfectionistic kids who hate to make decisions?"

Over the years, Bill has worked with dozens of kids and teens who hate the responsibility of making decisions, often due to the fear that they will make the wrong one. His advice to parents has been to say to their kid, "As you get older, I want you to be able to confidently make decisions for yourself. I know it makes you really anxious at this point, so I would be happy to make the decision for you. Before I do, though, I want you to tell me what, if you were going to make it yourself, your best decision would be." Letting them make good decisions is a long-term goal, and we don't need to force kids to do things before they're ready.

"What about kids who won't listen to reason when we discuss pros and cons?"

Again, we want kids to make informed decisions that aren't crazy. If children will not consider the relevant information, we don't support letting them make the decision.

"What about kids with ADHD, who we know have an immature prefrontal cortex? Or kids with other disabilities or problems?"

As much as we'd like to, we can't chronically protect kids from themselves. Bill consulted with the parents of a twenty-four-year-old young woman who had just finished her fifth year as a full-time student in community college but still had fewer than twenty-five credits, apparently due to a combination of ADHD and emotional instability. Her parents, understandably, had attempted for many years to exert a high level of control over their daughter's life and to protect her from herself in a variety of ways. Bill encouraged them to think differently about their role in their daughter's life. "What can we do to make sure that if we pull back, she will *want* to take steps to move forward?" they asked. "What happens if she gets discouraged and doesn't do it?" Bill reminded them that they can't make their daughter want what she doesn't want and they can't make her do what she doesn't want to do. He also pointed out that it couldn't be their responsibility to make sure that her life was successful, and that their job was to support her, express empathy, set limits when necessary, and model assertiveness.

"In the real world, kids don't get to make all their own decisions. Don't we need to prepare them for being told what to do and then doing it responsibly?"

You're right, there are plenty of circumstances in which kids (and adults) don't get to make their own decisions. But the equation here works differently than you might think. Giving kids more choice when you can makes it *easier* for them to accept authority when they need to.

"Doesn't this just open the door to everything becoming a negotiation? That is exhausting. Sometimes I just want my son to go along."

We get it. Parents are busy, and when in the midst of making breakfast and corralling the family to get out the door on time, you don't always want to collaboratively problem solve with your twelve-year-old, or go through the pros and cons of wearing sandals on a rainy day.

Overall, try to remember that negotiating is a great thing for your kid to know how to do. You want him to learn to advocate for himself and to practice those skills for the real world. If he's never able to "win" with his parents, he'll internalize that message. He may be more apt to sneak, lie, or cheat to get what he wants, or to give up pushing back on authority altogether, believing that he has no voice. To improve your legitimacy, you have to show your child that he is being heard. So give him credit for making good arguments, by sometimes changing your position so that he knows that a well-thought-out argument is in fact a worthwhile pursuit.

Also feel free to say, "You know, I love what a great negotiator you are. Some people get paid a lot to do what you do so naturally. But sometimes it's exhausting for me, and it's especially hard when we are crunched for time or when there's a lot going on. I'd be grateful if when I need you to, you could go with the flow, without the need for a discussion. If you can do that, it will help the morning run more smoothly and I will acknowledge that you've really helped out."

What to Do Tonight

- Tell your child, "You're the expert on you. Nobody really knows you better than you know yourself, because nobody really knows what it feels like to be you."

- Give your child a choice about something you may have previously decided for her. Or ask her opinion about something. (If they're young, you can frame it as, "Do you think we should do it this way or that way?")

- Have a family meeting where you problem solve together about what chores need to be done and who should do them. Give them options. Could they walk the dog instead of doing the dinner dishes? Take out the trash instead of cleaning the toilet? Do they want to do it each Sunday or each Wednesday? Morning or night? Keep a consistent schedule, but let them choose that schedule.

- Make a list of things your child would like to be in charge of, and make a plan to shift responsibility for some of these things from you to him or her.

- Ask your child whether something in his life isn't working for him (his homework routine, bedtime, management of electronics) and if he has any ideas about how to make it work better.

- Do a cost-benefit analysis of any decision you make for your child that she sees differently.

- Tell your child about decisions you've made that, in retrospect, were not the best decisions—and how you were able to learn and grow from them.

- Have a talk in which you point out that your kid has got a good mind. Recall some times when he's made a good decision or felt strongly about something and turned out to be right. If he'll let you, make a list together of the things he's decided for himself that have worked well.

- Tell your teen you want him to have lots of practice running his own life before he goes off to college—and that you want to see that he can run his life without running it into the ground before he goes away.

- Emphasize logical and natural consequences, and encourage the use of family meetings to discuss family rules or family policies more generally (e.g., no gaming during the week).

CHAPTER FOUR

The Nonanxious Presence

How to Help Your Kids Find a Sense of Control
by Finding Your Own

D O YOU REMEMBER when you first took the wheel of a car? It was probably a little scary but invigorating. Driving a car is the culmination of more than a decade's worth of empowering first moments, starting with learning to walk. Think of the toddler recognizing for the first time that he can take a step on his own. Suddenly he's racing everywhere—albeit unsteadily—with abandon. Or consider the ten-year-old who is given permission to bike to the store alone to buy candy or comic books. He feels like he owns the whole town. When a teenager first learns to drive, he imagines himself as Mario Andretti. He's breaking away, the road is *his*.

Now let's look at each of these moments from a parent's point of view. The toddler who is racing everywhere means that mom and dad need to be more vigilant, barricading stairs and cordoning off balconies. The ten-year-old biking to the store probably leaves his parents biting their nails in his wake—craning their necks out the window and struggling not to follow. The mother of the new driver may find herself imagining that scene from *Thelma and Louise*—any moment now he will be driving off the cliff and there's nothing she can do about it.

Parental anxiety isn't new. Parents have worried about their kids ever since having kids was a thing, but we believe it's worse now than before. Why? For one, we have a lot more information than we've ever had before. In days past, we had to be okay with not being able to reach our kids at every waking minute. Now it's almost a mandate that we know their every move. Barry Glasser, a top sociologist and author of *The Culture of Fear*, concludes that "most Americans are living in the safest place at the safest time in human history," but it doesn't feel that way because 24/7 news and social media inundate us with scary story after scary story about kidnappings, drug overdoses, and freak occurrences that, in their ubiquity, muddy our perspective.[1] This, combined with an increasingly litigious culture, has dramatically changed the way we think of "danger." Let your six-year-old climb a tree and you're considered careless. Let your eight-year-old walk to school on her own and you're positively neglectful.

And then there's the way parents have changed. We can worry about our kids because, on balance, we're no longer worrying about survival the way we once were. Our great-grandparents' fears were about illnesses like polio and cholera, or drought, or world war, or full-scale economic depression. There wasn't a lot of space left to worry about what Jimmy Jr.'s B average means for his chances for admission to a choice college, or why he wasn't invited to Suzie's birthday party. Many families still have to worry about getting food on the table, but even those of us who don't still find plenty to give us sleepless nights.

Our anxiety is seeping into our kids. Children don't need perfect parents, but they do benefit greatly from parents who can serve as a nonanxious presence. When we are not unduly stressed, worried, angry, or tired, we are much better able to comfort an infant, handle the behavioral challenges of young children, and respond to our teenager's limitations without impulsively saying or doing something hurtful. When we can be a nonanxious presence for our children, we do a world of good—just by not freaking out. In fact, a recent study showed that other than showing your child love and affection, managing your own stress is the best thing you can do to be an effective parent.[2] One first grader's mom cried every time they talked about his need for tutoring, so he told her, "Mom, you're going to have to get it together before we have these talks."

We recognize what a quandary we've presented you with. First, we push you out of your comfort zone, encouraging you to give your kids more control over their lives when that's likely the very thing that makes you anxious. And now we're telling you you'd better calm down about it. Put that way, it just sounds *mean*. But we have no intention of leaving you without tools and a way forward. So this chapter is intended not only to help you understand why being a nonanxious presence is so important, but to show you *how* to do it. Because here's the thing: you can't fake it.

Trickle-down Anxiety

Bad news first: anxiety tends to run in families. Up to 50 percent of children of anxious parents develop anxiety disorders themselves. This may make you think that if you have anxiety, even if it's treated, your kid is screwed.

That's not necessarily true. Kids come into the world with different susceptibilities to anxiety. Some aren't bothered by it—scientists call kids like this "dandelion children." Like dandelions, they're fairly impervious to their environment. Others are "orchid children," with a very high biological sensitivity to context. They are particularly sensitive to the parenting they receive. They flourish under parenting that is calm and nurturing, and struggle with parenting that is high strung. There are both positive and negative aspects to parenting orchid children. Though sensitive children are more susceptible to a negative environment, they also thrive in a calm and loving environment.[3]

One of the ways we pass on anxiety to our kids is through something called epigenetics, a new field that is still only partially understood. Epigenetics refers to the ways that experience affects genes by turning the function of specific genes on or off. So while children may be born with some genetic predisposition, it takes experiences to "turn on" the specific genes that ignite depression or anxiety.

Turning these problematic genes to the "on" position is all too easy to do, and it can happen in at least two ways:

1. Secondhand stress

There are some people whose presence just makes you nervous. For adults, it could be an overbearing boss, a perfectionist in-law, or a colleague who is constantly in panic mode. For kids and teens, it might be a strict teacher, that friend fretting about every last assignment, or, well, you.

Stress is catching, like an emotional virus. That may sound kind of kooky, but there's considerable evidence for what scientists call "stress contagion." Just like a cold—or a plague—stress spreads through a contained population, affecting and infecting everyone in its path. Who hasn't worked in an infected office and felt the debilitating effects of just one permanently stressed-out person? We all know that one family member can spread anxiety around the house until everyone is on edge.[4]

So-called secondhand stress can linger even longer than your own personal stress. Seen through the lens of control, this makes perfect sense. Stress most often results from feeling a low sense of control over events or the environment we live in, and the less control we experience, the more stressed we feel. If your sister thinks the mole on her arm might be cancerous, you feel justifiably anxious for her. What you can't do is force her to go to a dermatologist and have a biopsy to settle your fears. Her stress, while significant, is at least partially under her control. But you can't act to mitigate your own stress about the mole.

From the time babies are in the womb, they are influenced by their environment and sensitive to our stress. From then and throughout the early years of life, if a child's parents are highly stressed, the child's genes are affected—including genes involved in insulin production and brain development. Stress effects the gene expression of the fetus and young infants through a process called methylation. A certain type of chemical (called a methyl group) "locks" the gene that's supposed to turn off the stress response in the *on* position.[5] Changes in gene expression can continue to be seen right through adolescence.[6]

While stress in utero and in the first year of life have the most decisive impact on the developing brain, recent studies have shown that secondhand stress persists. For example, when parents are anxious about math, their kids are more likely to be anxious about math, too, but only if the anxious parents often help with the homework.[7] In other words, if you have math anxiety, your kid is probably better off if you don't offer your help. It works the other way, too. When your kid is upset, your amygdala reacts, which makes it even harder to be calm. This is why so many parents find themselves, ironically and often comically, angrily yelling at their kids for losing their temper.

So how does this happen? Where or how does the virus "catch"?

First, as we talked about in Chapter One, the amygdala senses threat and picks up on anxiety, fear, anger, and frustration in other people. It even picks up fear and anxiety in the smell of stressed people's perspiration. Second, the prefrontal cortex, the Pilot, includes what are called mirror neurons. As the name suggests, mirror neurons seem to imitate what a person is seeing, which is why they're important to emotions like empathy. (In people with autism, who have trouble imitating other people, the functioning of these neurons is atypical.) These mirror neurons are what make kids learn through observation, but they also help kids pick up their parents' anxiety. They will literally mirror what they're seeing, a process that starts in infancy. When parents of newborns are stressed, the babies cry and fuss more than if their parents are feeling calm and confident.

If you think you can hide your anxiety from your kids, you are deluding yourself. Psychologist Paul Ekman has made it his life's work to identify and catalogue our thousands of different facial expressions, and while there are many that we make intentionally to show others how we feel, we also have an involuntary expressive system that signals our feelings whether we want to share them or not. In an interview with Malcolm Gladwell, Ekman explained, "You must have had the experience where somebody comments on your expression and you didn't know you were making it. . . . Somebody tells you, 'What are you getting upset about?' 'Why are you smirking?'" Ekman points out the obvious—that while you can hear your voice, you can't see your face. "If we knew what was on our face," he said, "we would be better at concealing it."[8]

Kids see what you feel, even if you don't want them to. Then they mirror those feelings, even if you don't think you're projecting them, and they begin to feel those feelings, too. One of the reasons for this is that kids tend to be particularly bad at correctly interpreting what they're seeing. So whereas an adult might spend the evening in the company of her grumpy spouse and think, "He's grumpy, but it's not about me. I think I'll just leave him be," a kid is likely to think, "Dad is grumpy. I must have done something wrong. He's mad at me." If kids are stressed, that already immature interpretation function goes haywire. Kids are great observers but lousy interpreters. Ned's daughter, Katie, for instance, consistently perceives that people who are angry *near* her are angry *at* her. She is a classic orchid child.

Much of maturity is marked by increased emotional self-regulation. This is when the prefrontal cortex is conscious of what you're doing and in charge. You can inhibit. But when a kid senses a threat, say, in the form of a stressed or grumpy dad, he doesn't have a fully developed Pilot to say, "No big deal. The bumps will pass, and we'll just fly at a different altitude in the meantime." Instead, he panics. His amygdala takes over. And before you know it, he's stressed and grumpy, too. If this happens too much, his amygdala becomes larger and even more reactive. In Robert Sapolsky's words, if stress persists for a long time, the amygdala becomes more and more "hysterical."[9]

Now imagine the cognitive dissonance experienced when we can tell a person's words do not match the emotions he's feeling. As parents, if we are fully attentive, our kids cannot slip "I'm fine" past us when in reality they are not. So, too, we should be careful about telling our kids one thing when we are experiencing another. There's a concern about telling kids too much and burdening them with emotions they are not prepared to handle, but whatever you do or don't tell them, be mindful both of your child's ability to *feel* your emotions and of her fear, uncertainty, and doubt. In the absence of a story or explanation, people tend to create their own, and often the scenarios kids will come up with are more alarming than the truth.

The mother of a family Ned worked with was diagnosed with cancer. The parents wanted Ned to know, since their sixteen-year-old daughter Ayse, who was temperamentally anxious, was likely to have less support than usual. Her mom needed to attend to her treatment, and her dad would be busy supporting mom, taking care of Ayse's younger sister, and picking up other roles that her mom had to set down for a while. "But don't tell Ayse," they said.

"We don't want her to worry." Ned sat on that for a while before circling back and expressing concern that Ayse would pick up their worry. She'd spent her entire life reading their faces. It was territory she knew intimately. How could she *not* notice if something was amiss? What would Ayse think if she could feel something was wrong but her parents swore all was well? That a divorce was pending? That they were upset with her? It's hard to say. Ultimately, Ayse's parents did share the illness with her. Knowing what was going on and understanding the course of treatment reduced Ayse's uncertainty and doubt. It also allowed Ayse to *do* something. She helped her mom and dad by doing a few more chores and by driving her sister to soccer when her parents couldn't. The cancer was still scary and, though it is now in remission, it will always be part of their lives, an uncertainty they can never expunge. But knowing and being honest helped them all. By not having two truths—one the parents kept to themselves and one for their kids—the family was in sync, right down to the mirror neuron level.

When my daughter was just over a year old, we went to visit friends in Chicago. On return we were stuck on one of those long ground stops on the tarmac that so often bedevil summer travelers. My daughter, like the rest of us, was not delighted by her circumstances and articulated her displeasure as most infants do, which did little to add to the experience for me or the other couple of hundred lucky souls spending an extra two and a half hours slowly getting hotter. What I remember most is how stressed I was that my daughter was so upset, how embarrassed I was to be "that family" whose child couldn't be consoled. I wanted so desperately to soothe her but wasn't able to because I was too stressed myself. A nonanxious presence I was not. On airplanes, they tell you, "in the event of a loss of cabin pressure, put on your own oxygen first before assisting children." It's the same with stress: in the event of an increase of cabin (or school, or life) pressure, tackle your own stress first before attempting to help others.

—Ned

2. Behavior

The second way you can inadvertently turn your child's anxiety genes "on" is through your behavior. Let's suppose your anxiety is more of the social variety (the most common form of anxiety, by the way), which means you experience intense fear of being scrutinized and negatively evaluated by others in social situations. A study out of Johns Hopkins University found that parents who suffer from this form of anxiety tend to have difficulty communicating warmth and affection, are more critical, and generally express more doubt about their children's abilities than less anxious parents do. They are more apt to be overcontrolling and less likely to grant autonomy—behaviors known to increase anxiety in children.[10]

If this all sounds familiar, it's not insurmountable. Since behaviors can fire up unwanted genes, it stands to reason that we can prevent the ignition of those genes by avoiding certain behaviors. Johns Hopkins researchers conducted a study where they identified children who were at a high risk for developing anxiety. One group received a family-oriented therapy intervention program that focused on reducing factors that contributed to anxiety in kids and parents, such as parental modeling of anxiety. Only 9 percent of the kids in the intervention group developed an anxiety disorder in the next year, compared to 21 percent of the kids in families that were provided only with written instructions about managing anxiety, and 30 percent in families that got no therapy or written instructions. A study in 2016 replicated this finding, except that this time 5 percent of kids in the intervention group developed an anxiety disorder, compared to 31 percent of the control group.[11]

If you have unmanaged anxiety, tread carefully. Because of your anxiety, it will be harder for you to give up control when it comes to your kids, which may very well result in their rebelling, which will make your anxiety spike and your need for control even greater . . . which will make them further rebel. You see the negative feedback loop here? Though we offer some tools in this book, we also encourage parents suffering from anxiety to consult with a therapist. There are ways of retraining our minds to avoid negative feedback loops and to deflect potential sources of anxiety.

That ends the science portion of our program. There's also a common sense portion. When parents worry about their kids, it undermines the kids' confidence. Bill recently evaluated Robert, a sixteen-year-old with a social anxiety disorder. Bill asked Robert about his social life, in response to which he told Bill about things he likes to do with his friends. He also said that he often enjoys being with his family, but he quickly added that he sometimes wants to "get away" from them:

ROBERT: Mom's always worried about me. She's always worried that I'll do something bad. One night I didn't tell her where I was and she was really worried. My dad just said, "Have fun and don't get arrested."

BILL: How long has she worried about you like this?

ROBERT: She's done it for a while. I didn't notice it until last year when I tried to push her away a bit. She told me that when I was younger she would walk by my class to make sure I was getting along with the other kids.

BILL: When was that?

ROBERT: Fourth grade through sixth grade.

BILL: How did you react when she said that?

ROBERT: [*Shrugs*] Even if I'm shy and might not always get along with kids, she doesn't have to be worried about me all the time.

BILL: Do you feel like you have a good relationship with
    your mom?
ROBERT: I do when she's not on me all the time.

Bill hears the parents' end of this discussion, too. It's common for a mom or dad to weep quietly when discussing their child's difficulties and then say, "I just want him to feel good about himself." After passing the tissues and waiting for the feelings to settle down, Bill says, "It's hard to help Robert (or Tim, or Edward) feel good about himself if we're worried sick about him." It's common sense. If we're unable to accept our kids as they are, how can we expect them to accept themselves?

Calm Is Contagious

Just as our kids mirror our stress, they can also mirror our calm. You probably know calm people, those who always project an aura of well-being and are able to maintain a sense of control while accepting the messiness in the world around them. They are the ones you want to call in a crisis, or whose presence you crave when you're feeling edgy, because they somehow help level you out. Without preaching, without even doing much of anything, these people communicate calm and confidence to those around them, and help others develop a similar sense of balance in their own lives.

One of the reasons we know this is because we *are* this nonanxious presence to many of our clients. We think of ourselves as being a bit like Michael Clarke Duncan's character in *The Green Mile*, only instead of sucking up other peoples' cancer, our role is to remove their stress. It's as if we're saying, "Let me take that. I can handle it. You don't need that anymore." A mother recently told us that she comes to all our lectures because every time she hears the message that it's right (and safe) for her not to continually worry about her children or be on their case, she is able to "hold" the calmness and confidence, at least for some time. Another parent told Bill, "When I left your office the last time we talked, I felt so calm. I had Jill's life in such a positive perspective. The problem is that within an hour of leaving here, I talked to another parent from Jill's school and my anxiety level shot up again."

Ned's calming effect on his students and their parents is perhaps even more measurable. While he deliberately doesn't maintain statistics on score improvement for the kids he tutors, a rise of hundreds of points on a standardized test is not uncommon. The kids he tutors learn math and vocabulary, of course, but not one of them believes that a few math tricks or a new word list made all the difference between one testing and the next. Why, when kids have already tried classes and books and strategies, can a few sessions with Ned cause such a spike in scores?

The kids who come into Ned's office and sit across the desk from him come from all sorts of home lives. There are kids with doting parents and kids whose parents are workaholics. There are kids with anxious helicopter parents and kids with no parents at all. But no matter what kind and quality of attention they get at home, they invariably benefit from the nonanxious presence Ned provides. And, as a side effect, their scores benefit, too.

Students are constantly telling him, "If you could just come with me to the test, just be in the room with me, then I know I'd be okay." Ridiculous, right? How in the world would it help a kid remember the Pythagorean theorem or the meaning of "tumultuous" if Ned were just sitting there, across the room, staring at his shoelaces or twiddling his thumbs?

But he's tested this proposition. He'll give kids sections of a practice test, and sit calmly across the desk from them as they take it. Then he'll give them a test and leave the room, giving them the peace and quiet of an empty room. Finally they'll take the practice test in a more realistic setting, with other kids in the room tapping their toes and visibly wracking their brains. Can you guess when they do best? Of course you can. When Ned is there they feel calm, they remember the confidence he's expressed in them, and the things he's taught them come easily to mind. When he leaves, they're on their own, and their own negative thoughts have freer rein. They do worse. And when you add in other kids, other anxious presences, the stress attacks like the plague, jumping from kid to kid and escalating each time.

We love the term "nonanxious presence," but we didn't invent it. It was coined by Edwin Friedman, a rabbi, student of complex systems, and consultant.[12] In Friedman's view, we live in a chronically anxious and reactive society in which there are too few people leading our families, schools, and organizations who can serve as a nonanxious presence. He makes the case that groups work best when leaders are true to themselves and are not unduly anxious or worried—and thus do not communicate undue worry or fear to others. From Friedman's perspective, this is as true for families as it is for religious organizations or large corporations.

Scientists back him up. Remember the laid-back California rats (those who were sent away from their moms but then returned and were groomed)? Well, the same researchers later studied the effects of calm versus anxious parenting styles on the development of rat pups, and found that rat mothers with low stress levels spent a lot of time licking and grooming their pups. The pups they produced were calmer and explored more than rats who were licked and groomed significantly less. Why would this be? Because they're shown more love? That may be part of it. But we and others in the field believe that what those mama rats transmitted was a sense that the world is safe and you're free to move around and explore in it. It also changed the rat pup's genes involved in stress regulation.

It wasn't an issue of genetics—that calm mama rats produce calm baby rats. When rat pups who were born to low-licking mothers were "fostered" by high-licking mothers, they turned out to be calm—even though they were genetically vulnerable to being anxious.[13]

What these rat mothers were doing was making home the safe base we've been arguing for in this book. When your home is a calm space, free of excessive fighting, anxiety, and pressure, it becomes the place to regenerate that your kids need. They can go back into the world and better deal with fraught social dynamics, academic stresses, and challenges like tryouts or auditions, knowing that at the end of the day they have a safe place to recover.

Part of making home a safe base is remembering that it's your child's life, not yours, and that his problems are his problems, not yours. It's easier to adopt this philosophy when we're calm, and it's easier to be calm when we adopt this philosophy. When we're calm, we can let kids experience discomfort and learn to manage it themselves. We can allow children to experience their own painful feelings without rushing in to take responsibility for resolving them. When we're calm, we don't give our kids excessive power to take us up and down with them. When parents separate their happiness from their children's, when they accept that it's okay for mom to be happy and at peace even if her twelve-year-old is not, it's easier for them to offer the support their kids need. We often emphasize this point to parents whose kids are really struggling; while they almost never cause their children's problems, their responses become part of a family dance that often takes them out of the role of chief consultant and into the role of worrier in chief.

Remember from Chapter One that social support is one of the key factors for controlling stress. If a parent is anxious or critical, the kid doesn't feel this social support. It's an unfortunate double whammy: we're making our kids anxious, and then we're not doing our job of helping them.

A friend, Rosa, told us that when she was a new mom, she attended a support group in which all the women went around and shared what it was about their own moms they wanted to emulate and what they didn't. When it was Rosa's turn, she talked about how her mom was very loving and affectionate, which she appreciated, but she always took the ups and downs of Rosa's life too hard, so that Rosa learned to keep things from her to protect her. Rosa's mom would still be upset about something long after Rosa was over it, which effectively eliminated her as a source of support. As an example, Rosa talked about the time she came home from preschool and told her mom no other kids would play with her, after which her mom burst into tears. Of course, parents can swing too far the other way, too. Another new mom sitting next to Rosa laughed and said, "Our moms should have met because maybe they would have balanced each other out. My mom would have said, 'I don't send you to preschool to make friends—I send you to *learn!*'"

How to Be a Nonanxious Presence

To be—and not just fake being—a nonanxious presence, you have to get a handle on your stress. Make no mistake: you have just as much of a need for control as your child does. And sometimes wanting too much to be there for your kids can actually backfire. Much of the work involved in providing a nonanxious presence for your kid begins with you. Here are a few tips that we've found to be helpful for the parents we've worked with.

Make enjoying your kids your top parenting priority.

In a competitive, overly busy world, it's so easy to forget the basics: that enjoying your kids is one of the best things you can do for them, and for yourself. You don't have to spend every moment with your kid, or convince yourself parenting isn't hard when it is. But think for a moment about the giddy look we give babies when we see them in the morning or after a long day away. Think about the experience of being that baby: every time someone looks at you, they smile as if you're a miracle.

Your kid needs to feel the joy of seeing your face light up when you see him because you are genuinely happy to spend time with him. This feeling is incredibly powerful and important for his self-esteem and sense of well-being. Bill still remembers that when he went through a difficult period in his early twenties, he had a pair of friends who always expressed how happy they were to see him. This was forty years ago, and still it's seared into his consciousness.

This powerful memory helped shape Bill's thinking when he started to do psychotherapy with kids and families. He began to suggest to parents that they make enjoying their kids their top priority so that their kids would have the experience of being joy-producing organisms.

Once that priority of enjoyment is set, work backward. If you're not enjoying your children because of unresolved anger, focus on resolving that anger. If you're not enjoying your kids because of pressures from work, focus on relaxation strategies and cognitive techniques for minimizing anxiety. If the lack of enjoyment is due to marital conflict, investigate couples therapy. If you're not enjoying your kids because of their problematic behavior, work with a professional to help improve this behavior. If you're not enjoying your kids because you're not getting enough social support, socialize more. Or perhaps you're not enjoying your kids because you're spending *too much* time with them. Our highest goal in life isn't to make our kids feel good—but it's worth paying attention to what's blocking you from genuinely enjoying them and removing it.

Very early in his career, Bill did a consultation with Eric, a twenty-one-year-old "failure to launch" young adult who had had academic and behavioral difficulties in high school, flunked out of college twice, and was struggling to stay clean and sober. After Eric had recounted his struggles in school and the constant conflict that occurred between him and his parents in the teenage years, Bill asked, "Do you think there is something that your parents could have done differently when you were in high school that could have made life better for you?" After thinking for a long time, Eric said, "I think it might have helped if they had been happy to see me sometimes."

Don't fear the future.

Virtually all our anxiety as parents is about the future—over which we have relatively little control. We've seen parents' anxiety levels drop dramatically when we reassure them that, no matter what their kids may be going through, things will likely work out well. What makes it so stressful and painful when our kids aren't doing well is the "fear of getting stuck"—the fear that our kids will get locked into a negative place from which they won't be able to emerge.

When fear rears its head, remember to take a long view. Life isn't a race, and the world is full of late bloomers. We know hundreds of stories of children and teenagers who weren't doing well only to turn out to be happy and successful. Who your child is as a ten-year-old or a teenager is not who he will always be. The prefrontal cortex continues to develop rapidly in adolescence and into early adulthood, which is why Mark Twain said, "When I was a boy of fourteen, my father was so ignorant I couldn't stand to have the old man around. But when I got to be twenty-one, I was astonished at how much the old man had learned in seven years."

Most kids go through childhood, adolescence, and young adulthood without experiencing serious problems. And even if they do have problems, most of them still turn out well. If you worry constantly about the possibility that your child will fall into the small category of kids who chronically struggle, you're only making matters worse.

Commit to your own stress management.

In a survey conducted in the late 1990s, children and teenagers said that what they wanted above all—even more than spending more time with their parents—was for their parents to be happier and less stressed.[14] And this was in a period before ubiquitous smartphones, when the pace of life wasn't as manic as it is today. As the saying goes, "We're only as happy as our least happy child." The same is true for kids, who sense their parents' stress and unhappiness, even when they are not being yelled at, scolded, lectured, or ignored. We worry about our kids, and they worry about us.

So slow down. Exercise. Get enough sleep (not the four hours that one couple boasted to Ned they were sure to get every night, thus setting a great example for their son). Consider learning to meditate, if you don't already. One teenager who practices Transcendental Meditation with his family said that in his experience, "TM calms the mind and calms the mom." His mom is much more able to be a nonanxious presence at home since she's been meditating regularly.

Think about your default mode network and nurture your radical downtime—which we'll cover more in Chapter Six. It is very rare for adults today to have even brief periods of unplugged "downtime" in which they turn their attention within, even though there are hundreds of studies documenting the benefits of doing so. Stop splitting your attention, and concentrate instead on living in the present, and, as much as possible, being fully in the moment with yourself and your kids.

Make peace with your worst fears.

One of the most powerful questions anxious parents can ask themselves is, "What am I most afraid of?" Envisioning the worst-case scenario and letting it play out can actually be a calming process. Asking "What would I do?" and realizing that they would still love and support their child helps them let go and stop trying to control a situation they cannot control. Let's take this idea a little further by going over some of the fears we hear about the most.

"I'm afraid my child will get stuck."

Perhaps you're concerned that somehow, because of mistakes he's making now, he won't get a good education, won't have the skills necessary to be successful in life, will never develop true friendships, will never marry, and so on. First, think of the challenges you had in middle or high school. Are they still bedeviling you? Chances are you grew and changed, as will your kids if given a chance to do so.

Remember the question we asked in Chapter Two: Whose life is it? If any one of these things happened, would you still love your child and do everything you could to help him? Of course you would. Your responsibility is to love and support your child. It isn't your responsibility to protect him from pain. You can't.

"I'm afraid that if I don't insist on certain standards and show my disapproval, my child will think I'm okay with his bad behavior."

Many anxious parents tend to be hard on their children in part because they believe they need to until they are doing better—and that it would be dangerous to "let up" until then. This can lead parents to be constantly disapproving. But as we've already established, staying on kids continually about the same issues (table manners, cleaning up, brushing their teeth, doing their schoolwork) is counterproductive. In fact, kids are most likely to get stuck in negative patterns if we repeatedly try to change them and they resist. Their sense of control becomes dependent on their *not* letting us influence them. When our spouse, parents, siblings, or friends badger us about changing certain behaviors, doing so is absolutely the last thing we want to do.

"I'm afraid that if I let my guard down for a moment, my child will get hurt or even killed."

If your greatest fear is that your child will be abducted on the way to school or be the victim of an attack or car accident, our response is twofold.

First, remember that this is the safest time in which to live, and understand the skewed vision of the world these fears stem from. Crime rates and car deaths are all at their lowest in decades. It's our *perception* of the danger that's up.[15] We are trying to make everything safe and sanitized, but it's a fool's errand. Let's take the arena of playground equipment, as Hanna Rosin did in an article for the *Atlantic*.[16] Great efforts have been made to take away all risk from playgrounds, so that most play structures leave little room for exploration and creativity. Despite this, Rosin reported that "our close attention to safety has not in fact made a tremendous difference in the number of accidents children have."

Second, if you want to keep your children as safe as possible, the best thing to do is to give them experience and teach them judgment. Let them climb that tree and fall when they're six—it will teach them important skills about risk and about being in their bodies. Even if they break their arm and are in a cast, they will benefit from knowing that they have experienced and survived a scary incident and are stronger for it. According to Rosin's article, kids who injure themselves falling from heights are less likely to be afraid of heights at age eighteen. Experience is typically a better teacher than words. What's more, they'll *pay attention next time.* Your kids need practice managing and taking nonlethal risks. After all, life isn't exactly risk free—we take risks in love, in work, in finance all the time. Learning how to recognize and manage risk is part of growing up. Remind your children that you are not always watching them and that you cannot always keep them safe, so they will take some of that responsibility on themselves. They will be more careless if they take it for granted that you are always there. In the words of one of Ned's good friends Jennifer, don't try to carpet the world when it's far easier to give out slippers. Or, to quote a character from the film *Miss Peregrine's Home for Peculiar Children*: "We don't need you to make us feel safe . . . you made us feel brave and that's even better."

Adopt an attitude of nonjudgmental acceptance.

Werner Erhard made famous the phrase "What is, is" in the 1970s. Today, we may say "It is what it is" or "It's all good." This is another way of saying that it makes sense to accept the world as it is. When applied to people, it's a way to talk about loving someone, warts and all.

The common denominator in all emotional pain is a desire to change current reality ("I need my child to do better in school, to do better socially, to be less anxious, to eat more [or less, or better], to not be so addicted to video games and social media," et cetera). In their book *Rapid Relief from Emotional Distress*, Gary Emery and James Campbell recommended that we teach ourselves to make peace with reality by first honestly accepting it for what it is.[17] They advocate a formula known as ACT: Accept, Choose, Take Action. In the context of your kids it might look like this:

> I **A**ccept the idea that my kid is underachieving/doesn't have friends/can't read, and I see this as part of his path.

I Choose to create a vision of myself as a calm, compassionate parent who has a supportive relationship with my son.

I will Take action by offering to help, focusing on his strengths, setting limits where necessary, and modeling acceptance and self-care. I will also seek help from others if my child needs assistance with reading, math, or any area where a third party can help him more than I am able to.

Acceptance does not mean approving, condoning, or letting yourself be abused. It simply means acknowledging reality as it is rather than internally railing against it or denying it entirely. Accepting reality is the only alternative to counterproductive ideas like "I know how the world/my son/my daughter is supposed to be (and this ain't it)."

Acceptance is a powerful stance. For one thing, accepting your children the way they are conveys respect. Acceptance is also a choice, and choosing to accept that "it is what it is" increases our sense of control. It's the opposite of thinking that we have to change something we can't change. (Why does my son have ADHD? Why is my daughter anorexic? Why did it have to happen to me?) Finally, if we start with acceptance, we will be more effective at limit setting and discipline. Acceptance increases our flexibility and allows us to respond thoughtfully, rather than instinctively and reactively.

Consider that for all we know, our kids may well be exactly who and where they are supposed to be right now. This does not mean that we don't desire the best possible future for them. It simply means that, at this moment, there is no evidence that they are really off course.

There is a Chinese parable we like to share about a wise farmer. This farmer was very poor. He had only one son, and only one horse to till his land. One day, the horse broke away. The farmer's neighbor came by and said, "You poor man! You were already so poor and now you have no horse." The farmer said, "Maybe yes, maybe no. It's hard to say." The next week the farmer was out with his son, pulling the plow, and it was ugly—the work was tedious, slowgoing, and exhausting. But then a week or so later, the horse came back and brought two wild horses with him—apparently, he'd found a herd and two of the herd had followed him back. The neighbor said, "What incredible luck! Now you have three horses to work your land!" The farmer said, "Maybe yes, maybe no. Life is very long. It's hard to say." The farmer's son got to work trying to break the wild horses. He was thrown from one and broke his leg terribly. "You poor man!" the neighbor said while the boy was convalescing. "Maybe yes, maybe no," said the farmer. Not long afterward, while the boy was still bedridden, word came down from the emperor that China was going to invade the Mongols, and every family needed to send a son. But the farmer's son could not walk, so he could not go, undoubtedly sparing his life. The point of the parable is clear, and one we should take to heart in parenting: life is long, and you just don't know what will happen next.

What to Do Tonight

- Spend private time with your child, ideally without electronics. Take turns with each child if you have more than one, so that the ratio is one-on-one. It is remarkably healing for kids and will help you to enjoy them. It also makes them feel like they are your number one priority.

- If you're highly anxious, do something about it. Treating anxiety is one of the best things you can do for yourself and your family. Consider participating in cognitive behavioral therapy: you can learn very effective strategies for identifying and "talking back to" the distorted and unproductive thoughts that contribute to high anxiety. Learn to meditate. Take a yoga class. Be very regular in your exercise routine. Spend time in nature. Get more sleep. Socialize more with friends if it helps you feel calm.

- Avoid making decisions for your child based on fear. If you find yourself thinking, "I'm afraid if I don't do this now, then—" *stop.* Do what you feel is right now, not what you feel you have to because of what you're afraid will happen if you don't.

- If your child is struggling, schedule a short time every day for you to worry about his or her problems. Literally write it into your planner. This will let your brain know that it is safe not to worry all day long.

- Remember who's responsible for what. It cannot be your responsibility to see that everything goes well for your children at all times.

- If you are very worried about your teenager and have talked through the issues together many times, write your child a short letter summarizing your concerns and offering any help the child might need. Then promise that you will not bring the issue up again for a month. When you break your promise (because you will) apologize and recommit to it.

- Get out a piece of paper and draw a vertical line in the middle. In the left-hand column, write statements such as the following: "It's okay for Jeremy to have a learning disability," "It's okay that Sarah doesn't have any friends right now," "It's okay for Ben to be depressed right now." In the right-hand column, write down the automatic thoughts that come to your mind in response (likely rebuttal) to these statements. Then question these automatic thoughts. Ask questions such as, "Can I be absolutely sure that this thought is true?" "Who would I be if I didn't believe this?" This kind of self-questioning exercise, developed by author and speaker Byron Katie and others, can serve as a useful tool for discovering the thoughts that trap you into negative judgments.[18]

- Create a stress-reduction plan for yourself. Can you get more exercise? More sleep? What calms you down and how can you do more of it? Don't make yourself available to your kids at the expense of your own well-being. Wall off some "me" time.

- Model self-acceptance and tell your kids what you're doing.

CHAPTER FIVE

Inner Drive

How to Help Your Kids Develop Motivation

MOTIVATION IS A TRICKY THING. We want our kids to want to practice their instrument, to do well on their math test, to help us clean up the house, and to set the table once in a while. But what if they don't? We've spent quite a bit of time trying to convince you that you can't make your child want what he doesn't want. Which begs the question: what the heck can you do?

As it turns out, a lot.

First, let's get an important distinction out of the way. There are some things we need our kids to do simply because we need them to get done. While it isn't crucial for Ned's daughter, Katie, to practice the violin, Ned and Vanessa do need her to put on her seat belt, brush her teeth, and get dressed and ready in a timely way in the morning. If she doesn't, she's late for school, and they're late for work. There are countless scenarios that fall into this category, where children are not motivated to do something we need them to do for the good of the family, and their unwillingness creates stress for everyone else. Go to any quiet street around 7:30 on a school morning and you can hear the frustration and feel the stress emanating from the houses that line the block. In these "must-do" situations, most parents rely on the external motivational strategies passed down for eons: the carrot and the stick. Rewards can be effective and in some cases can even spark good habits. They can help encourage your kids to accomplish short-term goals, to modify behavior, and to ensure cooperation. They can get a kid started on something, by helping him take those all-important first steps. For some kids, especially kids with ADHD, rewards can get the brain to activate for boring tasks, and can help them buckle down to do tasks that are really hard for them to do, like going to bed on time or doing their homework. But these scenarios are not about developing motivation—they're about enlisting cooperation.

This short-term external motivation isn't the type we'll be talking about in this chapter. Our aim is to focus on the self-motivation necessary for the long game—the inner drive that we want our kids to have so that they commit to something and persevere, develop their potential, and take steps toward living the lives they want to live. Research over the last four decades has repeatedly demonstrated that incentives like sticker charts, consequences, and other forms of parental monitoring that are "laid on" children actually undermine this type of motivation. What we're trying to do is to help kids to motivate themselves and to realize that they have something important to offer the world. We want to help them learn to run their own lives and seek to make them meaningful.

The damage isn't done immediately; it happens over time. Studies show that rewards for things like grades or other achievements can lower performance, crush creativity, and lead to bad behavior, like a willingness to cheat on a test or take performance-enhancing drugs.[1] Significantly, these external motivators can reinforce the idea that someone other than the child is responsible for his life. Rewards can erode self-generated interest and lead to interest only in the reward itself. What's more, our clever brains see through external motivators; we've evolved in such a way as to detect them and to resist attempts to be coerced. We'll devise ways to get the reward without doing the job or assignment. This is why kids can get As in courses they hardly remember after a few months.

Our aim is to largely take away the carrots and sticks and to offer you instead a deeper understanding of the brain . . . which, happily, is all you really need.

What Makes Us Tick?

Grasping the way motivation works in our brains and bodies will go a long way toward helping you understand your kids. Lucky for us, psychology and neuroscience are in agreement as to how to "make" motivation, and have even offered up a recipe. Here are the key ingredients:

The right mindset
Autonomy, competence, and relatedness
The optimal level of dopamine
Flow

It's all in your mind(set)

The work of the renowned psychologist Carol Dweck on motivation and mindsets may be familiar to you, as it's gotten a lot of attention across fields over the years. She posits that when students have a "fixed mindset," they see their mistakes as coming from a lack of ability, something they're powerless to change. In contrast, when students have a "growth mindset," they focus instead on their own effort as a means to become more successful. A growth mindset offers students a sense of control, as they believe that it's in their power to get better and better at something—indeed, at anything. Dweck's studies have found that students with a growth mindset tend to see learning as a more important goal in school than obtaining good grades. Their motivation, in other words, is internal. They are not relying on someone else's pronouncement that they are worthy or smart. Promoting a growth mindset is one of the best ways to improve your child's sense of control, to foster their emotional development, and to support their academic achievement.[2]

To encourage a growth mindset, Dweck recommends praising effort and the various strategies kids use to solve problems, rather than their built-in ability. Say things like, "Your curiosity is really fun for me to see" over "You're so smart"; or "I'm really impressed with how hard you worked on that test" instead of "Fantastic grade!" In Dweck's words, "a focus on inner effort can help resolve helplessness and engender success."[3] A growth mindset is the MVP of the self-motivated child.

Self-determination

Because motivation is such a strong focus of our work, we have studied the best thinking on this topic. Dweck is one of our great teachers in this area, and so are eminent psychologists Edward Deci and Richard Ryan. Deci and Ryan have developed one of the best-supported theories in psychology, known as self-determination theory (SDT), which holds that humans have three basic needs:

A sense of autonomy
A sense of competence
A sense of relatedness

Autonomy, they argue, is the most important of the three for developing internal motivation, so let's start there. According to SDT, the best way to motivate a child (or an adult, for that matter) is to support their sense of control. Hundreds of studies of schools, families, and businesses have found that explaining the reasons why a task is important and then allowing as much personal free-dom as possible in carrying out the task will stimulate much more motivation than rewards or punishments. We now know that if teachers foster autonomy in their students, they will catalyze inter-nal motivation and a desire for challenge, and that if parents pro-mote autonomy and mastery, their kids will be more likely to explore their interests and extend themselves. The very best thing you can do to help your children develop self-motivation is to give them as much control over their choices as possible, including ask-ing them what it is they want to be competent at and in charge of.[4]

Competence is the next piece of the puzzle, and this can be misleading. Many parents put all their focus on a narrow definition of competence, thinking that if their son or daughter becomes in-credibly skilled at math, or at playing soccer, then his or her intrin-sic motivation will kick in. These parents focus so much on the performative aspects of competence that, through their nagging and plan making, they actually compromise the fulfillment of the other two needs, autonomy and relatedness. Think of self-determination theory as a three-legged stool. One extremely tall leg won't make you sit higher, it will topple the whole thing over.

But competence is important, too. None of us want to do some-thing we feel like we constantly stink at. Yet as Dweck revealed, competence is more about our feeling that we can handle a situa-tion than it is about being really great at something. It's about feel-ing consciously competent, not about having an "I'm the Best!" trophy on a shelf. It's an internal rather than external barometer of accomplishment. Supporting our kids in developing competence is our job as parents. "You worked really hard on that science test and I'm proud of you even if you didn't get the grade you wanted. I imagine it's clear to us both that you are getting better and are get-ting nearer to reaching your goal." Remember that you can't de-velop competence for them, and any attempt to do so will just undermine their own motivation.

Finally, relatedness refers to the feeling of being connected to others, of being cared about. When your child feels connected to his teacher, he'll want to work hard for that teacher. When Ned asks the students he coaches what their favorite class was the previous year in school, he always follows up their answer with another question: "Was it the class or the teacher?" At least half the time, the answer is, "It was the teacher. She was really great." Likewise, when your child feels connected to you, when you communicate unconditional love and he tells himself, "My parents care more about me than about my grades," then it is more likely that your child will internalize your values. Self-determination theory calls this "integrated regulation." It is a child's identification with the values and goals of the people who care for him and love him unconditionally.

If you believe in education and hard work, and want your children to as well, we don't recommend scolding them each time they come home with a subpar grade. Though you may think it's the best way to communicate values, it's actually counterproductive because it signals conditional love. Chances are that they are already irked by the grade, so offer a sympathetic, "I know this is upsetting to you. I know you worked hard on that. I'd be happy to talk through things to help you for next time, if you want." Note that this response is sympathetic (relatedness). You're also reminding your child that there are ways to get a better outcome next time (competence). And by ending it with "if you want," they see they are in control, that you're a consultant, not a manager (autonomy).

Dopamine: Your "get up and go" aid

Brain science backs up what psychologists have been arguing about motivation since the 1970s. As you may remember from Chapter One, the brain's reward system is fueled by dopamine, which activates and energizes the brain. When something really cool happens, and especially when you're anticipating something really cool happening, you have a surge of dopamine. This happens with animals, too—just think of how a dog responds when his owner reaches for the leash. He knows where it's hanging and that it means he'll get a walk. He's up and wiggling around excitedly, ready to go out. In fact, he can't really be still. We want kids to experience this high-dopamine state. When we find something boring at work, generally the dopamine level in our prefrontal cortex is too low to motivate us to get up and go and to sustain effort. The same is true when kids can't motivate themselves to do their homework.

For years we've listened to stories about kids like Savannah, lovingly described by her parents as the most gifted procrastinator in the world. "Savannah is maddening during homework time," they told Ned. "She puts it off and puts it off no matter how many times we tell her to just get it done so she can do something fun. It's so frustrating because we know she can do it. It's just that she chooses not to. There are times like last night, when her brother finished his work at seven thirty and Savannah still hadn't started hers at seven forty-five. Her brother really wanted to go out for ice cream, and so we told Savannah that the three of us were going to Ben & Jerry's and she could come too if she finished her work. She was done by 8:00. It took her fifteen minutes to do the work, and yet she'd chosen to avoid it for three hours."

If you think of the role dopamine plays in motivation—and in anticipation of pleasurable outcomes—stories like this make complete sense. The thought of doing homework didn't generate enough dopamine in Savannah's brain to get her going. The thought of a Ben & Jerry's ice cream made her dopamine level spike (much as Ritalin does for kids with ADHD), allowing her to focus on an otherwise uninteresting task and to finish her homework in record time.

Offering ice cream may help in the short term, but you can't do it every night. Besides, we've said that rewards are counterproductive to intrinsic motivation. So how do you help a child develop a healthy dopamine system? The answer is surprisingly simple: encourage them to work hard at what they love.

Sculpting a motivated brain

Prior to the mid-1980s, people didn't realize that the brain could be changed. We thought what you're born with is what you've got. It's relatively new knowledge that we're capable of forging new neural pathways, and that how and where we focus our attention makes a measurable difference in the way in which our brain develops.[5]

When kids work hard at something they love and find challenging, they enter a state of what's come to be called "flow," where time passes quickly and their attention is completely engaged, but they're not stressed. When you're in flow, levels of certain neurochemicals in your brain—including dopamine—spike.[6] These neurochemicals are like performance-enhancing drugs for the brain. You think better in flow, and you process information faster. To be fully engaged this way, the activity has to be challenging enough not to be boring, but not so difficult that it's overly stressful. Think of playing tennis against a partner who is not nearly at your level. Completely boring. If you're playing against someone who is vastly more skilled, it's so punishing it's not enjoyable. A partner with whom you're well matched? That's where you find your flow.

So when you see an eight-year-old highly focused on building a Lego castle, lips pressed in concentration, what she is actually doing is getting her brain used to being motivated. She is conditioning her brain to associate intense enjoyment with highly focused attention, practice, and hard work. Just as frequent exposure to high levels of stress can sculpt a young brain in ways that are unhealthy, frequent exposure to states of flow can sculpt a young brain to be motivated and focused.

Researcher Reed Larson has studied the development of

motivation in children and teens, and he's found flow to be the se-cret sauce.[7] In interpreting the results of Larson's results, the great neuroscientist Marian Diamond concluded that, "while 'wrapped up' in a favorite pastime, children report feeling excited and forget-ting their problems. The high internal motivation accompanying those feelings is a form of reinforcement for directed effort, learn-ing, and accomplishment that can't be achieved in any other way as successfully."[8] Think of it like cross-training. Maybe what you ultimately want is a kid who has the mental and leg strength to run a marathon, but playing jump rope or hopscotch is a great way to get those legs primed and ready.

Just as in sports, the training of the mind works on a progres-sion. That eight-year-old building the Lego castle was once a four-year-old playing dress-up. Playing dress-up involves high intrinsic motivation—the kid really wants to do it—but low attention, be-cause they can move on at a moment's notice to playing with Bar-bies. As the child gets older and participates in more challenging or structured activities that she has chosen, she'll reach the state of both high intrinsic motivation and high attention. In other words, that's when she'll experience flow.[9]

This process is true for the eight-year-old, and it's also true for a fifteen-year-old who may struggle in school but is passionate about skiing, or drawing, or playing an instrument. The best way to mo-tivate him for the things you think he should focus on is to let him spend time on the things he wants to focus on.

Bill knows this from a scientific perspective, and from one that's more personal. He was a 2.8 student in high school with little inter-est in being a top student. As we mentioned in Chapter Two, he became passionate about rock and roll in junior high, and in high school his band was the most important thing in his world. He spent long hours almost every night learning songs, teaching him-self chord structure, practicing his instruments, and singing—all fueled by his own love for music and being in a band. He often went into his "music room" at 7:00 P.M., telling himself that he'd quit at 8:15 so he could get at least a little homework done. Most commonly, what felt like 8:15 to him was actually 9:45, because he was in flow. What he later realized is that, as a teenager, he was sculpting a brain that was very familiar with a flow state and that would eventually be able to put "the pedal to the metal" when he found an academic discipline—and later a career—that turned him on.

"I Don't Have the Brain of a Middle-aged Man"

One of our favorite lines ever came from a thirteen-year-old whose father pushed her hard for good grades. She said, "My dad is the smartest person I know. But his methods don't work for me. I don't have the brain of a middle-aged man."

This girl was wise beyond her years. We see this disconnect all the time, where parents are driven crazy by the way their kids work and don't grasp that they are wired differently, that what works for a thirteen-year-old isn't what would work for them. Ned had a student, Grant, whose mom drove him to school every day. His school was nearly an hour away from his home. Grant had a great mind— he was curious, clever, a top debater. He was also a remarkably skilled procrastinator. He did everything at the last minute, including typing his papers in the car. On the way to school. On his phone. It made his mom nuts. But the daily rush (both of the hurrying and chemical type) compelled him to get it done. He had all As, but didn't achieve them the way his mom would have liked.

"It would be so much easier if he would simply start his papers in advance and do a little bit each day," she lamented, and she was right. It would have been easier—for her. Which Ned (gently) suggested.

"What do you mean?" she asked.

"Well," Ned said, "this is a teenage boy you're describing, right? Chances are it's been a very long time since you've been a teenage boy. His brain works differently. He's a kid trying to get the work done, and he knows he works best under pressure—or can only work under pressure."

"But it drives me crazy to watch him waste hours and then have to rush to get things done," said his mom.

To which Ned suggested with a smile, "Maybe you shouldn't watch."

The tension between Grant and his mother is one of the most common we see, in part because men and women on average process dopamine differently. Girls are generally more interested by— and more consistently motivated to achieve in—school. They tend to have higher standards and to evaluate their performance more critically. They are more concerned about pleasing their parents and teachers.[10] Girls generally have more empathy, which leads them to develop a greater fear of disappointing their teachers. Their dopamine levels tend to kick in earlier and to stay with them longer, so that some will go so far as to finish a paper two days early. They're less likely than boys to need the stress of performing under a tight deadline to get them started. In fact, they are more likely to panic under the stress of a too-tight deadline, activating their amygdalas so that they're no longer working effectively.

Two years ago Ned was tutoring several kids at the same school who all had history term papers due the same week. The Friday before it was due, he saw three girls from the school. "How's the paper going?" he asked the first. "Oh, pretty well," she said. "I just have to finish my footnotes." The next girl had a similar story. "I've written it," she said, "but need to edit it a couple more times." The same exchange happened with the third girl. The next day, the boys rolled in. "Hey, Oscar, so how's the paper going?" Ned asked the first. "Oh, yeah," he said. "Right! I've been working on it . . . I mean,

I've got some ideas. . . ." The next boy said, "I still have to get it all written, but, I mean, yeah!" and the third reported essentially the same progress. These boys weren't stressed, keep in mind. They just hadn't gotten to it yet. Girls are not boys. Boys are not girls. And while there are notable exceptions and not everyone fits the gender mold, girls tend to like to be on top of things and to feel stressed when they fall behind or have too many things on their to-do list.

Then, of course, these girls grow up and many of them become moms. It's moms who most frequently oversee their sons' homework. The result? What we've come to think of as the Dopamine Wars.

Gender can be a factor, but motivation also functions quite differently for kids with ADHD, anxiety, or depression. Kids with ADHD simply don't have the dopamine levels of other children, so they need some help jump-starting their motivation, in whatever form that may be.[11] For parents who have a child with ADHD, rest assured that we'll address things like medication, incentives, and exercise, which can help kids focus and get their work done, in more detail in Chapter Eleven.

Finally, it can be helpful to remember that what motivates one child will not necessarily motivate another. Some kids are motivated largely by a desire to have close personal relationships or to help people, while others are energized by the desire to achieve at a high level or by a love of learning new things and gaining new skills. Kids can even want the same things for very different reasons. Many kids love video games or sports not for the stimulation of the game or the thrill of winning but for the enjoyment of playing with their friends. Some students strive for good grades for personal satisfaction, while others drive themselves academically because of their long-term goals. Similarly, kids may run for high school student council for a variety of differing reasons: because they want to learn about government; to help solve problems that affect their friends; to build their college resume; to experience a feeling of prestige; or to satisfy their desire to "be in charge."

When parents pay attention to these differences, they can help their kids understand what motivates them—and what's truly important to them. This knowledge can also help parents understand why their kids will sometimes make decisions that seem to be ill-advised—like deciding to go to the local public school with all his friends when he has the option of attending an elite, more academically challenging high school.[12] One student we know chose not to continue on with her academically intense high school when administrators told her she'd have to give up some extracurricular activities she loved in order to make more time for homework. "I'm only fifteen," she thought. "Why would I give up things I love to do now?" She switched schools, graduated with distinction, and is now thriving in college. It's not the most academically prestigious college, but it was her first choice. She was never motivated by rigorous academics, and was smart enough to know it early on.

Common Motivation Problems and How to Approach Them

We see kids at extreme ends of the motivation spectrum. Some are such perfectionists, so driven to grab the brass ring, that they make themselves sick with stress. At the opposite end, some don't seem to care about anything, or appear to act against what they know to be in their own best interest.

We have found that kids at both ends of the spectrum suffer from a low sense of control. How best to approach them varies quite considerably. Here are the four most common motivation problems we see, and our suggestions for helping kids to solve them.

The Saboteur: *"My kid just can't seem to motivate himself to do what he knows he needs to do. It's like he's deliberately sabotaging himself."*

We see a lot of kids who might be described this way. They may want to do well at school, or in the school band, but they can't seem to put in the hours necessary to get the job done.

If this is your child, you can help your kid to see how things that don't seem so important now may be important to their long-term goals. Most parents have tried to connect the dots for their kids by the time they come to us, and we know that it isn't easy. If a kid's primary interest is in socializing with friends, encourage that interest and help him see how it will serve him professionally one day— he might have a fulfilling career as a teacher, psychologist, negotiator, lawyer, or sales director. But also tell him that most careers that place a strong emphasis on interpersonal skills require at least a bachelor's degree, and in many cases a graduate degree. So if he wants to interact with others for a living in a meaningful way, he'll have to learn to work hard to develop his academic capabilities.

You can also help him find his own reasons for working hard at the things that are important to him. We often try to help kids see the distinction between things they feel like doing and things they want to do. To illustrate this, Bill will ask them to think about new parents. He tells kids that when his daughter was a baby and it was his responsibility when she cried in the middle of the night to bring her to her mother to be fed, he never once felt like getting out of bed. But he wanted to do it because it was important that his daughter not suffer (and that he and his wife eventually get back to sleep). Using this logic, we encourage kids to tell themselves, "Even if I don't feel like doing my work, I want to do it because it's important for me and for my future." Not surprisingly, kids often find that telling themselves "I want to do it" is more motivating than telling themselves otherwise.

Every success coach or productivity guru will tell you that if a child can visualize himself accomplishing a goal he has chosen for himself, it tricks the brain into thinking he's done it. The same is true of writing goals down—it's powerful reinforcement, and if that goal is there in your child's handwriting it's a great reminder that it's his goal, not yours.[13] Writing goals down also helps people operate more from their prefrontal cortex instead of responding or reacting to what feels like an immediate demand or pressure. Writing down our goals reminds us to play the long game. Let's imagine your child is an Olympian and she writes down and pins to her bulletin board the fact that she would like to win four gold medals. When she is hungry and wants a piece of pizza, she sees her goal and will be more likely to go for a healthy plate of chicken and veggies over greasy Domino's. Not that Olympians are your average teen—most goals need to be more reachable and immediate for motivation to kick in—but you get the point. We encourage kids to put their written goals on a piece of paper in their backpack where they'll often come across it, or to stick them on their bedroom wall. Ned had a student whose goal was to transfer to Georgetown, and so he wore Georgetown gear all the time to remind himself to work hard.

You can also help your saboteur cultivate discipline in the area he's interested in. If a kid enjoys, say, baseball, but doesn't work on it outside regular practices, you can say something like, "Hey, I know you love baseball and I know you'll practice for hours if somebody's with you. Would you like me to find a high school player to work with you a few days a week, or schedule practice with a friend?" If your kid develops his skills, he'll develop a brain that is used to working hard to become better and better at something that's important to him.

These are fairly simple suggestions. We recognize that for many saboteurs, they won't be enough. Many kids who fall into the saboteur category have a dopamine deficiency problem, and helping them connect the dots or visualize goals won't go far enough to light up their brains. If your child has an unusually strong aversion to doing homework, we recommend having them evaluated to rule out ADHD, anxiety, sleep difficulties, and learning disabilities. Some additional strategies for igniting the saboteur include:

- Frequent exercise. Even short bursts of exercise can activate the brain enough to get started on something, in part by increasing dopamine in the prefrontal cortex. Physical activity is physically activating.

- Social support. Finding an older kid to serve as a homework coach, or helping your child join a study group of mildly more academic peers, can help his focus. For adolescents, we're particularly gung ho about peer-to-peer support, because teens are developmentally wired to be attuned to their cohorts. Research has also shown that kids often learn better from other kids than they do from adults, and that when a homework coach is an older kid, the one being tutored has a dopamine spike.[14] Another argument for outsourcing: if you have a tendency to be controlling, or even if you aren't but your child perceives that you are, his saboteur instincts will kick in.

- Stimulation. Some saboteurs need music in the background to help them accomplish tasks that they'd otherwise avoid. Music can serve as white noise and block out distraction. It can make a boring activity less so. And it can ease anxiety. For others, quiet is better. Your saboteur may have to experiment a bit to see which suits him. There's also recent evidence that chewing gum can improve activation, processing speed, and work production.[15]

- A healthy, high-protein diet and enough rest. (You've heard this a zillion times so we won't belabor the point. But it's true.)

- Circuit training. Saboteurs often do well when they work intensely for short periods marked by a timer and then take a prescribed break. If you think about it, "takeoffs" and "landings" are memorable in lectures and lessons. But in the middle, our brains meander. So twenty minutes of science, twenty minutes of Spanish, and twenty minutes of social studies, with breaks in between, repeated twice, may have better impact than forty consecutive minutes of each. Adding more starts and stops encourages the brain to be more attentive and motivated. Suggest circuit training as an option, and ask your kid if she wants to set her own timer, or if she wants you to serve as coach, setting a stopwatch and calling out, "Time!"

- Incentives. Yes, we've told you external incentives are bad for developing intrinsic motivation. But sometimes incentives are okay, so long as the child understands that your goal is to enable his brain to activate (by increasing dopamine) so that he can accomplish what otherwise may not get done. You might say to kids as young as six, "I know your brain just can't wake up without a little incentive. So I'm happy to offer something for your brain to wake up." It also helps to be a little creative with the incentives. Remember Savannah, who wouldn't do her homework until Ben & Jerry's was held out to her? Her parents might say the next night, "Savannah, I get that it's really hard for you to get motivated enough to study for your vocabulary test. If you want, I'd be happy to help you come up with a way to activate your dopamine so you can get going. Here's my suggestion: What if we do a practice quiz? If you don't get seventeen out of the twenty words right, you have to do twenty push-ups. If you do get seventeen out of twenty right, I have to do ten."

The Enthusiast: *"My kid is motivated—just not about school."*

Over the years, Bill has seen hundreds of kids who had relatively low academic motivation but were extremely motivated about something else—crafting, music, sports, or making *Star Wars* replicas.

What he says to the parents of these kids is that so long as they are working hard at something they really enjoy doing, he's not worried, because he knows they're shaping a brain that will eventually enable them to be successful. And Bill tells kids, "Working hard to get better and better at something that's important to you is one of the best things you can do for your brain." (An exception here may be video games, which aren't all bad, but require more nuance. We'll get into the impact of technology on the developing brain in Chapter Nine.) He tells the kids that it would be good if they could apply this sense of total immersion to something school related, and that he believes they are fully capable of doing so.

Ken Robinson is one of the leading thinkers in the area of finding your passion, and his book *The Element: How Finding Your Passion Changes Everything* emphasizes the importance of looking for that intersection of passion and skill. While it's not a book that will necessarily capture the imagination of your average seventh grader, parents can share its stories—from that of Simpson's creator Matt Groening, who had little interest in school but was always fanatical about drawing, to famous choreographer Gillian Lynne, who could never sit still in class as a child but thrived in a dance school. Stories like these can provoke a healthy discussion about what it means to want something and how to connect the dots to get there.[16]

Sebastian was a high school junior at an extremely demanding suburban high school when he came to Bill's office for testing. He had a 2.3 cumulative GPA, which, he said, was as low as it was because he did "no work at all—seriously, I never do any work." He described his skill at "manipulating" his teachers to get them to give him passing grades. Sebastian assumed that he had a very limited future because of his school performance. He thought he probably would not be able to get into college, and would end up working a bunch of low-paying jobs. But he was passionately involved in a local county rescue squad. In fact, he was staying up most of the night on Thursdays and Saturdays helping people with true emergencies.

To Sebastian's surprise (actually shock), Bill asked him if he had ever thought of dropping out of high school. "Why would you say that?" he asked.

"It seems like a waste of your time," Bill said, "not to mention of your teacher's time, to spend six hours a day doing something you care so little about, and spending so much of your energy resisting, lying, faking, and manipulating your teachers." Then Bill said, "Why don't you think about doing rescue work full time?" He told Sebastian that he hadn't actually screwed up his whole life by being a poor student—that kids can flunk all their classes in high school and then, if they decide they want an education, start at a community college (which are open enrollment), and once they have about thirty credits they can apply to virtually any college without having to show their high school transcript. Bill asked Sebastian to think about what would be in his own best interest and said they'd talk again.

When Bill met with Sebastian's parents the following week to discuss the test results, he was a little nervous, particularly when he learned that both parents were university professors. Bill thought there was a pretty good chance they would not be pleased by his conversation with their son. To his surprise, they started the meeting by thanking Bill for talking so frankly with Sebastian, who had left the office in a much more energetic and upbeat mood than they had seen him in for some time. They went on to say that he had announced a new plan that involved starting at a local community college and ending up with a degree in fire science from one of the major universities in greater Washington, DC. Later, Bill learned that on his own initiative, Sebastian had explored the possibility of dropping out of school but he had learned that if he did so, he would no longer be able to participate in the rescue squad. Newly informed and now motivated, he immediately started to do better in school. He agreed to work with a good tutor and gave up his all-night gig with the rescue squad on Thursdays. But he also saw school in a different context. Bill heard from Sebastian's mom two months later. She said his GPA was now 3.6 and asked if Bill could see Sebastian's sister, who had always been a good student but who, after Sebastian's turnaround, was nervous about the fact that, unlike her brother, she did not have a true passion.

While this story had a happy ending, it begs the question: what can you do if you parent a kid like Sebastian?

As a rule-out step, we'd recommend that if he is not at all motivated for school, you have him evaluated for a learning disability, depression, anxiety, or ADHD. Assuming that is not the case, treat him respectfully, but also give him an accurate model of reality. You'd be surprised at how many kids will listen to your suggestions if they feel you're taking them seriously. So if your son says he wants to get an athletic scholarship and play baseball for Duke, ask him how he wants to get there. Suggest sitting down together at the computer and researching academic requirements and statistics on recruitment. Help him explore what he needs to do to accomplish his goal.

If supporting kids in the pursuit of their nonacademic interests is a good move, then withholding those interests as a punishment is quite obviously a bad one. We get where the impulse to withhold sports or extracurricular activities comes in—there's only so much time in the day, and if your high schooler can't find the time to do his homework because he's too exhausted by everything else, what message are you sending about priorities if you let him put extra-curriculars above academics?

This logic sort of makes sense. But the science doesn't back it up. Remember, if a kid isn't motivated by school, he's not motivated by school, and you can't make him want to do better. Taking away something that does motivate him isn't going to solve the problem, and may, on the contrary, further dampen his motivation.

The Eeyore: *"My kid isn't motivated to do anything. He doesn't seem to know what he wants."*

It's common for teenagers to go through periods of diminished motivation, reminding you perhaps of Eeyore from Winnie-the-Pooh stories. If it goes on for more than two or three weeks, or comes on shockingly suddenly, then there may be cause for concern. Request a thorough medical evaluation to rule out medical causes for apathy and, if necessary, a psychological or psychiatric assessment to screen for depression and/or drug use.

Once you rule out more serious problems, you can encourage Eeyores to get involved in service activities and negotiate limits on TV and video games. You can expose them to things you think they might enjoy. But the most important thing you can do is express confidence that they will find something they love to do. We recognize that this is tough to swallow, but it helps to remember that finding a passion is not something you can do for your kid.

You can also emphasize the importance of self-awareness. It's astonishing to us how many kids have never asked themselves what it is they want, or have never had someone ask it of them. They're too busy either trying to please others, or rebelling against others' control. But they need to think for themselves about themselves. They need to consider their special talents and life purpose. They should ask, "What do I want? What do I love to do?" You can help them ask these questions, even if you can't supply the answers. Hard as it may be to accept this, it's your child's responsibility to find interests and motivation in life.

Help your kids pay attention to what they're good at. Many Eeyores will dismiss their natural talents: "Oh, anybody can do that," they'll incorrectly assert. "If I'm good at it, it must be easy." They often overlook their talents and focus instead on other areas that are someone else's greatest strength. When they find themselves lacking, it just justifies their gloomy outlook.

If they don't feel they have an area of obvious strength, they should ask, "What can I do at least as well as most people?" This can then lead to other bigger questions like, "What might be my purpose? What do I need help with? How can I get myself to do what I want and/or need to do?" It's at the intersection of interest, talent, and self-awareness that kids are able to find a sense of direction. What they find in their youth may not be the area they ultimately develop, but it's an important step.

Bill worked with a girl with language-based learning disabilities from the age of five through her second year in college. When Lette was fourteen, her mother expressed concern that although Lette did her homework adequately and generally did what her parents asked of her, she did not seem to have any true passions in life. Bill told her that while we should from time to time make suggestions about things we think may be of interest to our kids, this is not the kind of thing one can force. It has to happen on its own—and often happens in unforeseen ways.

When Bill saw Lette's mother again six months later to discuss a school-related issue, she said, "Oh, by the way, Lette has gotten involved with the Washington Animal Rescue League and seems to really enjoy it." Over the next several months, Lette became deeply invested in her work there and by the end of the year she could list all the shelters and rescuable dogs in the greater DC area. Bill knew better than to be surprised. A situation that may seem hopeless will often change because life changes. Opportunities come out of nowhere.

Rescue work became a true passion for Lette, who found in it a meaningful way to apply her love of animals. Three years later, as a junior in high school, she did an internship in early childhood education. What she found was that she was able to apply the same dedication and absorption she had devoted to animal rescue to her work with young children. Lette then became a highly motivated student of child development and preschool education. She recently graduated from college with a degree in early childhood education and is enjoying her first job as a teacher of young children.

Many Eeyores are homebodies who resist doing anything new or different and have a narrowly defined comfort zone. They often prefer to read or play solo or do video games rather than engage in more active tasks, and they are commonly reluctant to put themselves in unfamiliar social situations. Many parents say that if they didn't nag their Eeyores continuously they'd never get out of the house.

It's very hard to resist the tendency to nag Eeyores repeatedly; however, this never motivates them to try new things. It may be helpful to know that Eeyores commonly lack flexibility and confidence in their ability to adapt to new situations, which can lead to anxiety about trying new things. Also, because these kids are rarely "social naturals," they may have anxiety about the social demands placed on them outside the home or the classroom. Helping Eeyores thus requires a combination approach:

1. Stay calm and focus on maintaining a strong relationship with your child—which frequent cajoling undermines. Remember that some people have fewer interests and smaller friendship groups throughout their lives, and are perfectly happy.
2. Ask your child if she would like to feel more comfortable in new situations—to feel less nervous about them. If she says yes, you could suggest that she work with an expert who knows how to help kids feel more confident about taking on new challenges.
3. Tell your child that you feel it is your responsibility as a parent to expose her to the world and that you would rather

not have to nag her constantly to try new things and ask her what she would suggest you do. Negotiate a reasonable "compromise" between your desire for your child to be active and engaged most of the time and her desire to do as little as possible that's unfamiliar or challenging.

4. Physical activity can be motivating to all kinds of kids. See if you can interest your Eeyore (with a short-term reward if necessary) in engaging in an individual sport that most kids don't do, like fencing, rock climbing, or judo.

The Hermione Granger: *"My kid is stressed out of her mind. In her view, it's Yale or nothing."*

Some kids will get caught up in a competitive school environment or are wired to acquire as many accolades as they can. Harry Potter's friend Hermione Granger falls squarely into this category. Most often, the pressure they feel comes from their parents or teachers, although kids also infect each other with anxiety and competitiveness.

Hermiones are intensely—even unhealthily—driven to excel or to live up to someone else's expectations. Their motivation is largely fear based, as they experience anxiety about not being able to achieve the high goals they've set for themselves—or that others have set for them. They tend to have a very low sense of control and to feel "existentially impotent," to borrow the words of Julie Lythcott-Haims, former Stanford dean and author of *How to Raise an Adult*.[17]

Obviously, if the pressure is coming from mom and dad, the solution is simple: stop pressuring them. Even if you are proud of your child, she may come to believe that she is loved because of her accomplishments. Most commonly, this is just an issue of communication that needs to be repaired.

But if you have told her, "Look, I don't care about your grades or where you go to school," and still she is anxious and fearful, the fixes are more complicated.

We recently gave a talk about the effects of stress and sleep deprivation on the developing brain to a classroom of highly stressed and exhausted eleventh-grade AP English students. The students were courteous, took notes, and asked good questions, and they seemed to like the idea that they would ultimately be more successful if they were not chronically tired and stressed. When the talk was over, however, their teacher pulled us aside and said, "Every one of these kids think that if they don't get into Yale, they'll end up working at McDonald's." This is very similar to what we were told by an English teacher at an elite independent school in Washington, namely that by the time the kids hit ninth grade "they're all terrified" at the thought of not getting into a prestigious college.

So how do you even begin to fix this? How do you encourage internal motivation for a kid who is so reliant on external signs of achievement? First ask her if she'd be willing to hear some information that might help her to work with a lot of motivation but maybe a little less fear and anxiety. If she is, tell her the truth: that where you go to college does not make an enormous difference to your success in life. Share proof of this with her. Researchers Stacy Berg Dale and Alan Krueger have followed the career trajectories of the same class of high school graduates for decades. Among students who had comparable SAT scores, whether or not they went to an elite college made little difference in their earning potential. This was true whether they applied to and were rejected from the same elite schools, or whether they were accepted to the elite schools but chose to go to another, less selective college.[18] Another study from Gallup and Purdue University found that the type of college students attended (e.g., public versus private; highly selective versus less selective) made very little difference to their workplace engagement and well-being. The factors that best predicted well-being were those more intrinsic to the college experience itself, such as: 1) having a professor who showed personal interest in them, stimulated them to learn, and encouraged them; 2) having an internship or job in college that allowed them to apply what they were learning; and 3) being actively involved in extracurricular activities or projects that took a semester or more to complete.[19] Also, a study conducted in 2013 through the Pew Research Center found that graduates from public and private colleges reported equal levels of life satisfaction, including satisfaction with family life and personal finances, as well as job satisfaction.[20] What these studies suggest is that if you're bright and motivated, it doesn't much matter where you go to school. For some kids, knowing this makes it a bit easier to pay attention to what's really important to them.

You can also share the big-fish-little-pond theory with your Hermione. This idea, developed by Herbert Marsh,[21] holds that you see yourself in a more positive light if you perform well in relation to your peer group. So, being a standout at a lesser-known school is often better in the long run than getting lost in the crowd at a more competitive school. In his book *David and Goliath,* Malcolm Gladwell told the story of a high-achieving student determined to go into science at Brown. She found the environment at Brown demoralizing, and let go of her science focus. At another, less competitive school, she may have given her natural interest more of a chance to bloom. Gladwell wrote, "Rarely do we stop and consider . . . whether the most prestigious of institutions is always in our best interest."[22] Ask your child to think about whether it may be good for her to be a bigger fish in a smaller pond.

Help your Hermione see that while it can be frightening to fail at something, a poor grade does not translate to a permanently closed door. In fact, it can be liberating—as we saw with one friend of ours who failed an AP Music Theory class her freshman year of high school. While she was terrified initially, it ended up freeing her from a paralyzing fear of not achieving a GPA of 4.0. When she saw that the worst-case scenario actually didn't destroy her or close off her future, she was more empowered to take risks and more capable of living her life without feeling that a monster was chasing her around every turn. And that, ultimately, made her more successful.

When Bill's kids were in elementary school, he made a point of telling them that there was a low correlation between grades in school and success in life. He said that while he would look at their report cards if they wanted him to, he was much more concerned about their development as students and as people. They generally seemed to believe him and were happy that their mother and he were not on them constantly about their grades. Then one night when Bill's daughter was a junior in high school, she came to hear one of his lectures about the adolescent brain, at which he shared a number of the ideas discussed in this book. On the way home, she said, "I bet you don't really believe that part about high school grades not being so important for success in life."

Bill asked her why she thought this. She replied that her teachers and school counselors had always spoken about how important it was to be a good student (which she was). Bill assured her that, based on considerable research, he did believe it. To prove it, he offered to pay her a hundred dollars if she got a C on her report card, in any subject. He did this because he would have been perfectly happy for her to have the experience of having a C on her transcript and to see that her world did not end, that all her options for the future did not foreclose, and that she could still create a meaningful life. (She never took him up on it.)

Ned tells every Hermione he encounters (and he comes across a lot of them) that the most important thing she can do is develop the brain she wants for the rest of her life. Does she want a brain that's so stressed and tired that she is easily anxious and depressed thereafter? Does she want a workaholic brain? Or does she want a brain that is powerful, but also happy and resilient? Like Ned does, you can say, "You're clearly bright enough to do this. The question is whether it's healthy for your long-term development and consistent with your highest values." Then encourage her to think about her highest values, what's truly most important to her, and ask her to consider whether, when she thinks about them, she's driving herself in the right direction. Then help her set goals that are values based, because when we set goals we're in control of, our minds are happy. We'll talk much more about goal setting in Chapter Ten when we discuss the mental strategies that help kids succeed.

What to Do Tonight

- Support autonomy, support autonomy, support autonomy.

- Explore where your child's true inner motivation lies. You can do this by asking when in life he or she feels "really happy." Kids with a healthy self-drive will commonly think of times when they perform well in school or in sports, are engaged in pleasurable pastimes, or do something fun with their friends or family. In contrast, kids who are obsessively motivated or have difficulty sustaining motivation and effort will often say that they feel happiest when they have no responsibilities, when nothing is expected of them, and when they feel no pressure.

- Make a point of speaking with your kids about what it is they want in life. What do they love to do? What do they feel they're good at? If there's a reason they're here, what might that be?

- Help your child articulate (and write down) goals. We will explore this in more depth in Chapter Ten. For now, simply the act of voicing where she wants to get is a remarkably constructive step.

- Encourage flow in any activity by giving your kids the space and time they need to do what they love.

- Teach and model a love of challenge and persistence in the face of difficulty. Attribute positive motivational qualities to young kids (e.g., "I've noticed that you don't give up on things.").

- Teach your kids not to be overly preoccupied with pleasing others. If they're focused on external feedback, consider occasionally saying something like, "Everybody feels good when they're successful at things and get positive feedback from other people. It's completely normal. My experience, though, is that the wisest thing is to evaluate your own performance and to focus on getting better at doing the right thing."

- If your child doesn't seem to have a passion, remember that there are many people and experiences that will positively influence their lives. Seek out mentors or role models in different fields, and expose them to a range of careers and life choices.

CHAPTER SIX

Radical Downtime

I N INDIA'S ANCIENT Vedic tradition, it is said that "rest is the basis of all activity." Rest, activity, rest, activity. Everything we do requires this alternation. We see this in sports and fitness, where interval training has taught us that much of the benefit of exercise comes from the body's recovery during rest. We see it in the world of yoga, where each practice ends with the body lying perfectly still. And we see it in the realm of the brain, where daydreaming, meditation, and sleep give the brain rest—consolidating new information and skills in memory and making the brain healthier when it returns to a period of activity. The brain has at least forty resting-state networks, and while we won't go into all of them in this book, the fact that so much of the brain activates when we're at rest strongly suggests that rest should be taken seriously. We think of this deep resting of the brain as "radical downtime."

It's hard to argue that our balance of rest and activity is optimal. Our culture does not settle down easily. A recent series of studies found that 64 percent of young men and 15 percent of young women chose to self-administer a mild electric shock rather than sit quietly with their own thoughts for six minutes.[1] We do not know how to be without doing. Teens, adults, and increasingly even young children don't sleep enough and don't spend enough time on self-reflection, contributing to their feelings of being overloaded and overwhelmed. Parents will describe themselves as "crazy busy," and a high percentage of the kids we see feel stressed, pressured, and tired.

There are many forms of downtime. Anything that is relaxing or rejuvenating, like gardening or reading, we're all for. Yet as the pace of life goes faster, we need to radicalize our downtime. Radical downtime does not mean playing video games, watching TV, surfing YouTube videos, texting with a friend, or participating in organized sports or activities. It means doing nothing purposeful, nothing that requires highly focused thought. This is one of the most powerful things we can do for our brains. It is enormously important as an antidote to the mind-scattering and mind-numbing effects of 24/7 technology and multitasking. Radical downtime allows you to process a backlog of stimuli. Think of the many activities, tasks, and interactions of daily life as snowflakes that fall on your brain in quick succession, making big, unruly piles that seem impossible to navigate around. Radical downtime is the snowplow that comes through and evens them out, giving order to your life so that you can ski on a smooth surface and avoid the gulfs and occasional avalanches that may result from snow piling up in uneven ways. In this chapter, we will delve into two powerful forms of radical downtime: daydreaming and meditation. Sleep is a mammoth piece of radical downtime, and we devote all of Chapter Seven to its importance—and elusiveness—in modern life.

A Wandering Mind: The Benefits of Daydreaming

For as long as scientists have studied the brain, they have been captivated by the question of what the brain does when it's focusing on a task or processing external stimulation. Only recently did they turn to seriously consider what it's up to the rest of the time. In the mid-1990s, neuroscientist Marcus Raichle noticed that certain parts of the brain go dark when we're focused on a task or goal. In

1997, he and his colleagues at Washington University grouped to-gether and analyzed these parts of the brain and gave them a name: the default mode network. It wasn't until 2001 that Raichle pub-lished a study that showed what makes the DMN light up: a brain that is alert, but not focused on a task.[2] Over the past decade, Raichle has led a new wave of research that suggests that the unfo-cused downtime that activates the default mode network is abso-lutely critical for a healthy brain.[3]

Every time we blink, our default mode network activates and our conscious networks take a brief rest. Even simply closing your eyes, taking a deep breath, and exhaling can help refresh the brain. When your default mode network is active, you think about your-self, about your past and future, and about problems that need to be resolved, all of which are crucial for developing a sense of self. You consider the experiences and feelings of other people, a process that is important for the development of empathy. The default mode network is where the all-important work of personal reflec-tion takes place. It's what makes you a thoughtful human being. It allows you to organize your thoughts. It grounds you. Imagine you get into a spat with a friend who said something insensitive. In the hustle and bustle of that day, you don't have a chance to think about it, other than to know that it was irritating and that you're mad. Then, the next morning in the shower, you think, *that actually wasn't such a big deal.* I wonder why she said that? Maybe she was having a bad day. I can even sort of see what she had in mind. Every time you replay the scenario, it matters a little bit less. But it takes time to replay the scenario, and if you don't allow yourself downtime, you just hold on to the anger without seeing what it might become. If the brain develops according to how it is used, how can we develop an understanding of ourselves and of other people other than by thinking about ourselves and other people?

When we replay scenarios excessively, or when doing so is

painful and we engage in negative thought loops, that's not mind wandering, it's ruminating. This is an important distinction. You really need *unstressed* periods of downtime every day.

When we are in a healthy headspace and have a few minutes of downtime, the DMN allows the brain to analyze and compare, to solve problems, and to create alternate scenarios. But here's the thing about the DMN: it cannot activate when you're focused on a task. Researcher Mary Helen Immordino-Yang describes two alternating brain systems: 1) a task-positive or "looking out" system that's activated when we're engaged in goal-directed tasks, and 2) a task-negative or resting system that is for "looking in."[4] When we're focused on external tasks that require concentration, ranging from finding an address to studying for an exam, we shut off our daydreaming, "looking in" part of the brain. And when we daydream, our ability to "look out" and to do an explicit task evaporates.

Our culture values getting things done. But research shows us just how important it is to do that mind wandering. Jerome Singer, a legendary cognitive psychologist, was the first scientist to suggest that the mental state in which the mind is allowed to wander freely is, in fact, our "default" state. Singer further argued in his 1966 book, *Daydreaming*, that daydreaming, imagination, and fantasy are essential elements of a healthy mental life. These elements include self-awareness, creative incubation, autobiographical planning, consideration of the meaning of events and interactions, taking another person's perspective, reflecting on your own and others' emotions, and moral reasoning.[5] All of this leads to what we think of as "aha!" moments. The musician, bestselling writer, and neuroscientist Daniel J. Levitin emphasizes that insights are far more likely to come when you are in the mind-wandering mode than in the task-focused mode. It is only when we let our minds wander that we make unexpected connections between things that we did not realize were connected. This can help you solve problems that previously seemed to be unsolvable.[6] (As Carlo Rovelli pointed out in *Seven Brief Lessons on Physics*, Einstein's breakthrough on relativity came shortly after a year spent in Italy "loafing aimlessly" and attending occasional lectures.)[7]

The more efficient the DMN is at toggling on and off, the better you become at processing life events. When it's time to pull yourself out of that daydream and to turn back to the many constant stimuli of life, your brain is primed and ready for action. People with an efficient DMN do better on tests of cognitive ability, including measures of memory, flexibility of thought, and reading comprehension. People who are efficient at toggling their DMN on and off also have better mental health.[8] It's like having an efficient stress response, which turns on quickly when needed, and turns off quickly when not. In people with ADHD, anxiety, depression, autism, or schizophrenia, the DMN does not function efficiently. It's harder for them to toggle back and forth between looking in and looking out, resulting in too much daydreaming or excessive self-focus. When we ruminate, we're not toggling efficiently—we're getting stuck in thought when there's something in front of us we should be focusing on instead.

We live in a world where "boredom" is a dirty word, and people often compete to see who's busier, as if their sense of self-worth could be measured by how little time they have. This hyperproductivity trickles down to our kids. Think of your typical American family driving somewhere in the car: the kids want to listen to something, watch something, or play a game. They've forgotten how to look out the window, chitchat, or daydream. Psychologist Adam Cox noted that whereas fifty years ago kids might be bored after a couple of hours with nothing to do, nowadays kids become bored after *thirty seconds*, while most adults feel the need to check their phones in the four seconds it takes to slow down and stop at a stop sign.[9] Boredom is unsettling for hyperstimulated teens, whereas the "chaos of constant connection is soothingly familiar."[10]

The answer here is that less is more. Alternate periods of connection and activity with periods of quiet time. When you're waiting for a doctor's appointment, or for your bus to arrive, do you immediately pick up a magazine or check your phone? What if you just sat there for a couple of minutes instead? When you're driving, or walking or running for exercise, are you listening to Spotify or to a podcast? What if you listened to your own thoughts instead? What would you think about? We need to be more intentional about downtime now that stimulation is everywhere. Whereas hiking or camping was once a respite, soon there will be nowhere to go where you can't be connected. We need to actively choose to not take our phones with us, or to turn them off.

If there is one thing we hope you will do differently after reading this, it is *let* your kids do nothing. We parents are sometimes as much of the problem as the ubiquity of technology. One of the Ned's most overachieving and stressed-out kids eloquently expressed what so many kids feel. "All I want is a couple of hours to myself. To do what I want, which is to do nothing. But if I have a free block of time, my parents swoop in to fill it. 'Shouldn't you be doing more test prep or studying something?'" We schedule them in activity after activity so that they can keep up with other kids and never be "wasting time." But that free time to daydream is actually essential.

Child psychologist Lyn Fry recommends that parents sit down with their kids at the outset of a summer break and have them make a list of all the things they'd like to do on their own during their free time. If they complain of boredom, they can refer to their list.[11] *They* are the ones who have to figure out how to spend their time, without their parents filling it in for them. And they just may spend that time thinking about who they want to be. Learning to tolerate solitude—to be comfortable with yourself—is one of the most important skills one acquires in childhood.

My son Matthew is what people used to call "dreamy." When he was four or five, we were having breakfast together before school, and I looked up from the paper to see Matthew staring across his bowl of cereal into space.

"What are you doing?" I asked.

"I'm listening," Matthew answered.

"Oh, okay," I said, a little confused as it was pretty quiet as far as I could tell. "Can you eat your cereal before it gets soggy?"

"Sure," Matthew said, but a minute or two later he was still staring into space.

"What are you listening to?" I asked. I was worried about how long it was going to take him to finish his cereal.

"Songs in my head," he said.

It occurred to me then, as it has again many times since, that in interrupting Matthew's reveries, I was asserting that my grown-up agenda of packing him off to school was more important. But research now shows that Matthew's daydreaming may be as important for cognitive development as any other thinking that kids do. And now when my friends wonder where Matthew's musical ability comes from, I think about all the good that daydreaming did.

—Ned

A Meditative Mind

At a recent workshop for mental health professionals, Bonnie Zucker, the author of two excellent books on childhood anxiety, gave a presentation on the treatment of anxiety. She asked the three hundred professionals in the audience if they meditated on a regular basis. A handful raised their hands. Dr. Zucker then said, "Meditation is so powerful that I ask all of you who don't yet meditate to learn meditation—and then call me in a year to tell me how it's changed your life."

We couldn't agree more. Practicing meditation is increasingly important as changes in the world lead to higher levels of anger and fear, and as advances in technology quicken the pace of life, giving us little time to simply "be" with ourselves. Although kids and teens rarely beg their parents to find them a meditation teacher, research indicates that when children and adolescents establish a practice regularly, meditation benefits them in the same ways as it does adults. In this section, we'll briefly discuss mindfulness and Transcendental Meditation, the two forms of meditation that are used most widely with children and teens, and explain why we recommend building meditation periods into your kids' days.

Mindfulness

Jon Kabat-Zinn is the scientist whose mindfulness-based stress-reduction (MBSR) program has played the largest role in helping mindfulness gain popularity and scientific respectability. He defines mindfulness as "paying attention in a particular way: on purpose, in the present moment, and nonjudgmentally." The basic mindfulness meditation practice involves focusing awareness on the breath and noticing thoughts as they arise. The goal is to focus on the moment-to-moment experience, without judging or reacting. You monitor the content of your thoughts and your reactions to them. Other mindfulness practices include scanning the body for areas of stress, and mindful eating and walking. Some mindfulness practices encourage the development of ethical values such as patience, trust, acceptance, kindness, compassion, and gratitude.

Mindfulness comes in many forms. Psychotherapists use it to help kids learn to regulate their emotions, and schools are implementing programs like Goldie Hawn's MindUP and Mindful Schools, which introduces mindfulness to students in low-income elementary schools in Oakland, California. Mindfulness in schools sometimes includes guided meditations, visualizations, affirmations, breathing exercises, mindful yoga, exercise set to music, and writing and visual art exercises for promoting positive self-expression. Because of the wide range of practices included under the mindfulness umbrella, mindfulness interventions have been used with students from preschool to college. The eminent neuroscientist Richard Davidson is currently studying the introduction of mindfulness practices to children as young as four.

Research on the impact of mindfulness on children is still in the early stages, but studies have shown that in the school years these practices can lower levels of stress, aggression, and social anxiety, improve executive functions such as inhibition and working memory, and contribute to stronger performance in math.[12] Studies on adults also show changes in brain activation and even in gene expression—the turning on and off of specific genes.[13]

We recently spoke with Josh Aronson, a professor of applied psychology at New York University and acclaimed researcher whose work we've drawn on throughout this book. Aronson is currently conducting research using the mindfulness app Headspace with disadvantaged students in inner-city schools. He told us that after twenty days of practice, kids reported experiencing things they had never felt before. Some said they felt comfortable in their own bodies for the first time and have begun seeing beauty in nature. One boy reported that on his way to school, his typical thoughts would include things like, "Will I get held up or shot by a drug dealer or a cop who thinks I'm a troublemaker? Will I pass my classes, and will my friends be able to pass their classes so that they have a chance for a future?" After meditating for ten days, he said he noticed for the first time how beautiful everything looked on a sunny day. "Before meditation, I'd never looked up," he said.

Aronson argues for building meditation into the school day so that it becomes part of the social structure. If other kids are doing it, most kids will go along with it and most, once they get the hang of it, will benefit from it.

Transcendental Meditation (TM)

We both practice Transcendental Meditation. Meditators are given a mantra, which is a meaningless sound. When a practitioner silently repeats his mantra, the mind settles down and experiences quieter levels of awareness. Eventually, the mantra leads the meditator to the depth of the ocean of the mind, which is completely peaceful and silent. You get to a place of full alertness but with no thought. This is the "transcendental" part of Transcendental Meditation, as you transcend the process of thinking altogether. Although transcendence is the epitome of doing nothing, over forty years of research has found that this experience of deeply quieting the mind and body improves physical and mental health, as well as learning and academic performance.

The physiological state that TM produces in children, teens, and adults is known as restful alertness. It is distinct from sleep or from simply resting with your eyes closed. A number of studies have found that the depth of physical relaxation one can reach during the practice of TM is, in several important respects (e.g., oxygen consumption, basal skin resistance), greater than that obtained during sleep.[14] This deep rest allows the nervous system to recover from the negative effects of stress and fatigue. It also makes the stress response system more efficient, so that it responds sharply and adaptively to stressors but turns off quickly. With a more efficient stress response, young people are able to "let things go" and recover faster. Some studies have suggested they can do this as much as twice as fast, thereby increasing their stress tolerance and resilience, both of which are powerful predictors of academic, career, and life success. A marked increase in the coherence of brain wave activity accompanies the state of relaxed alertness. This in turn is associated with improved attention, memory, and abstract reasoning ability.[15]

Alpha waves are relatively slow brain waves that are associated with relaxation. We can see someone's brain waves when they're hooked up to electrical sensors, as Bill was as part of his training in biofeedback at the University of Tennessee. The sensors were attached to Bill's skull, and he was asked to close his eyes. Three or four seconds later, the doctor who was monitoring him said, "Holy moly."

Bill's eyes popped open and he asked, "What's wrong?"

"Nothing," the doctor said. "The second you closed your eyes, you had this beautiful burst of alpha waves." Bill told him he had been meditating for twenty-five years. The doctor said, "That's obvious." It provided validation that all those years of meditating actually led to a brain that functioned differently. Bill found this particularly affirming in light of the fact that he used to be one of those people whose very presence stressed people out.

Many years of research on TM has shown that kids who meditate for as little as ten or fifteen minutes twice a day will experience a significant reduction in stress, anxiety, and depressive symptoms and express less anger and hostility.[16] They sleep better, think more creatively, are healthier, have higher self-esteem, and do better in school and on tests of cognitive and academic skills. While TM involves no attempt to control the mind, it increases practitioners' internal locus of control. It does this, in part, by allowing the brain to refresh itself, which enables it to keep things in perspective. It also reduces the extent to which we feel overwhelmed and allows our minds to work more efficiently, increasing the effectiveness with which we tackle challenging situations and our confidence that we can handle the big and little challenges life throws our way. The Quiet Time school program, in which students meditate for fifteen minutes twice a day, has made a profound impact on students in underserved urban schools, many of whose lives are filled with violence, fear, and trauma.[17]

While we know that meditation benefits kids, we don't believe in trying to force students to meditate. It is like trying to force a dog to drink—it just doesn't work. It's also antithetical to everything we've espoused in this book. In our experience, many older children, adolescents, and young adults will meditate on their own if they are taught to see meditation as a tool that can alleviate their physical or emotional pain and/or improve their school performance, or if it is part of the daily routine practiced by the whole family. Because of the enormous importance of peer approval to adolescents, teens are more likely to meditate regularly with the support and approval of other young people. We suggest that you talk to your children about meditation and invite them to learn. If they are interested, ask them to give meditation a good try (meditating every day, or twice a day, for three months). Talk to your kids directly about the benefits of meditation, or enlist a pediatrician or family friend who meditates to talk to them. Help teens think through how a meditation practice could be incorporated into their schedule, and gain their full buy-in before starting a meditation trial. You can also help them recognize the changes that result from meditation. This will help them take ownership of their meditation and encourage them to maintain a regular practice. Lest you fall into "do as I say, not as I do," we suggest that you try out meditation first yourself and invite them to join you.

But that's about all you can do. When he was a teenager, Bill's son asked if Bill was disappointed that he didn't want to meditate. "I didn't learn to meditate because my parents did," Bill told him. "I learned because it appealed to me. If it doesn't appeal to you, don't do it."

When Bill first explored meditation, he was told that it would allow him to do less and accomplish more because a deeply rested brain can work so much more efficiently than a tired and stressed brain. He didn't think meditation would be a waste of time exactly, but he didn't think it would save time either. But he quickly learned that he could accomplish more even though he was taking twenty minutes twice a day to meditate. This is something he continues to experience forty-two years later. When he finishes with all his clients for the day, the last task he needs to complete is to organize and put away files and test materials. The process can take thirty minutes if he doesn't meditate first, in part because he ends up making five or six trips to the storage area to put things away. If he meditates first, he generally makes only two trips to the storage area. The routine takes only ten minutes, and the increased clarity and efficiency continue into the evening. It isn't magic. His focus is clearer, his thinking more efficient, and he makes fewer mistakes.

Elizabeth, a nineteen-year-old college student, came to my office for testing after struggling academically in her first year of college. She reported a history of anxiety and depression that began following the traumatic death of her father two years earlier. She acknowledged that mild depression, frequent marijuana use, and difficulty sleeping contributed to her significant trouble "making herself" attend classes and study on a regular basis. In the course of our discussion, I suggested to Elizabeth that she consider TM as an alternative to marijuana, as meditation would likely help to quiet her mind, improve her sleep, and over time heal the emotional pain associated with her loss—without the negative effects of smoking pot.

She agreed to try. She stopped smoking marijuana for fifteen days (a prerequisite for learning TM) and started to practice meditation regularly. She quickly noticed that she felt calmer inside and that she was able to sleep better. Within several weeks, she also noticed that she was feeling happier and had a strong desire to pursue her true passion—visual art. Her pot-smoking friends commented on the "natural high" Elizabeth seemed to get from meditation. As she began to feel better, she started taking community college courses to reestablish her academic record and volunteered as a teaching assistant at a local art school. She urged her mother to learn TM to help with her own grief and even considered becoming a TM teacher so that she could teach other young people to meditate. Elizabeth eventually decided to transfer to a major university with an excellent visual arts program, and she is currently pursuing her education and training with great energy and enthusiasm.

—Bill

What Parents Often Ask Us

"My kid's teacher says he daydreams all the time in school. How do I know he doesn't have ADHD?"

Kids with ADHD do engage in extensive daydreaming when they're not interested in what's being presented in class. If your child's teacher says that your child daydreams more than the others and raises concerns about distractibility, disorganization, and trouble completing tasks, and/or about impulsivity or excessive physical restlessness, then contact your pediatrician about a possible evaluation for ADHD.

"How can I tell if my child has anxiety? He's a huge daydreamer, and I hear they are linked."

Those who daydream constantly and don't have ADHD mostly do so for one of two reasons: either they're unhappy with the world around them and prefer to spend most of their time in their own head, or they get stuck ruminating over something that happened or that they're afraid will happen. Most kids who daydream excessively show other signs of anxiety, too. If you think your child daydreams a lot but you don't see any other signs of anxiety (such as difficulty sleeping, physical restlessness, headaches, agitation, perfectionism, excessive concern about how she's judged), then it's likely not a cause for concern.

"Which is better for kids, TM or mindfulness?"

It's hard to make a direct comparison. While TM is a highly standardized program, mindfulness incorporates many different practices that are taught in many different ways. Nonetheless, our general view is that there are great benefits to both. Mindfulness practices can give children and teens important tools for self-understanding and self-regulation that they can use on a daily basis. It can also help kids cultivate kindness and compassion, both of which are increasingly important as the stresses of life make empathy and altruism harder for young people to experience. As for TM, we believe that the profound state of restful alertness produced by TM is incredibly valuable, and that the twice-daily practice of TM can help lower levels of stress and anxiety, improve learning, and contribute to a positive school climate.

Practically speaking, mindfulness offers some advantages. It can be learned at a relatively low cost and can be adapted even to very young children, which is why mindfulness practices can now be found in so many schools across the country. Also, it isn't necessary for students to learn mindfulness practices from trained teachers.

Transcendental Meditation is a standardized technique taught by highly trained teachers, which means it can be implemented with fidelity in virtually any school. It is usually more expensive to learn, however, and Quiet Time programs can be more challenging to implement, as TM can only be taught by a certified teacher. It is encouraging, though, that the David Lynch Foundation and other donors have raised money to enable thousands of students in underserved schools across the country to learn and practice TM.

While TM, mindfulness, and daydreaming are critically important to the developing brain, the pièce de résistance of radical downtime, the foundation on which so much of our lives depends, the activity we should spend a third of our lives engaged in, is *sleep*. Sleep is so important, it is the star of our next chapter.

What to Do Tonight

- Look for opportunities during the day to let your mind wander. This could mean just sitting quietly for a few minutes looking out the window or at the clouds. It could also mean engaging in activities you can largely do "mindlessly" (e.g., mowing the lawn) that enable you to "be with yourself."

- Talk as a family about the importance of going off-line and giving yourself truly free time. If they're open to hearing it, tell your kids that it's only when they aren't focused on anything in particular that they can really think about themselves and other people. Also tell them that discoveries and insights will often come when you let your mind wander, and that they need downtime to solidify the things they're learning in school.

- Ask your child, "Do you feel you have enough time to yourself, time when you're not studying, doing sports, texting, or talking to other people? Do you have enough time just to chill?" If your child says no, help him to think through when he might find a few times in his day to sit quietly and let his mind wander. Think out loud with your kids about the challenge of building in enough time for yourself.

- The next time you're driving with your child, instead of turning to technology, say, "Do you mind if we take a couple of minutes to just take in the scenery?"

- Consider learning to meditate yourself. The University of Massachusetts Medical School has a Center for Mindfulness with great resources (umassmed.edu/cfm), as does the University of California, San Diego (health.ucsd.edu/specialties/mindfulness/Pages/default.aspx), and the University of Wisconsin-Madison (centerhealthyminds.org). You can also visit the main TM Web site (tm.org). If you're interested in TM, attend an introductory lecture at your nearest center, and see if your middle- or high-school-age child would be willing to come along. Let your kids know about the dozens of celebrities who practice and endorse TM, including those who are popular with teenagers (currently Katy Perry, Kesha, Margaret Cho, and Hugh Jackman) to pique their interest.

- If you're interested in mindfulness, you could try a mindfulness app with your child, such as Headspace or Mind Yeti, which can be particularly useful at times of stress. For younger kids, check out Lauren Alderfer's book *Mindful Monkey, Happy Panda* and Eline Snel's book and CD combo *Sitting Still Like a Frog*.

CHAPTER SEVEN

Sleep

The Most Radical Downtime

I N THE EARLY YEARS of the twentieth century, adults in America slept nine hours a night or more. The spread of electricity and technology changed everything. Now we sleep on average two hours less. Sleep experts say that if you're tired during the day or need caffeine to keep you going, you're not getting enough sleep. And if you need an alarm clock to wake you up, you also need more sleep. By those measures, many of us are seriously sleep deprived.

Most of the teenagers we see tell us they feel tired during a significant portion of the school day. In fact, a study of sleep patterns in adolescents concluded that more than 50 percent of teens fifteen and older sleep less than seven hours a night, and that 85 percent get less than the eight to ten hours that is generally recommended for adolescents. Ages fourteen to fifteen appear to be a major turning point at which students start to become significantly sleep deprived.[1] In the 1990s and early 2000s—before smartphones exacerbated the problem of sleep deprivation—the dean of pediatric sleep researchers, Mary Carskadon, found that half of the teenagers she studied, who averaged seven hours of sleep a night, were so tired in the morning that their EEGs looked like those of people with narcolepsy.[2] The problem is most acute with teens, but many of the kindergarten and elementary children Bill tests yawn all morning and say they're used to feeling tired "all the time."

"Children learn from kindergarten on about the food pyramid," said Dr. Carskadon. "But no one is teaching them the life pyramid that has sleep at the base."[3] Everything in nature rests. All animals and insects sleep, even fruit flies. If you give a fruit fly caffeine, it will hop around frantically for a few hours, but it will eventually crash and "sleep in" to make up for the lost sleep. Lab rats will die as quickly if you prevent them from sleeping as if you don't feed them.[4] Sleep optimizes the functioning of the brain and the body. Without sleep, a vicious cycle takes place. Because your sense of control is weakened by a lack of sleep, the more tired you are, the harder it is to get yourself to go to bed, and the more tempting it is to just stay where you are and watch one more episode of *Homeland*. Your ability to inhibit your YouTube binge-watching habit or to stop yourself from checking your phone evaporates. You're also much more likely to eat an entire pint of ice cream at 11:00 P.M., when you're tired, than at 9:00 A.M., when you're fresh. Our bad habits are exacerbated by insufficient sleep. It would seem on the surface to be easy enough to address, but the cycle of sleep deprivation is actually hard to break because if you're tired you'll be more anxious, and if you're more anxious it will be harder to sleep. This is a big problem, because sleep is arguably the single most important thing for healthy brain development.

Many parents are aware of the importance of sleep and want ideas about how to help their kids get more of it. They're frustrated, because they can't control how much homework their child is assigned, how early school starts, or the fact that their kids' soccer games don't start until 8:00 P.M. But what makes them really want to tear their hair out is that they can't *make* their child sleep. We'll delve into these quandaries and more, but first, let us explain how sleep contributes to a strong sense of control.

Sleep and the Brain

We are passionate about sleep, and though we lead pretty busy lives ourselves, we are vigilant about getting enough sleep to wake up without an alarm clock (for Bill it's seven hours, for Ned it's eight to eight and a half). Our zealousness stems from an understanding of how foundational sleep is to everything else. It's like the foundation of a house—easy to neglect because it's not very sexy or interesting, but without it, everything falls apart. Add a rainy winter and soggy ground to the weak foundation, and you're looking at a catastrophe. Sleep is brain food. And so on those nights when you consider staying up to answer one more e-mail, or if your daughter wants to take on just one more commitment, consider these powerful sleep statements, share them with your kids, and let them guide your decisions.

Sleep deprivation is a form of chronic stress. According to Bruce McEwen, a leading researcher on stress, sleep deprivation produces similar effects on the mind and body as chronic stress. These include higher cortisol levels, increased reactivity to stress, higher blood pressure, and decreased efficiency of the parasympathetic nervous system (which serves a calming function). Sleep deprivation produces inflammation, impacts insulin production, decreases appetite, and depresses mood. McEwen discovered that chronic sleep insufficiency (getting six hours of sleep or less per night) is like acute sleep deprivation in young adults. There is no difference in performance on cognitive tasks between older adolescents who sleep four to six hours per night for six weeks and those who get no sleep at all for three days.[5]

When our stress response system functions normally, our cortisol levels are highest when we wake up in the morning and lowest before we go to bed at night. Cortisol helps give you the kick you need to get out of bed. But in people who are highly stressed, this pattern can often be reversed. Their cortisol levels will be high at night, when they're trying to settle down, and low in the morning, when they're trying to get up. The same is true of many sleep-deprived kids.

Emotional control is dramatically impaired by sleep deprivation. If you don't sleep enough, your amygdala becomes more reactive in response to emotionally charged events, mimicking the brain activity of people suffering from anxiety disorders.[6] Many of the negative characteristics we associate with teens, like moodiness and poor judgment, may actually be the result of sleep deprivation. Ned gently asks his students, "Do you ever notice how when you're really tired, your mom is *so* on your case and your best friend is being *such* a jerk—on the same day?" This is because sleep deprivation decreases your flexibility, weakens your ability to see things in context, and impairs your judgment. Sleep-deprived teens are much more likely to use caffeine, nicotine, alcohol, and drugs to cope with the mood swings they could deal with more effectively by getting enough sleep.[7]

Sleep loss is like a "negativity bomb." This is according to distinguished sleep researcher Robert Stickgold, who performed a study in which the subjects, half of whom didn't sleep for thirty-six hours, and half of whom were well rested, were shown positive, negative, and neutral words (e.g., "calm," "grief," "willow") and asked to rate their emotionality. After two nights of recovery sleep, they were given a surprise memory test. Those from the "rested" group remembered 40 percent more of the words they'd been shown and retained the positive and the negative words fairly evenly. Those who were sleep deprived remembered fewer words in general and many more of the negative ones. Their recall of positive words decreased by half and of negative words by just 20 percent. "This result suggests the rather horrifying possibility that when you are sleep deprived, you effectively form twice as many memories of negative events in your life as of positive events," Stick-gold concluded, "producing a biased—and potentially depressing—memory of your day."[8]

Sleep deprivation, like chronic stress, can trigger anxiety and mood disorders in children who are already vulnerable to getting them. When you don't get enough sleep, the connections between the prefrontal cortex and the amygdala are weakened.[9] Your Pilot is asleep but your Lion Fighter is awake. This disconnect between prefrontal cortex and amygdala is seen in PTSD, depression, bipolar disorder, and other psychiatric syndromes.[10] There is a strong correlation between insufficient sleep and depression. Men and women with sleep apnea are two and a half times and five times more likely respectively to have major depressive disorder than peers who sleep well. The use of a CPAP (a device that keeps your airways open at night) significantly reduces symptoms of depression. The fact that girls' risk for depression triples after puberty may be related to the fact that it gets harder for them to get enough sleep.

Sleep deprivation has physical implications. It impairs blood sugar regulation and contributes to obesity. Studies of children in Japan, Canada, and Australia found that kids who get less than eight hours of sleep per night have a *300 percent* higher obesity rate than kids who sleep ten hours.[11] In Houston, a study of teens showed that the chance of obesity increased 80 percent for each hour of lost sleep.[12] If teens are sleep deprived, they're also likely to get sick a lot more, as sleep deprivation suppresses immune function.[13] Sleep loss also leads to a significant decrease in cancer-killing cells, enough for the American Cancer Society to classify night-shift work as a probable carcinogen.[14]

Sleep is critical to learning. There's almost nothing more important to learning than being well rested. Simply put, it is far more effective to teach someone for four hours after they've slept for eight than to teach them for eight hours after they've slept for four. It doesn't take much sleep deprivation to impact thinking and cognitive performance. As part of a study of minor sleep restriction, sixth graders were asked to sleep either one hour more than usual or one hour less than usual, for three nights. The students who slept as little as thirty-five minutes less than others functioned like fourth graders on cognitive tests, effectively losing two years of cognitive power.[15]

Consider what happens when we sleep. The brain "replays" experiences, sending signals back and forth repeatedly from the cortex to the hippocampus, integrating and consolidating memories. Recently learned material plays on a screen in your mind, making it seep in more deeply and connecting it to other things you have learned in the past. Sleep refreshes the whole brain and improves its ability to pay attention, making it optimally receptive to new learning. During non-REM sleep (sleep without rapid eye movements), scientists see short bursts of electrical activity called "sleep spindles" that help the brain move information from a short-term storage site in the hippocampus to the long-term locus of memory in the cortex. This so-called slow-wave sleep helps to solidify new memories and saves information we've learned. Sleep expert Matthew Walker likens it to hitting the "save" button. Electrical waves travel from one part of the brain to another in what Walker calls a "slow synchronized chant," helping to connect pieces of information in different parts of the brain, relate them to one another, and build a tapestry framework of understanding.[16]

In an early sleep study by Robert Stickgold, participants played *Tetris* for seven hours over the course of three days. When awakened just after falling asleep, 75 percent reported experiencing visual images of the game, suggesting that the brain was continuing to work on mastering *Tetris* skills during sleep (an important skill to master if ever there was one). Stickgold concluded that people who slept after learning and practicing a new task remembered more the next day than those who stayed up all night after learning the task.[17]

You don't have to be a high school student for the impact of sleep on learning to be relevant. Last spring, Bill decided to learn Hebrew at the encouragement of his wife, Starr, as she had been studying it for a couple of years. He made decent progress in the first week or so, studying for a few minutes in the morning before he left for work. One evening Starr suggested that they study Hebrew together at 8:45 P.M. While Bill felt perfectly alert and could easily have held a conversation, played the guitar, or discussed a case with a colleague, it turned out that he was too tired to learn. He slowly sounded out a few three-letter words on the first line of his workbook and then proceeded to the second line. After laboring for a couple of minutes to decode what seemed to be a new and harder set of words, he looked back to the first line and realized that the words on the second line were exactly the same as those on the first—but he was too tired to remember them. By 8:45 at night, he was trying to learn with a brain that was functioning at 10 percent capacity at best. If he *had* to learn the words, he suspected it would take him several hours, whereas if he went to bed and returned to them in the morning, he knew he could do it in twenty minutes. And yet this level of mental inefficiency is where many students do most of their learning!

Not surprisingly, sleep and grades are intertwined. Numerous studies have shown a correlation between students' self-reported shortened sleep time and weaker academic performance. Later school start times have led to decreased absences and tardiness, reduced sleepiness in school, and improvement in mood and feelings of efficacy.[18] According to a recent study of nine thousand high school kids by Kyla Wahlstrom, when start times were pushed back to 8:35 A.M. and later, grades rose a quarter step. The later, the better, Wahlstrom says. You'll see stronger results when you change a school's start time from 7:30 to 8:30, for instance, than from 7:30 to 8:00.[19]

When You're Rested . . .

When you're well rested and not stressed, the prefrontal cortex helps regulate your emotional systems in a top-down way. If you sleep well, the connection between the prefrontal cortex and other systems is refreshed and strengthened, enabling our trusty Pilot to regulate our thinking and behavior.

Every once in a while, Ned will see a kid who is not only getting top grades and putting in a sterling performance in outside activities, but who is also happy and unstressed. When he asks about sleep patterns (because he *always* does), the student will say something like, "Oh, yeah, I'm in bed by ten. I just cannot function well when I'm tired." Now it's possible that these kids are just more efficient and learn more easily, so that they can complete their work and get to bed at sensible hours. But it's more likely that they're more efficient and learn with greater ease precisely *because* they're well rested. (It's also true that poorly regulated kids very frequently have trouble sleeping, a problem we'll discuss in Chapter Eleven.)

Put simply, sleep heals. Rapid eye movement sleep—where most dreaming happens—takes the sting out of emotional experiences. When we're in REM sleep, all stress-related neurochemicals are absent from the brain—the only time this happens in a twenty-four-hour period. According to Matthew Walker, during REM sleep the brain reactivates emotions and problematic memories and brings them back to the mind through reflective dreaming in a neurochemically safe, stress-free environment. This is the science behind the old saying that sleep makes things "look better in the morning."[20]

Just about everyone experiences a greater sense of control after a good night's sleep. But here's the clincher: to fall asleep, you have to let go. You have to give up control to gain it. And clearly, you can't do this for someone else. So how can you help your children get enough sleep? There are as many obstacles to sleep as there are reasons to prioritize it, and the challenges vary considerably based on the age of the child. For that reason, we have decided to devote the remainder of this chapter to the questions we most commonly hear from parents, and how we answer them.

"How much sleep does my child need?"

Generally, preschoolers need ten to thirteen hours of sleep every day (one hour often comes in the form of a nap). Six- to thirteen-year-olds need from nine to eleven hours. Teenagers aged fourteen to seventeen need eight to ten hours. And young adults from eighteen to twenty-five years old need seven to nine hours.[21] This is a general guideline, and Judith Owens, one of the top pediatric sleep researchers in the world, suggests that, like most other human needs, the need for sleep probably varies according to a bell curve.[22] Some people need more sleep to function effectively than others. To determine whether your child is getting enough, consider: Does he wake up on his own? Is he tired during the day? Is he restless or irritable during the day? Use these considerations to guide you as you help your child get the sleep he needs.

"How can I tell if my child has a sleep problem that requires a doctor's help?"

There are a few common sleep problems that parents should be aware of. At the top of the list are insomnia and sleep-related breathing problems, such as sleep apnea. If your child snores or has trouble falling asleep or staying asleep, you should consult your pediatrician and, if necessary, a sleep specialist, as you will want to rule out physical conditions such as asthma, allergies, and enlarged tonsils or adenoids that could be interfering with your child's sleep. Insomnia can be a problem for children as young as four or five. For teens, insomnia is very prevalent, as is a phase-delay sleep syndrome, where they don't feel tired until 1:00 or 2:00 in the morning and need to reset their biological clocks. Insomnia is frequently linked to ADHD and autism.[23] You will also want to rule out stress, anxiety, or depression in the sleep-challenged child. If your child does not have ADHD or autism, but has trouble settling down or needs an adult in the room to help her sleep, this is considered a form of insomnia that has behavioral roots. It's worth getting a recommendation for a cognitive behavioral therapist or a behavioral sleep specialist, as early interventions can be effective.

"I get that sleep is important, but school starts so early, and my daughter's extracurricular events plus homework have her up way too late. I hate to make her quit her extracurriculars—she loves them! What can I do?"

We hear concerns like this *a lot*, and see it for ourselves. One of Ned's students, Kelly, was a varsity athlete in three sports and took AP U.S. History, AP English, and AP Calculus. Her mom was understandably concerned about Kelly's lack of sleep.

"You're involved in a lot," Ned said to Kelly one day. "How are you doing?"

"It's okay," Kelly shrugged. "I'm just really tired and pretty stressed."

"I can imagine," Ned said. "Your mom sounded concerned about how you fit it all in. Just out of curiosity, what time do you get to bed?"

"Usually two or three A.M."

"Wow. Can you walk me through your day? As serious as you are as a student and an athlete, you're making it awfully hard to do your best, whatever that is, with so little sleep."

"Well, I usually have five hours of homework," she said.

"In my experience, when we're a little more rested, we can do homework a bit faster. Maybe you could get the work done in only four hours and get more sleep. But, still, why two or three A.M.?"

"I have lots of activities," she said.

"Beyond three varsity sports? What else do you do?"

"Well, let's see. There's the Best Buddies program. And I do Model UN. And I'm a leader of my school's Social Action Program. And I'm on the Honor Committee. Oh, and I'm a student ambassador, a student tutor, and peer mentor. I go to therapy. And I play club lacrosse and am part of an exercise program for kids with special needs."

We wish we were making this up. Of all the things Kelly needed to learn, foremost among them was how to make good choices. Ned said he couldn't tell her that any one of those things was something she shouldn't be doing. But she had less to give to each activity because she was involved in so many. An important part of high school is learning that you can't do it all and knowing that your own well-being has to come first.

With high-achieving kids like Kelly, or with perfectionists, Ned often gives the following pep talk, which you can feel free to use as your own:

I know how conscientious you are. You've made all these commitments and will never let anyone down. You'll stay up later and work harder to get everything done. And so you will sacrifice yourself. You cannot be doing your best at anything if you're chronically tired. One of the things you don't know yet is that you don't have to be superior at everything. You need to figure out what you want to specialize in and put your time and attention there. Consider dropping one of your extracurriculars or settling for a lower grade if there's one class you both don't like and know consumes a disproportionate amount of time. Reinvest that time in yourself, your sleep, and the classes or activities that really matter to you. Don't look at it as letting someone down if you say no to an opportunity—instead, you're giving someone else a chance to step up.

"When I tell my teenage son he needs more sleep, he argues that he doesn't need the nine and a half hours I think he does. He says that he feels just fine with less and that most of his friends are sleeping seven hours a night or less. How can I tell how much sleep he really needs?"

The fact is that adolescents experience a normal sleep phase shift after puberty, the result of which is that most are unable to fall asleep until about 10:45 P.M. (and their brains stay in sleep mode until approximately 8:00 A.M.)[24] Compounding the problem is that teens are more sensitive to the effects of light—and use more technology at night.

The key, especially with teens, is to negotiate in a respectful manner. Many kids resist changing their sleep patterns because they don't want to hear "I told you so" from their parents. It is important to approach the subject in such a way as to validate their knowledge of themselves. You could say something like, "You may be right. You may be one of those kids who needs less sleep than most people. Let's see if that's the case. I want to support you in making good decisions for yourself." As Helene Emsellem, sleep expert and author of *Snooze . . . or Lose!* points out, at the end of the day, if teens aren't interested in changing their bedtimes or being less tired during the day, there's no point in trying to make them embrace sleep-enhancing interventions.[25]

So start with the presumption that your child knows what it feels like to be tired, and how good it feels to get a good night's sleep. You can acknowledge that some people need less sleep than others, and that he may be someone who only needs eight or eight and a half hours. You can also say that most kids can't really judge very well how tired they are or how much sleep they need, and invite him to do an experiment. On some weekday when he's home from school, have him lie down in a dark room at 11:00 A.M. How long does it take him to fall asleep? If he's out within a few minutes, it's a sign of serious sleep deprivation. Another idea is to recommend doing a "study." Suggest that he stay up until he thinks it's time to go to bed for three nights in a row and then rate how he feels during the day. He can rate himself on a scale of 1 to 5 according to his alertness, focus, academic productivity, mood, worry, frustration, and/or ability to get along with others. The next three nights, encourage him to go to bed early enough to get the amount of sleep you think he needs. Have him chart how he feels during those days, too. What does he see? If he really feels no difference, he may be right.

"It's clear that my daughter is chronically tired, but I can't get her to buy in to the idea that she needs to sleep more. She says that sleep is a waste of time. What should I do?"

There's no question that this is a fine line to walk. On the one hand, you want to respect her autonomy and refrain from making sleep an issue of control. You can't make your child sleep, nor can you make your child want to sleep more than she does, but you can promote a quiet slowing-down routine in the evenings. If your child is resistant, you can say, "If you're having trouble falling asleep, my responsibility is to help you with it, to make sure you're in a dark room when your doctor says you should be in bed."

The evidence that sleep is important is irrefutable. Some strategies you might use in your consultant role include:

- Often when the advice comes from a third, nonparental party, kids are more willing to take it seriously. With a school-aged child, tell her that you want to get her pediatrician's advice about sleep—or the advice of another adult the child respects. If you have a teenager, ask her if she would be open to your sharing articles about sleep with her.

- With school-aged kids and younger, you can enforce an agreed-upon lights-out time. Remind them that as a responsible parent, it's right for you to enforce limits on bedtime and technology use in the evening (more on this later).

- Because technology and peer pressure can make it very difficult for teens to go to bed early, say, "I know this is hard for you. I'm not trying to control you. But if you'd like to get to bed earlier and need help doing it, I'm happy to give you an incentive." An incentive is okay in this case because you're not offering it as a means to get her to do what *you* want her to do, but to help her do what she wants to do on her own but finds challenging. It's a subtle but important distinction.[26]

- For older kids, make privileges like driving contingent on getting enough sleep—since driving while sleep deprived is so dangerous. How to chart their sleep is more complicated. Reliable tools for assessing when a child falls asleep and how long he stays asleep, such as the actigraph, require extensive training and are not something parents can use at home to track their kids' sleep. Moreover, Fitbits are unfortunately unreliable in gathering data. But you can ask your child to keep a sleep log where she records what time she turned out the lights, and (in the morning) how long she thinks it took her to fall asleep, and whether she was up during the night. She may not know how long it took her to fall asleep; that's okay. Just ask,

"Was it easier to fall asleep than last night or harder?" Helping kids figure out if they've gotten enough rest is a process, and trust, communication, and collaborative problem solving are key to that process.

- Encourage your child to do screen-time homework earlier and save reading homework for later so she gets less late light exposure.

- Ask questions such as "If you knew you'd be better at everything you do if you slept an extra hour and a half, would that change your sense of how important sleep is?" And "If you knew you'd be at risk for developing depression if you didn't sleep enough, would that change your mind?"

- Talk to her about your own attempts to get to bed earlier. Ask, "Would you be open to us supporting each other in getting the sleep we need? I'll remind you and you remind me?"

"My sixth grader seems to consume a lot of caffeine. She drinks several sodas and a Starbucks coffee every day, though she hasn't gotten into energy drinks—yet. Should I be worried?"

The simple answer is yes. We worry about the significant increase in the consumption of caffeinated beverages in teenagers, and despair that some of these products are marketed to children as young as four. Many teens consume up to 800 milligrams of caffeine a day, which is equivalent to around eight cups of coffee. (The Mayo Clinic recommends a maximum of 100 milligrams of caffeine per day for adolescents and no caffeine for children.)

The effects of caffeine on children's development have not been well studied, but we do know that children can develop a tolerance, which contributes to habitual consumption.[27] And caffeine stays in your system for hours. If you have caffeine at 10:00 A.M., for instance, at 4:00 P.M. half of it is still in your system.[28] Though kids metabolize what they consume faster than adults do, it's nonetheless concerning to have a stimulant in their systems for so long. Our recommendation is to not serve caffeinated foods and beverages to children, with the exception of some chocolate and an occasional soda. If they are intent on feeling "grown-up" like their friends, suggest decaf as Ned does. (Though there is still some caffeine in decaf.)

It's unlikely that you could keep your teenager from consuming sweet caffeinated drinks even if you wanted to. The best course, then, is to talk with your teen about the effects of caffeine, which can be positive in the short run but negative in the long term. When sleepy teens use caffeine, they sleep even less. And they experience the same side effects adults do: jittery nervousness, racing thoughts, anxiety, increased heart rate. These symptoms are exacerbated when you drink a lot of caffeine in a short period of time, or chug energy drinks.

Ask your child to pay attention to his level of alertness and tension or nervousness after consuming caffeine. When adolescents really pay attention, some report that caffeine keeps them awake but does not make them more alert or clearheaded. Let your kids know that there are other ways to increase alertness and energy (such as sleep and exercise). Tell them that staying well rested without the use of stimulants is a great challenge for most *adults* in our society, too. Ultimately, it is their responsibility to figure out how to manage their own energy. Bill tells kids that if they can figure out how to stay well rested and not be dependent on stimulants, they'll be way ahead of the game as they move into young adulthood.

"I'm a night owl, and I know my kid is, too. It's tough to fight that tendency and get to bed at a reasonable hour."

We agree, it's not easy to get to bed early when you've got your circadian rhythm working against you. There's a study we love to cite on this subject. The researcher, Kenneth Wright, studied young adults after a typical workweek, and then after a week camping without electric light and digital technology. After a week of normal life, melatonin (a drowsiness hormone) onset was about two hours before the subjects went to sleep, which was usually around 12:30 A.M. After a week of camping, the melatonin onset moved up by approximately two hours—and so did bedtime. This study also found that camping reduced individual differences between the sleep schedules of "late sleepers" (night owls) and early sleepers (larks). The biological clock of night owls is often delayed by exposure to electronic media and electric light. In short, if you and your child are night owls, you will need to pay particular attention to the amount of light you expose yourself to from dinnertime on, and start your wind-down process earlier than someone who is a lark. There are also glasses you can buy to reduce the effect of blue light on your system, and now many devices have a mode for reducing blue light built in. But the stimulus of online news, movies, or e-mails will still often get in the way of a good night's sleep, so be sure you're paying attention to more than just light.

"My teenager has to get up at six thirty on school mornings but sleeps until twelve thirty on weekends. Is that okay?"

Advice varies on this point. If on weekends we get up significantly later than our normal wake time, we're going to experience the mental confusion and "feeling off" that we feel when we're jet-lagged. For that reason, many sleep experts suggest that teenagers not get up more than two hours later on weekends than they do on school days—and that they take short naps instead if they need to fill the tank. Others, like Danny Lewin, a behavioral sleep specialist at Children's National Medical Center's Division of Sleep Medicine, feel that negotiation and flexibility is the name of the game, and we agree. Talk to your teenager about the ideal sleep schedule and figure out what works best for you and your child. Let him know that if he sleeps in more than two or three hours later than he does on school mornings, he'll have that jet-lagged feeling and it will make it much harder for him to fall asleep on Sunday night. But if he's listening and weighing the pros and cons, let it be his call.

What to Do Tonight

- Make sleep a family value, and set a family goal of sleeping more. Ned always tells his teenage students, "Pay yourself first," a lesson adopted from financial planning that involves putting money into your savings account before you pay your bills. He tells kids "you'll need to sleep something in the neighborhood of sixty-three hours a week (nine hours a day), so plan that and then plan what you'll do the rest of the time." It's good advice for you as well as your kids. Talk to your kids about your own sleep-related challenges, and let them know if you've found things that have worked for you. Tell them you're open to their suggestions.

- Assess whether your child has an effective wind-down routine before bed. If not, read about what experts call good sleep hygiene, or sleep habits. Try getting ready for bed before you're really tired, as it's harder to inhibit the desire to do one more thing or watch one more episode when you're tired. Encourage your teens to try the same thing. Dim lights and pull shades at least thirty minutes before a child's bedtime, which will trigger melatonin production. Try using blackout curtains and/or relaxation tapes. Also try warm milk, which actually does have a sleep-inducing effect. If necessary, talk to your pediatrician about the use of melatonin, which can be very effective for highly anxious kids and for kids with ADHD. Encourage exercise during the day, particularly if falling asleep in the first place is hard.

- If your child is a light sleeper or struggles to fall asleep, consider a white-noise generator.

- If your child is an athlete, do a Google search for studies that document the incredibly powerful effect sleep has on athletic performance. A study of Stanford basketball players found that they all ran faster and shot more accurately after several weeks of training when they got more than eight hours of sleep a night.[29] Let your kid know that, on the advice of sleep specialists, many NBA teams have eliminated morning shootarounds to give players more sleep.

- Talk as a family about creating technology-free zones in the bedroom at night. Danny Lewin recommends that kids (and parents) leave their devices charging in the kitchen thirty to sixty minutes before bedtime. (This gives us a chance to resist our phone only once, rather than all night.) Lewin also encourages negotiating with teenagers in a respectful way. If no phones in the bedroom seven nights in a row is too much for your teenager to manage, how about five? Then you and your child can discuss the difference between what happens when the phone is in the room and when it isn't. If your child insists that she needs her phone because she uses it as an alarm clock, go to the store immediately and buy her an alarm clock. Get her the most high-end kind she wants. It's money well spent.

- Suggest that your high school child ask her friends or other kids in her grade who *do* get eight-plus hours of sleep a night how they do it. Kids commonly learn more from each other than they do from adults.

- If your kids are tired, remind them to be patient with themselves and with others. Help them recognize that their emotional reactions will be different when they're tired—and that they'll be more irritable with you and with friends.

- Ideally, we want kids to learn to calm themselves. But there are some—particularly those with ADHD or anxiety problems—for whom it's too hard. Some kids need to listen to music (but not on their phones) or even to have the TV on to fall asleep. Though it's not ideal, it's not worth fighting about if it works.

- Encourage your sleepy teenager to take a twenty-minute power nap after school or during study hall. Naps shouldn't be longer than that, otherwise they can cause grogginess and throw off sleep rhythms for the night. Think of them as a little pick-me-up to get through to bedtime.

- For kids who have sleep disorders and/or are suffering from severe sleep deprivation, consider having a doctor write a letter recommending that they be permitted to miss first period. Also check out the sleep tool kit on www.racetonowhere.com/sleep-page.

- If your kid's circadian clock is off, exposure to bright light early in the morning can be an effective tool, but consult with an expert on sleep before trying light therapy. Also, if weather permits, go camping. We constantly encounter kids who struggle with sleep the whole year, and then summer camp gets them back on track. For the duration of the camp they're in bed at 9:30 P.M., because there's no electric light or digital technology. A camping trip won't be feasible if it's in the middle of winter, or if you live in the northern parts of the world where the sun doesn't go down until very late. But it's a very effective technique when you can swing it.

- Continue reading about sleep. Books we recommend are Helene Ensellem's *Snooze . . . or Lose!* and Dr. Richard Ferber's *Solve Your Child's Sleep Problems*.

- Assess the extent to which school commitments—and particularly homework—are undermining your child's efforts to get to bed. This last is not a simple matter—which is why your child's school environment is the subject of the entire next chapter.

CHAPTER EIGHT

Taking a Sense of Control to School

W E SEE A LOT OF KIDS who hate school. Not coincidentally, a student's sense of control lowers with every year they attend.[1] In order to help our kids manage their school lives, we need to first spend a moment thinking about what school feels like from their vantage point. They transition from lots of free choice in the youngest grades to mandatory homework, standing in line, having to ask permission to use the bathroom, and needing to do what's asked, exactly as it's asked, almost every moment of the day. Where is the autonomy there?

From preschool through to college, we want kids to have a school experience that is engaging, and inventive. School should provide a mixture of stimulation and downtime. It should encourage kids' natural curiosity and allow them to be in a state of flow for long periods of the day. In an ideal school, teachers have autonomy and kids have choices. This type of school environment provides a nearly perfect model of an internal locus of control. Unfortunately, whether you go public or private, this isn't the direction schools are going.

Recent trends in education make it hard for teachers to teach and students to learn. Teachers are losing autonomy to "teacher-proof" instructional techniques. Many full-day kindergarten programs begrudgingly allow only one ten-minute recess, based on the misguided assumption that cutting recess time will increase instructional time and raise test scores. As early as first or second grade, kids are bogged down by homework. By high school, they feel defined by: 1) their grades, 2) their standardized test scores, and 3) their college admissions—all of which depend on external validation. Some adult somewhere to whom they can rarely make an appeal is sorting them. Do you remember that TV commercial where people walk down the street with their credit scores floating above their heads? "I am not a number." we all want to cry. With the perception that school is a Sorting Hat with the mindset of an actuary, is it any wonder how stressed some students are?

For more than two decades, school reform has been driven by an agenda that appears to be uninformed by even the most basic research into what we now know about the functioning of the brain or the healthy development of the child. Educational leaders and policy makers aren't asking, "What do children need for healthy brain development?" "How do they learn best?" or "When's the optimal time to teach him or her to read or do algebra?" Rather, they seem to be asking, "What do we need this child to be able to do in order to meet our school, local, or national standards?" Most reform has been focused on what to cram into children's heads—and testing them ad nauseam to see what sticks—rather than on developing their brains. What this means is that we do more but accomplish less. Educational reforms fail because they hinge on policies that lower the sense of control of students, teachers, and administrators alike, predictably leading to greater stress, lower student engagement, and ever more teacher dissatisfaction and burnout.

We understand that we can't change school policy in this book (we'll save that for the next one), but we can give parents information that will help them be effective advocates for their kids. We can also give educators—who we very much hope will be reading this chapter—some concrete actions to change a child's educational experience even if they can't change the system as a whole.

So while this chapter isn't a comprehensive treatment of school policy issues, we believe that recognizing the importance of a sense of control can guide our thinking about the all-important place where our kids spend upwards of seven hours a day nine months of the year.

Get Them Engaged

One of the greatest challenges educators and parents face is getting students engaged in their own learning. Particularly in middle school and high school, a large segment of students is doing as little as possible to get by. Even some top students take what Ned calls a "station-to-station" attitude, refusing to do anything that doesn't contribute to a grade.[2] We're not raising curious learners who are motivated to develop their own minds. We're raising kids who are overly focused on metrics and outcomes.

The best thing you can do to facilitate engagement in the classroom may be to give your kid autonomy *outside* of it. Edward Deci and Richard Ryan, whose self-determination theory we discussed in Chapter Five, found that parents who were more supportive of their kids' autonomy had children who "reported more well-internalized regulation for schoolwork and more perceived competence and were rated by their teachers as having greater self-motivation, competence, and classroom adjustment."[3] They also received better grades and performed better on standardized tests.

What happens inside the classroom matters, too, and supporting autonomy within the teaching environment doesn't have to be difficult. It can be as simple as encouraging teachers to give their students choices ("Do you want a pajama party or a special show-and-tell day?" "Would you prefer an in-class essay or a take-home essay?" "Do you want to work on this in class or at home?" "Do you want to work on this individually or with a partner?"). It also helps to offer more than one way to demonstrate mastery of material, seek student feedback, encourage them to explore strategies that work for them, and more generally explain *why* they're being asked to do things and what you hope they will gain from them.

We know that if a kid connects with his teacher and relates to him or her, he will try harder and do better. We also know that there are some good teachers, some great teachers, and some not-so-good teachers. Not every teacher will connect with every kid. And then there are teachers who don't really connect with *any* kids. Part of the problem stems from the fact that teachers themselves often have little autonomy, making many grumpy and dissatisfied. There is evidence that teachers teach better and feel less stressed when they have a choice about what they teach and how they teach it. Unfortunately, recent research has indicated that teacher autonomy has reduced in the past decade.[4]

As a parent, there are several things you can do if you feel the student-teacher relationship is not gelling. For starters, you can try to help your kid connect with his teacher, urging him to start a conversation about something he's studying in class or to ask the teacher about his own interests as a kid. If it's a really bad match, you can speak to the principal about moving your child out of that teacher's class, though doing so can be tricky. But perhaps the most effective thing you can do is to emphasize to your child that *he* is responsible for his own education. It's not his teacher's job, it's not his principal's job, and it's not your job. If he doesn't have a handle on sixth grade math but needs to know certain things to be able to do prealgebra in seventh, the fact that he had a crummy sixth grade math teacher will be of little consolation. We're not suggesting that you tell your struggling son that it's his fault. Rather, acknowledge that only 10 percent of teachers will be in the top 10th percentile, and tell him that you can't expect to have the Teacher of the Year every year in every subject. Help your child strategize as to how he can take control of his own learning, with or without the teacher's help. Otherwise he's in a frustrating situation, knowing he isn't learning and feeling helpless to change it.

What will make your child want to learn even if he doesn't connect with his teacher? Will he decide to do well in order to prove his teacher wrong? Great. Will he decide to do well so as never to have to take a class from that teacher again? That's great, too. Emphasize that he doesn't have to be limited by a poor teacher. School aside, this is an important life lesson.

You can also offer practical help. If your child isn't learning, try to find a tutor or educational games to engage him in math or science. For middle school and high school kids, you could encourage them to check out the Khan Academy or other online tutoring sites to help them master material they're being taught in class. You could even encourage them to learn some of the material *before* the teacher addresses it in class, so they feel "I've got this" during the next lesson. That's a much better place to be than having to play catch-up to unscramble the confusion of the day's lesson. You can also encourage your kids to learn on their own and to teach what they've learned to someone else—a parent, a sibling, or a fellow student. This builds self-esteem, is empowering, and is the best way to truly master complex material.

Reduce Academic Stress and Pressure

In Chapter One, we talked about what stress does to the brain's emotional functioning. Here we want to talk about stress specifically as it affects learning.

One of the first things Ned noticed in his tutoring career was that kid after kid would do very well on practice tests, and less well when they took the actual SAT or ACT (American College Test). He read widely and talked to scientists and psychologists to understand why this was, and this is how he came to discover the Yerkes-Dodson Law. In the early 1900s, two psychologists, Robert Yerkes and John Dodson, proposed that performance increases with physiological and mental arousal up to a point, after which it starts to decline. We need a certain level of arousal—from curiosity, excitement, or mild stress—to reach our optimal level of mental acuity. But when we're *too* stressed, we can't think straight. Our brains become inefficient. The different approaches Ned's students took to their term papers offers a perfect illustration of the Yerkes-Dodson Law in action. Girls have, on average, a curve that shifts to the left, and boys one that shifts to the right. What this means is that optimal levels of stress for girls often isn't enough to motivate boys, and optimal stress for boys can be overwhelming for many girls. (Remember, these are averages—every kid is different. Some girls are more boylike and vice versa.) As a parent, it is worth remembering that what works to motivate *you* may not work for your kid, and what seems like no big deal to you may be really overwhelming for your child.

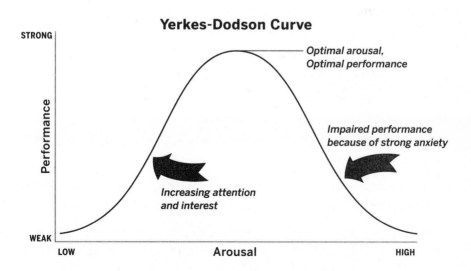

Yerkes-Dodson Curve

STRONG

Performance

WEAK

LOW — Arousal — HIGH

Optimal arousal, Optimal performance

Impaired performance because of strong anxiety

Increasing attention and interest

If you consider the Yerkes-Dodson curve in relation to school, you may see a third of kids in the optimal state of learning, called "relaxed alertness," a third overstressed, and a third bored to sedation. Over the years, the Yerkes-Dodson Law has been supported by research studies again and again.[5] Students learn and perform best in an environment that offers high challenge and low threat—when they're given difficult material in a learning environment in which it is safe to explore, make mistakes, and take the time they need to learn and produce good work. When students know it's all right to fail, they can take the kinds of risks that lead to real growth. They can develop brains that are capable of performing at a high level, and of being happy.

Many of the kids we see aren't learning in this environment. They're learning in a brain-toxic environment, where their days consist of stress and fatigue, often accompanied by high levels of boredom. You know that classical description of war as "interminable boredom punctuated by moments of terror"? Many schools have become pastel versions of this. As a result, many students aren't learning well and are suffering from stress-related symptoms.

Too much stress floods the prefrontal cortex, which we introduced in Chapter One as the fussy Goldilocks of the brain. The prefrontal cortex needs a delicate balance of dopamine and norepinephrine to run effectively. Without a fully operational prefrontal cortex, students lose their ability to focus and sustain attention, and their three core executive functions—inhibition, working memory, and cognitive flexibility—are impaired.[6]

Working memory is probably the most crucial of all the executive functions when it comes to learning. It's what allows you to hold information in mind while manipulating or updating it. Working memory allows you to relate the present to the past and future, enables you to make connections, and is key to creativity. You could say that working memory *is* learning. Some experts say that working memory will become the new IQ—because it predicts academic success and life outcomes better than IQ.[7] When kids are stressed and their working memory is impaired, it's hard for them to integrate information and to grasp and retain the thread of a narrative. Think of the brain like the RAM memory in a computer that lets programs run (rather than storage on the hard drive). A large cognitive load—too many things on your mind—is like having too many browsers open. At some point, the computer starts to slow down or to crash. Too many stresses, and so does the brain.

Ned has a clever little math trick that he plays with kids (try it yourself if you'd like but do it in your head, not on paper) to demonstrate working memory. He says quickly, "Take 1000. Add 40. Okay? Add another 1000. Add 30. Add 1000. Add 20. Add 1000. Add 10. What'd you get?" When he asks people what number they got, most everyone says 5000. (The answer is 4100.) Ned has a friend who's a bond trader on Wall Street—so a real math geek—and she, too, said 5000. This has nothing to do with math but rather with how brains work, and how hard it is under the best of circumstances to keep multiple pieces of information in our head while building on it. Add stress in there, and you're toast. Some while ago, Ned worked with a family whose daughter was *really* struggling. School was tough, but the ACT was hell. Suffice it to say, stress was swamping her. Ned prefaced the above trick by telling her he had a math trick that "everyone fell for" (trying to make it safe for her) and would like to show her the kind of mistake we often make on tests, mistakes that test makers create by deliberately tricking us. He didn't even get halfway through the above numbers before her eyes filled with tears, as math—really anything tied to school—had become so deeply threatening. Calm, not calculations, was what her brain most needed.

Remember, we're not *supposed* to be able to think clearly and logically when we experience a threat. We're supposed to run like hell, to stand and fight, or to play dead. If your kid is terrified that his strict teacher is going to call on him and he'll be embarrassed in front of the class, he's not thinking at all about whatever she may happen to be teaching at the moment. Survival will always trump learning.

Although we want schools to challenge our kids, they should do so in an environment that feels accepting and encouraging. What this looks like will vary depending on the circumstances, but the questions are the same: Do our kids feel safe in school, physically and emotionally? Do they have a sense of control over what they're doing in the classroom? Is it safe for them to make mistakes?

Also, remind your children that what's important is that they develop themselves, not that they get perfect grades. As we discussed when we covered Hermiones in Chapter Five, help your child keep perspective. Finally, one of the best things you can do to minimize academic stress is to not take it on yourself. And if you do, apologize, as the mom of one of Ned's students did. She wrote a letter to her daughter that was so moving that we asked if we could include it in the book. It said:

Tonight I failed you, and I would like to ask your forgiveness. I know my actions cannot be justified, but I would like to explain what happened.

This afternoon I saw one of your classmates' moms, and she questioned me about your performance on the math test yesterday. I shrugged and said that I did not know about a math test. When she shook her head disapprovingly at me, I felt the shame of a negligent mom. My ego got tangled up and confused. When I came home, I fired questions at you about test prep and results. I told you I wanted to check your homework and see your grades. Incredulous, you stared at me with tears in your eyes.

You have always been an intellectually curious and creative child. You are helpful and inclusive, diligent but noncompetitive. I allowed a mom who was trying to ascertain if her child had better results than my child get in the way of my relationship with my child.

I promise that I will never again ask how you scored on a test, never check your homework or grades online, and never even look at your report card unless you choose to show me that.

You are not a number or a letter to me; you are my dear gift who deserves my respect. I hope I can re-earn your trust and respect.

I love you.

Mom

We also think it's important for students and adults to work together to make school less stressful. We support the creation of stress-reduction teams that include students, teachers, administrators, and parents—with the goal of exploring ways to make school less stressful for *everyone*. (The first time Bill lectured a school faculty about the effects of stress on the brain, the assistant head of school cornered Bill after the workshop and voiced concern about his own brain, given how stressful life as a school administrator was.) These teams can focus on ways of increasing student and teacher autonomy, creating more opportunities for downtime during the school day, and modifying homework policy (like removing homework requirements during vacations).[8]

Homework: Inspire—But Don't Require

We have seen hundreds of kids who feel crushed by homework. In the last thirty years, there has been an enormous increase, especially for children in the early grades.[9] A recent study found that students from kindergarten through third grade had up to three times more homework than was recommended by the National Education Association and the National PTA, with kindergarteners averaging thirty-five minutes per night.[10] Teenagers at elite high schools averaged over three hours of homework every night, while middle schoolers came in at two and a half hours. Yet only 20 to 30 percent of the students surveyed reported that they perceived their homework to be "useful or meaningful."[11] Why are young kids piled up with homework when, despite ninety years of research, there is no compelling evidence that homework contributes significantly to learning in the elementary school years? And why are high schoolers expected to put in so many hours when research shows that homework's efficacy is limited at best? Small amounts of homework (one to two hours a night) can contribute to academic achievement for middle and high school kids, but any more than that backfires when it comes to actual learning.[12]

When kids are tired and stressed, they do more but accomplish less. Homework often creates tension between kids and their parents, almost invariably weakening their relationship and undermining the kids' sense of autonomy. It confuses the means and the ends. Bill routinely sees kids who ace their tests and clearly master the material—but get Cs and Ds because they don't turn in their homework.

Our motto is "Inspire—but don't require." We want teachers to inspire kids to want to learn outside the classroom. Several studies have shown that when kids have some control over the topics they study, they're more likely to be engaged in the work and to complete it, a compelling reason for most homework to be voluntary and ungraded.[13] We believe in recommending assignments and encouraging kids to do them—or an alternative task that would contribute to mastering the objectives—but not requiring or grading them. When teachers offer assignments, they should explain how students will benefit from doing them and should seek their students' feedback and suggestions. This is a very different approach from "Read pages 20–50 of textbook B by tomorrow and answer the ten study questions." In the best of all possible worlds, teachers would say, "If you can work on this for twenty minutes at some point after school, your brain will make new connections when you sleep tonight that will help you understand and remember what you've learned. But if you're too tired or stressed, do something else. You can always turn back to it when you feel fresher."

Finnish students—who have among the highest educational outcomes in the world—have the lightest homework requirement, rarely receiving more than a half hour per day.[14] The most prominent spokesman for Finnish education, Pasi Sahlberg, reports that many primary and lower school students finish most of their homework before leaving school and that fifteen-year-old students in Finland do not use private tutors or take additional lessons outside of school.[15] He points out that this makes the performance of Finnish students even more astonishing, as students in many Asian countries who perform comparably in reading, math, and science spend much of their time outside of school being tutored and taking additional classes.[16]

Over the years, Bill has spoken to many teachers who either don't assign homework, make it optional, or assign it only if the students are not keeping up. These include teachers in Montessori schools, public middle school teachers, and an International Baccalaureate economics teacher who, ten years ago, started recommending weekly readings but not requiring homework assignments. His students have performed at least as well in the last ten years as they did with homework (and have continued to perform above average on their IB exams). Ned deliberately assigns very little homework. He has no interest in busywork. He wants the kids he is seeing to work hard on what they believe helps them. If they arrive for tutoring and tell Ned they didn't have time to complete their homework, he thanks them for their honesty, expresses his belief that they must have had more important uses of their time, and lets them know he is happy to help them schedule time to complete the work, if they wish.

Let's suppose your school takes the anti-Finnish approach. If you have options, you can try to switch to a school that focuses on brain-centered learning instead, a school that aims to develop inquisitive learners, not score seekers. You can step in if you feel homework is becoming onerous or if it's unduly stressful for your child. Schools like to say they use evidence-based policies, so ask your principal for the evidence behind the school's homework policy. Try using one of our favorite lines from Sara Bennett and Nancy Kalish's book *The Case Against Homework*: "It's not working for my child." You'd be surprised by how willing teachers are to make adjustments if homework has really become a problem.

You can also give your kid a pass to just let it go. If a teacher is assigning too much homework, and interventions haven't worked, you could talk through the pros and cons of just not doing it. Which is more important? His happiness and well-being, or his grade with this particular teacher? To us, the answer is clear.

Teach Kids When They're Ready

Our friend Marie's daughter Emily just entered kindergarten. Emily went to preschool, where the curriculum revolved around things like petting rabbits and making art out of macaroni noodles. Emily isn't all that interested in learning how to read, but she loves to dance and sing and can play with Barbies for hours. Emily's older sister, Frances, was reading well before she started kindergarten, and the difference between them worried Marie. Emily's grandparents thought it was a problem, too, and hinted that perhaps she should be reading to Emily more often. When Marie talked to another mom about it, her friend shared the same concern about her own two daughters, wondering if it was somehow her fault for not reading to her younger daughter enough. Would these younger siblings be behind the moment they started kindergarten?

This scenario drives us crazy because it's grounded in fear, competition, and pressure, not in science or reality. Not only are parents feeling undue pressure, but their kids are, too. The measuring stick is out, comparing one kid to another, before they even *start* formal schooling. Academic benchmarks are being pushed earlier and earlier, based on the mistaken assumption that starting earlier means that kids will do better later. We now teach reading to five-year-olds even though evidence shows it's more efficient to teach them to read at age seven, and that any advantage gained by kids who learn to read early washes out later in childhood.[17]

What was once advanced work for a given grade level is now considered the norm, and children who struggle to keep up or just aren't ready yet are considered deficient. Kids feel frustrated, embarrassed, and experience a low sense of control if they're not ready to learn what they're being taught.

The fact is that while school has changed, children haven't. Today's five-year-olds are no more fundamentally advanced than their peers were in 1925, when we started measuring such things. A child today can draw a square at the same age as a child living in 1925 (4½), or a triangle (5½), or remember how many pennies he has counted (up to twenty by age six). These fundamentals indicate a child's readiness for reading and arithmetic. Sure, some kids will jump the curve, but children need to be able to hold numbers in their head to really understand addition, and they must be able to discern the oblique line in a triangle to recognize and write letters like K and R. The problem is that while children from the 1920s to the 1970s were free to play, laying the groundwork for key skills like self-regulation, modern kindergartners are required to read and write.

Brain development makes it easier to learn virtually everything (except foreign languages) as we get older. Work is always easier with good tools. You can build a table with a dull saw, but it will take longer, be less pleasant, and may ingrain bad building habits that are hard to break later on. One of the most obvious problems we see from rushed academic training is poor pencil grip. Holding a pencil properly is actually pretty difficult. You need to have the fine motor skills to hold the pencil lightly between the tips of the first two fingers and the thumb, to stabilize it, and to move it both horizontally and vertically using only your fingertips. In a pre-school class of twenty we know of in which the kids were encouraged to write much too early, seventeen needed occupational therapy to correct the workarounds they'd internalized in order to hold a pencil. Think of it: 85 percent of kids needed extra help, parents spent extra money, and parents and kids felt stressed because some adult thought, "Hey, wouldn't it be swell if we taught these four-year-olds to write?" without any regard to developmental milestones.

We see this early push all the way through high school. Eighth graders take science classes that used to be taught to ninth graders, and kids in tenth grade read literature that used to be taught in college. In Montgomery County, outside Washington, DC, the school district attempted to teach algebra to most students in eighth grade rather than ninth grade, with the goal of eventually teaching it to most kids in seventh grade. It was a disaster, with three out of four students failing their final exam.[18] Most eighth graders don't have sufficiently developed abstract thinking skills to master algebra. Historically, kids started college in their late teens because they were ready; while there have always been exceptions, on the whole fourteen-year-olds weren't considered developmentally ready for rigorous college work. Ironically, in the attempt to advance our kids, our own thinking about these issues has regressed.

Ned fields requests from many parents who want their kids to start SAT prep in the ninth grade. Ned tells them that it's a mistake to spend their kid's time and their money for him to teach them things that they will naturally learn in school. It's far better to wait for them to develop skills and acquire knowledge at school, and then to add to that with some test preparation in their junior year. Starting test prep too early is not just totally unnecessary, it is actively counterproductive. It's like sitting your fourteen-year-old down to explain the intricacies of a 401(k) plan. It's not going to register.

Bill routinely deals with the aftermath of early academics gone wrong. He has seen many kids who shut down or cry upon being asked to read because they've experienced it as so threatening in the past. When kids fail again and again, they internalize failure. Bill recently spoke with a child psychologist whose four-year-old daughter felt like a failure because she couldn't write in her journal as well as her classmates.

The central, critical message here is a counterintuitive one that all parents would do well to internalize: earlier isn't necessarily better; and likewise, more isn't better if it's too much. To counter the effects of too-early learning, here are some things you can do:

- Where possible, choose schools that are developmentally sensitive in their curriculum and appropriate for your child. Some kids will do really well as big fish in small ponds. It gives them the confidence to tackle the currents without being afraid of being swept away. They get to grow strong and feel strong. So what if there are bigger fish in bigger ponds? Help your children find the right curricular environments for them.

- Relax and take a long view, even if no one else around you is. Most kids who learn to read at five aren't better readers at nine than those who learn to read at six or seven. Bill remembers vividly the mild panicky feeling he and Starr had when their daughter was five years old and some of her friends were starting to read. Even though they knew that kids learn to read much easier at age seven than at age five, and that pushing academics too early was harmful and produced no lasting benefit, Bill and Starr wondered if they were jeopardizing their child's future by letting her fall behind her peers. They briefly considered pulling her out of her nonacademic kindergarten. But they stuck to their guns and left her in a school that did not push and did not give her any homework until the fourth grade. Despite an unrushed start, she received her PhD in economics from the University of Chicago at the age of twenty-six and is a successful economist. Bill loves telling that story, not to brag (okay, just a little), but to emphasize that it is difficult to buck the tide even when you know the current is carrying you the wrong way.

- Remember that any gains from rushing development will wash out. Parents often tell Bill that their third grader is doing fourth- or fifth-grade math—but he never hears twenty-six-year-olds brag that they're more successful than most twenty-eight-year-olds.

- Don't go overboard on AP classes. You are doing your child no favors if you let her take more APs at the cost of her mental health and sleep. There's a reason why kids get more out of *Moby-Dick* in college than in high school. When we consider the enormous differences in the maturation of their prefrontal cortex—and the associated development in their capacity for abstraction and emotional maturity—it should come as no surprise that the majority of students will understand and appreciate novels written for adults better when they're older. The same is true for complex scientific theories and data, quantitative concepts, and historical themes, which are easier for most kids to grasp when they are college aged. This isn't to say that some students aren't ready for college-level courses when they're fifteen. The problem is that when this becomes the default for most students (I'll never get into college if I don't have five AP classes) it's destructive.

Test Kids the Right Way

Both of us test kids for a living, so we're not against tests. We live and breathe tests, and think that, when done right, they can be incredibly useful tools.

Neuroscientists are fond of saying "neurons that fire together, wire together." What we do repeatedly *with deliberate effort* more readily becomes etched in our brains. Henry Roediger, a University of Washington psychologist who is an expert on testing, thinks that while the word "test" has a very negative connotation, it's still one of the most powerful learning tools available. As he observed, when you struggle to recall a fact or concept, the act of doing so strengthens your memory of it, unlike simply reviewing notes. "Testing not only measures knowledge but changes it," he said.[19]

Testing also helps you recognize what you're missing, and helps teachers know where to spend their time. There's nothing like objective feedback to clarify or confirm perceptions about what you do (or don't) know. Testing can also mitigate test anxiety. Testing yourself, alone or in a study group, will put you under some pressure, and getting used to mild pressure is a useful stepping-stone to the stress of the actual exam.

That said, we have significant problems with standardized testing in schools as it exists today. Many of the policy makers who espouse these tests are politicians, not inspiring educators. They talk a lot about things like accountability, raising the bar, narrowing the gap, and "racing to the top," and very little about the research that shows that a heavy reliance on standardized testing is an ineffective way to improve educational outcomes. Our favorite Finn, Pasi Sahlberg, looked at the test-based approach that so many nations around the world use and showed that test scores in these countries are actually declining. By contrast, Finland chose to emphasize highly trained teachers, collaboration, school-based curricula, and a leadership style among educators built on trust. Finland's scores improved.

Also consider testing from the teachers' point of view. It forces them to teach to the test, giving them little autonomy. It makes them fear for their job, as their contract often depends on the test scores of their students (over which they have little direct control). They may look at their fellow teachers as competitors rather than collaborators (Is the other ninth grade teacher getting all the top kids in the class?) and at their students as potential obstacles to their advancement. They may encourage a kid be held back, as they are not incentivized to think as much about his overall well-being as his potential test scores. Most often test results are used to evaluate teachers and school districts in the aggregate. All of this gets in the way of the teacher's ability to do his or her job effectively and to connect with students.

Anything that makes kids, parents, and teachers more stressed and lowers their sense of control is bound to fail. An overly strong emphasis on testing makes education narrower and more frustrating. Every student should have something to look forward to every day, and test-driven education puts this at risk by squeezing out time for elective classes and focusing those hours on test prep instead. Many kids shine most brightly in classes that aren't core academic subjects (or in activities that aren't classes at all)—like art, music, shop, and drama. These are never "station to station" and always about trying to make a product or performance better, bit by bit. From a motivational perspective, your kid may not love geometry, but if he knows that he has chorus, band, art, or shop class coming up, where he really gets to be creative and enjoy what he's doing, it sure makes learning the Pythagorean theorem more palatable.

In the 2014–2015 school year, more than 650,000 students opted out of taking standardized tests in school. We wouldn't recommend opting your child out of the test if he wants to take it, but talk to him about the pros and cons and let him choose.

If your child opts in to standardized testing, you can still com-municate what value the tests have and what value they don't have. Tests like the Educational Records Bureau (ERB) or the Common Core should only be used to assess skills and knowledge and to help guide teachers. They are not a label for your child's intelligence. Make sure she knows it.

Ways to Bring a Sense of Control to School

In sum, schools should focus more on nurturing healthy brain de-velopment and less on test scores. They should be exploring how to make the school experience less stressful, to promote self-understanding and self-regulation in students, to maximize self-motivation by promoting autonomy, and to maximize engagement by incorporating the arts into all aspects of teaching.[20]

There are a number of programs that are leading the charge for a reduced-stress school environment. These include the Quiet Time Program we talked about in Chapter Six, which was first imple-mented in 2009 at Visitacion Valley Middle School, an underfunded urban school in San Francisco. Most students practice Transcenden-tal Meditation for fifteen minutes twice a day. (Others read or rest during "quiet time.") When Bill toured the school in 2011, the assis-tant principal said that prior to the program's launch, there would have been thirty kids standing around outside the school counselor's office because they'd been tossed out by their teachers for fooling around in class. In just two years, there were none. Many other schools in California and around the country have adopted Quiet Time programs, and are seeing remarkable results.[21] While Quiet Time is often used in underfunded schools, it is just as valuable at the other extreme. As an administrator from an elite girls' high school in Chicago told Bill, she adopted the Quiet Time Program because "I just couldn't send one more stressed and depressed kid to the hospital."

Some schools promote self-regulation by teaching their students about mindful awareness or by incorporating mindfulness practices schoolwide, through programs like Zones of Regulation. In this program, children are taught to ask themselves how they're feeling in their body and to recognize certain signals. When children are in the "red zone," they are feeling intense and emotional. The "yellow zone" is also a heightened state, but they have more control over their actions. In the "green zone," they feel calm, alert, and focused. This is the optimal state for learning, the place where kids are challenged but not unduly so. And then there is the "blue zone," where a child is bored, tired, or sad. We've seen classes of first and second graders come in from recess hyper and frenetic, only to have their teacher explain that it was time to get into the green zone, and encourage the class to take some deep, focused breaths together in order to calm their bodies down. And it worked.

Other schools are substituting fitness training for traditional high school PE classes in order to take advantage of the tremendous cognitive power of vigorous exercise, or placing a strong emphasis on Carol Dweck's approach to developing a growth mindset in students. We support all these programs—and other approaches that promote the development of a healthy sense of control.

The approach to your child's education that we're advocating won't always be embraced. In some regions of the country (and, indeed, of the world), the ultracompetitive school, the multiple AP classes, and the race to the finish feel as inevitable as the Starbucks on every street corner. In their conversations with Bill over the years, many driven teenagers who are taking medication for depression have implied (as have their parents) that if they managed to get into an elite college, it would be worth everything they had done (i.e., compromised) to achieve that end. It's not. As Robert Sapolsky has said, depression is the cruelest disease. For kids to become depressed because they're too tired and stressed and have been driven for too long is too high a price to pay for that admissions letter. Getting in is only one piece of the college experience. The most crucial question, which we will turn to later, is what happens when you get there.

What to Do Tonight

- Teach your kids that they are responsible for their own education. Kids should feel in charge, not that school is being done "to them." Note this is very different from blaming kids who are struggling.

- If your child is not learning from his teacher, acknowledge this without blaming the teacher. "Mr. Cooper is doing the best he can. He just doesn't know how to teach you the way you learn." Encourage your child to think of what will motivate him to master the material being taught in the class anyway.

- Remind your child of the big picture, that grades matter less than the ways he or she develops as a student and person.

- Resist the pressure to push your child if he's not ready, be it reading in kindergarten, algebra in eighth grade, or AP classes in high school.

- Create an advocacy group made of up teachers, parents, and kids to talk about what you can all do to make school a less stressful experience. Consider advocating for brain-friendly experiences in school such as exercise, the arts, and meditation.

CHAPTER NINE

Wired 24/7

Taming the Beast of Technology

P ARENTS HAVE ASKED us a lot of questions over the years. Some are anchored to a particular cultural moment: *How should I talk to my ten-year-old about terrorism?* A few seem to come up over and over: *How can I help my child who doesn't like to read work around his dyslexia? How can I get him to do his homework?* But if we made a graph of the questions we hear most often over time, it would show the rapid rise of one in particular: *How can I get my kid to stop playing video games every second he's not in school?*

It was tough enough for parents in the 1980s and '90s, when games had to be connected to the family television or purchased cartridge by cartridge for a prized handheld device. At least then consoles and televisions could be locked away and were off limits during dinnertime, sleep time, and schooltime. But now that a critical mass of young people have their own smartphones—about 73 percent of thirteen- to seventeen-year-olds, according to a recent Pew study[1]—it's gotten a lot harder to get kids to limit the time they spend on video games, texting, and social media. By the time they're seven, most American kids have spent the equivalent of one full year 24/7 in front of a screen.[2] While only 35 percent of teens socialize in person after school, and almost as few speak on the phone to one another, 63 percent exchange text messages daily.[3]

Kids between the ages of eight and ten use screens seven and a half hours a day, which is high enough, but then that number jumps to eleven and a half hours for kids ages eleven to fourteen.[4] This means that most of this generation's social and cognitive development is happening through a screen. Technology addiction is the new norm for young adults, many of whom will actually panic if they are unable to use social media for as little as a few hours.[5] Some parents are left befuddled by it all. Adam Pletter, a psychologist and the creator of a program that educates parents about the technologies their kids are using, points out that making decisions about kids' use of technology is unlike other parenting decisions because parents know relatively little about the tools they're placing in their children's hands.

One father of a technology-addicted seven-year-old recently approached Ned after a presentation. He was beside himself with concern for his son, who spent every waking moment—and many when he should have been sleeping—playing video games.

"I've begged him. I've threatened him. I've bribed him. Nothing," he said. "He's in his room all day. He doesn't talk to me or his mother or his brother, he just yells things at strangers on the computer."

The game itself wasn't his main concern; it was the fact that his son was isolating himself and wasn't talking to anyone in the family.

Technology is an incredible tool with the great power to enrich lives, but the things it displaces—family time, face-to-face interaction with friends, study time, physical activity, and sleep—are invaluable, and the way technology trains the brain to expect constant stimulation is deeply troubling. In Adam Alter's book *Irresistible: The Rise of Addictive Technology and the Business of Keeping Us Hooked*, he makes the condemning point that many of those who work in technology and best understand its power don't want their kids using it.[6] Many of them send their kids to Waldorf schools, which ban technology from the classroom and make a point of actively discouraging it at home up until the age of twelve. The king of tech himself, Steve Jobs, was careful to limit his kids' technology use, and wouldn't get iPads for his own kids. Chris Anderson, the former editor of *Wired*, told Nick Bilton of the *New York Times*: "My kids accuse me and my wife of being fascists and overly concerned about tech. . . . That's because we have seen the dangers of technology firsthand. I've seen it in myself, I don't want to see that happen to my kids."[7]

Devices are constantly evolving. Technology moves fast, and we're learning more about its impact all the time. But we already know more than people realize about what constant technology use does to young people's brains. Some think video games can save the world, and others are convinced that technology is poisoning us. This chapter will explore the science behind both points of view.

Technology can be daunting (Snapchat replaced Instagram which replaced Facebook and now I don't even know what's up. . . . Or is it WhatsApp?), frustrating (My kid was doing better until the latest Minecraft came out; now it's like we're back to square one), and it can inspire a feeling of helplessness (How can I deny my kid a phone when everyone else her age has one?). We've heard it all. But it also represents a great opportunity. Think of it as a beast that, when tamed, can bring joy and possibility into your child's life. Learning to tame the beast is a powerful skill—one that will stay with them for years to come. The key is to teach your kids how to stay in charge.

Teens find it thrilling to be constantly connected. Forget love letters or surreptitious notes: they can now reach one another instantaneously, anywhere at any time. A friend with an au pair marveled at how technology eased the au pair's transition to a new country. She was just eighteen and far away from home for the first time but she could join WhatsApp groups to conveniently meet up with other au pairs (an instant community) and post photos to Instagram so her parents and friends back home could keep up.

You don't have to be living across the world from your family to benefit from social media. Shy kids are often more forthcoming when they interact online, and kids can get help with schoolwork through study groups and note sharing.[8] Others who might feel marginalized or alienated can connect online with a community of people who are more like them.

Even as recently as a few years ago, it seemed like children and teenagers who spent a lot of time on video games would have nothing to show for it as they got older, but the landscape is changing as video games are now part of a $20-billion industry. This means that there are many jobs and that gamers can make a living doing something connected to their passion. At video-game competitions, the total "purse" might be worth millions of dollars. Bill consulted with a brilliant twenty-one-year-old who spent many hours a day playing an interactive strategy game. He was in the top 1 percent of players in the world, but in his words, he was nowhere near being good enough to play professionally. His plan was either to become an agent who represents top game players, or to get the training and experience necessary to be able to do play-by-play commentary for the gaming competitions.

Many video games are "hard fun," exercising cognitive skills like pattern detection, eye-hand coordination, and hypothesis construction, which may explain why a study at Beth Israel found that laparoscopic surgeons who played video games for more than three hours a week made 37 percent fewer surgical errors than their non-gaming peers.[9] Daphne Bavelier, one of the preeminent researchers in this area, points out that action-game players have to make fast decisions, divide their attention, and then switch quickly to a single narrow focus of attention. In the lab, she and her team have found that people who play action (first-person shooter) video games between five and fifteen hours a week have a better ability to perceive salient details and to remember landmarks. Gamers are better able to filter out irrelevant information.[10] Bavelier has reported that gamers also appear to be more efficient at multitasking. (Though this is still not as efficient as doing one thing at a time.)[11]

Game designer, speaker, and writer Jane McGonigal, an unabashed advocate, argues that people who game extensively develop four useful characteristics: 1) urgent optimism—the desire to act immediately to tackle an obstacle, accompanied by the conviction that they can be successful; 2) enhanced sociability—research suggests that we like people better after we play a game with them, even if they've won, because playing a game together builds trust; 3) blissful productivity—we're happier working hard to win than we are relaxing or goofing around; and 4) epic meaning—gamers love to be attached to awe-inspiring missions. These four superpowers, says McGonigal, result in "superempowered hopeful individuals."[12] Just imagine what we could accomplish if we could channel this energy for the good of the planet.

From a brain science perspective, video games produce spikes in dopamine and induce a state of flow. They require kids to focus and to think hard for long periods of time. For many children, electronic games are the single most powerful venue through which they experience a sense of control. Game designers have long programmed games that induce "total immersion" by adjusting the difficulty of the game to the skill level of the player—creating a perfect setting for concentration, effort, and involvement. They also offer up a safe environment in which mistakes are never shaming and are instead a means to learn new skills and become a better player. Scientists have concluded that gaming satisfies the needs for competence and a sense of control—and that multiplayer games satisfy the need for relatedness. (It's worth remembering what we learned in Chapter Five, that all these things are important drivers of motivation.)

But much work is still to be done in this area, and there is no compelling evidence yet that the sense of control and motivation one feels when playing video games translates to real life. And with the exception of the improved surgical ability, there is no evidence that gamers will complete non-game-related tasks or assignments with greater focus or accuracy. Even McGonigal acknowledges that the four qualities of gamers don't show up much in the less action-packed world we actually live in.

What we do have evidence of is that technology is changing our brains. The most recently evolved, "plastic" parts of the brain change in direct response to experience. Because of technology, today's kids have a better memory for visual images and a greater facility for learning how to navigate and decode the digital world by doing it. Digital bombardment has changed the way that children process visual information, and even how they read. Reading used to be linear—there were no distractions, it was just line after line, page after page after page. Now anyone who spends significant time on a computer reads differently. They look for keywords, for links. They skim. Maryanne Wolf, a scientist whose book *Proust and the Squid* is one of the best books written about reading and the brain, has seen these changed patterns in her own brain. After a day of computer work, she tried to read a lengthy and complicated novel. "I couldn't force myself to slow down so that I wasn't skimming, picking out key words, organizing my eye movements to generate the most information at the highest speed," she said.[13] This change of reading style is affecting everyone, but children—who are growing up with iPads instead of books, with Wikipedia instead of the encyclopedia—are most impacted.

Research psychologist Larry Rosen and education consultant Ian Jukes have concluded that, due to their exposure to technology, kids' brains work "completely differently" from their parents' and from kids' brains of previous generations. One of the manifestations of this change is that many kids can't stand a minute of boredom or tolerate doing just one thing at a time.[14] Interestingly, though, the more primitive parts of our brains are not much different than they were a hundred thousand years ago. Our stress response is about the same as when our ancestors faced off with woolly mammoths and saber-toothed tigers. Our amygdala still activates and starts the same freeze-flight-or-fight response. The brain systems that help infants develop secure bonds with their parents still depend on face-to-face interaction. The ones that run our biological clocks and determine our need for sleep also haven't changed much. What this means is that while technology may be changing parts of our brains for the better, it's chipping away at things that the other parts of our brain need. Which leads us to the downsides.

Technology's Downsides

In 1881 (yes, that far back), a physician by the name of George Beard offered up a theory as to why more and more Americans were suffering from nervousness. His main culprit was technology: new "conveniences" were making life go faster—like the railroad and telegraph—and making people pay more attention to small details—like the pocket watch.[15] It's well known that technological breakthroughs commonly create more work rather than freeing up time. Consider the steam iron. It aimed to make life more convenient by making ironing easier . . . only now instead of ironing just once a month, people began ironing every week and even every day. We do more of something if it's easier, whether it's e-mailing rather than sending a letter, or texting rather than trying to reach someone on the phone. Technological breakthroughs almost by definition must make life more stressful, because they quicken the pace and raise the bar of what can be accomplished. Beard was on to this even before the greatest technological breakthrough in history: the use of electric light, which enabled us to live outside of nature's rhythms.

But if you can imagine the stress that a pocket watch caused (according to Beard, watches "excite the habit of looking to see the exact moment, so as not to be late for trains or appointments"), then it's no wonder that with tweets coming in at the speed of rain, our stress levels are many times what they were in 1881. A typical adult checks his smartphone forty-six times a day.[16] Eighty percent of teens report they check their phones hourly (which in our experience seems low), and fifty percent say they are addicted to their phones.[17]

So how do we help our kids foster the self-control not to look at Snapchat every couple of minutes? Moderating technology use has proven to be tricky even for adults, and kids' brains haven't yet developed to the point of being great at resisting compulsion or distraction.

When you refresh your e-mail, look at your text messages, or check your Instagram account, you get a hit of dopamine, and an especially big one if you encounter something positive. This taps into a basic psychological construct: intermittent reinforcement. With intermittent reinforcement, you don't know if you'll be rewarded for something each time you do it, but you might be, and the anticipation drives you. This is the reason why dog trainers advise a "jackpot" rewards system: if you want a dog to perform a task, don't give him a treat each time he does it—give it to him every third time, or every fifth time, and make it a good treat. He never knows when a treat is coming, or what's coming. So when you say "Come!" he might get nothing, or he might get a piece of flank steak. Anticipation is addictive, so he'll come every single time. The same phenomenon is at work when people sit at slot machines for hours, and when kids check their texts. That incoming text could just be from their mom, reminding them to be on time. Or it could be from a guy or girl of interest. Every text contains the possibility of being juicy. So it will probably come as no surprise that adolescents are more influenced by the whiff of what's possible than people at any other time of life. Also, kids often tell us that what makes it so hard to resist checking their devices is FOMO, or the fear of missing out.

If you're a kid, the formula begins to look like this: the more technology you use, the poorer your self-regulation.[18] The more technology you use, the worse your executive function (your Pilot). This matters a lot; self-regulation and executive function are about twice as good predictors of academic success as IQ at all grade levels, including college.

That's the 360-degree view of the problem. But let's take what we know about technology and dopamine generally and apply it to the areas where it affects kids specifically. We have five main areas of concern about technology and our kids:

1. Screen time is an independent risk factor for many of the things we don't want for our kids—or for ourselves.

The research of Larry Rosen and his colleagues has shown that time in front of a screen is positively correlated with increases in 1) physical health problems, 2) mental health problems, 3) attention problems, and 4) behavior problems.[19] Similarly, in her troubling recent article, "Have Smartphones Destroyed a Generation?" Jean Twenge (whose research we discussed in Chapter One) argues that smartphones and social media are making the current generation of children, teens, and young adults "seriously unhappy." Her research suggests that despite their constant connections through media, contemporary young people increasingly feel lonely, tired, and left out.[20]

Screen time has a whole host of physiological effects that make it different from other sedentary activities like reading or drawing, and make it an independent risk factor for many physical and mental health problems. In children, every hour of screen time is associated with increased blood pressure, while every hour spent reading is associated with decreased blood pressure. These effects are independent of how much time kids spend exercising. It's not enough to run laps for an hour if you're then going to sit in front of a screen the rest of the day.[21]

Screen time brings violent news—from live shark attack footage to police shootings—home like never before. A study in the *Proceedings of the National Academy of Sciences* looked at the stress responses of people who had direct exposure to the Boston Marathon bombing, and those who were exposed to six hours-plus of media about the bombing. Believe it or not, it was the latter camp that reported the higher levels of stress.[22] You can be scrolling through your Facebook feed and, whether you're looking for it or not, see a link to some sort of violent death or crime. It's unsettling for adults, so imagine the impact on kids.

2. Social media takes control away from you and gives it to your peers.

Social media's reliance on quantifiable lists of friends, likes, and follows worries us, particularly with girls. A recent study found that increased time spent on Facebook is associated with a decreased sense of well-being.[23] If you post a photo of, say, your sandwich, and it gets seventeen likes, you might feel great. But what if the next day a new photo of your sandwich garners only six likes? It's all too easy to get sucked in by a swirl of questions: Did I choose the wrong sandwich? Bad photo? Are my friends not paying as much attention to me? Maybe I upset them, acted too needy, or am I losing my connection to them? It may seem silly to those of us who grew up with Polaroids instead of Instagram, but for a generation that does so much of its socializing online, those highs and lows are just as real as our feelings when a friend embraces or snubs us in person.

It's hard to imagine a purer externalization of the locus of control. Instagram and the like are akin to a real-time 24/7 beauty pageant, and any of your 867 online friends can tell you you're not so hot today by firing off a snarky remark or just neglecting to like your latest post. Social media turns our attention from our own experience (Did I enjoy my sandwich? Or the people I actually had lunch with?) to what other people think of our experience. Adolescents are already inclined to care deeply about what their peers think of them. By making more of their lives public, they give up the few parts that belong solely to them.

In a powerful *Washington Post* piece, Jessica Contrera followed thirteen-year-old Katherine Pommerening, whose phone was the social nexus of her life. Like many teens, Katherine would carefully cull through the photos she wanted to post on Instagram, choosing the ones she thought would garner the most likes: "Over 100 likes is good, for me," she said. She described the importance of a "tbh," which stands for "to be heard" or "to be honest." "If someone says, 'tbh you're nice and pretty,' that kind of, like, validates you in the comments. Then people can look at it and say, 'Oh, she's nice and pretty.'"[24]

It's no wonder that heavy social media users—any one of whose hundreds or thousands of friends or followers can reflexively pass judgment—disproportionaly suffer from anxiety, depression, and narcissism.[25] It's a bleak reality, and one that kids don't necessarily even want. In a recent poll of thirteen- to thirty-year-olds, most reported feeling defined by their online social profiles, exhausted by always having to work at it, and yet utterly unable to look away.[26]

3. Technology sucks time away from activities the brain needs to develop a healthy sense of control.

Technology keeps kids from getting the things that we know they need for healthy development: sleep (at least 84 percent of teen cell phone users have slept right beside their phone, and teens send an average of thirty-four texts per night after going to bed),[27] exercise, radical downtime, unstructured child-led play, and the real-life, face-to-face social interaction with friends and parents that is such a powerful antidote to stress.

While social media is a greater concern for girls, video games tend to be a bigger problem for boys. Video-game developers are geniuses of motivational science. They know just how to keep you engaged and rewarded enough so that it's hard to stop. And as we've already seen, adolescents are particularly vulnerable to not being able to stop because they haven't yet fully developed that all-important self-control. Leaving aside the argument that first-person shooter games cause more aggression (which we believe they do) and the benefits kids reap from playing video games (which are real), they are highly problematic and even addictive for approximately 10 percent of the kids who play them.[28] This is especially true for multi-player role-playing games such as *World of Warcraft*, which are immersive and promote a sense of relatedness to other players, including players in other countries and in different time zones. One of Bill's colleagues evaluated a twenty-three-year-old young man a few years ago who, according to his parents, hadn't left their basement in four years. He spent all his waking hours playing *World of Warcraft*. The family actually moved from Massachusetts to Maryland as part of a strategy to get him to make a clean break.

Technology is highly implicated in sleep problems. A study published in the *Journal of the American Medical Association* looked at data from twenty studies involving more than 125,000 children ages six to eighteen. If a child had access to a screen at bedtime at least three times a week, the researchers saw an 88 percent increase in the child's risk of not getting sufficient sleep and a 53 percent increased risk of poor sleep quality. The findings held up even if the devices weren't used. Just having a phone or a tablet in the bedroom increases sleep problems.[29] As the study's lead author Ben Carter told the *New York Times*, "The most important point is that we need a communitywide strategy to empower parents so that it becomes an acceptable routine to remove devices prior to bedtime."[30]

> I got my first glimpse of how addictive video games are when I was giving a lecture on sleep and sleep disorders to a group of parents and professionals. During the question-and-answer session, one mother stood up and said that her adolescent son had been uncommonly tired and almost impossible to wake up for several weeks. As a result, she scheduled an extensive sleep evaluation through the sleep disorders clinic at a local pediatric hospital. The evaluators told the mother that during the assessment her son had admitted that he had been setting an alarm for 1:00 A.M. and playing an interactive role-playing game with players from all over the world until 4:00 or 5:00 A.M.—and then telling his parents that he had insomnia and was unable to sleep. The diagnosis was "feigned sleep disorder."
>
> —Bill

4. Technology appears to lower empathy.

Staring at a screen instead of a person is having a measurable effect on our kids' levels of empathy. There's been a 40 percent drop over the last thirty years in levels of empathy reported by college students, most of which has occurred in the last ten years.[31] This can easily be connected to a decrease in face-to-face communication. Think about it: if someone is cruel online, he doesn't have to deal with seeing the object of that cruelty in the flesh.

Sherry Turkle, a research psychologist at MIT and the author of *Alone Together* and *Reclaiming Conversation*, calls what's happening a new "silent spring." Where Rachel Carson saw an assault on the environment, Turkle sees an assault on empathy. She reports that 82 percent of Americans say that communicating via media has reduced the quality of their conversations. When she was interviewing people for *Reclaiming Conversation*, again and again they would say, "I'd rather text than talk." But it's through conversation and face-to-face interaction that we learn intimacy and empathy.

5. Technology offers easy access to pornography, leading to a more violent sexual culture.

Technology's dark underbelly keeps getting darker. Porn is available everywhere, and seeps in where it is not welcome and at moments when we are not looking for it. Nancy Jo Sales, author of *American Girls: Social Media and the Secret Lives of Teenagers*, argues that pornography is normalizing a new kind of sexual violence. Consider what are called "slut pages." If you don't know about them, you should. Slut pages are when someone, typically a boy, collects nude photos of girls in his school and posts them online. It's not a consensual sharing, and sometimes occurs without the girls' knowledge. For this reason, among others, we strongly recommend letting your child know that you will be checking her texts and social media until you feel comfortable that she's safe. This practice is completely consistent with giving kids a sense of control, by the way. First of all, you're letting them know instead of checking their phone on the sly; and second, you're signaling that there are some areas where they still need training wheels. As we covered in Chapter Three, giving kids a sense of control doesn't mean that you let go of all restrictions and rules, and in order to feel safe themselves, kids need to know that you're there to help them navigate deep waters. There is perhaps no deeper water than technology.

Taming the Beast

Now that we clearly understand what we're dealing with—the good, the bad, and the ugly—we can fashion an approach to helping our kids tame the beast so it works for them and not against them.

The principle of "It's your call" still applies to technology: be very thoughtful about setting parameters, work with your kids to set them, and let them work within them.

Kids want their parents to help. Most recognize that their tech use can get out of control. But at some point they're going to have to learn to self-police their limits. You can't exactly go to college with them if they're struggling to manage their gaming or social media use. You have to step back over time. It's a progression, and here are some of our best tips for teaching your child (and perhaps yourself) how to tame the technobeast:

It starts with you.

Recognize that you may very well have unhealthy habits when it comes to technology—most people do. In a British study, 60 percent of parents worried that their kids engaged in too much screen time, while 70 percent of kids felt their parents used technology too much.[32] You have to model responsible use of technology. Talk to your kids about the universal struggle to regulate technology use, including your own. Offer tips that have worked for you or other people you know. Give your kids permission to call you out when you check your phone when they're trying to talk to you. Apologize. Show them you're working on it. When a friend of ours was on vacation with her family, she gave her phone to her husband to stash out of sight. She knew if she had access to it, she'd be too inclined to check her e-mail, taking her out of the moments she wanted to focus on her family.

Seek to understand.

Although children often will adapt to the mores of their parents, many teens won't. Rather, they adapt to the mores of their peers. They need to learn to work successfully within the world they will inhabit, not the world you were raised in. They will have to navigate a whole set of social rules and manners that may be foreign to you. Seek to understand them, so you can respectfully help your child shut her technology down when it's time.

If you are the parent of a teen, understand that online is where your child most often socializes. Just as you wouldn't interrupt your daughter when she was midsentence with a friend and say, "Stop talking this moment," you can't tell her to stop typing when she's midtext.

When it comes to video games, we hear so many parents say things like, "He's wasting his life away playing video games." The conversations they're having with their kids take on a disrespectful tone. Instead, play video games with your kid. Try to understand what's appealing about it. You might be surprised. Acknowledge that you "get" it, that it's fun, and that you know it's important to them, but also that it's important not to become dependent. Showing an interest and being knowledgeable will help you to effectively negotiate limits and intervene if problems arise. We're much better able to influence our kids when they feel respected and emotionally close to us. Learn about their interests for these reasons, but most important, because doing so matters to them.

Get back to nature.

When Bill's son took part in a three-month outdoor leadership education program after college, he returned saying that he hated his phone. Having lived three months without it, he loved the freedom of not being available, of not being interrupted, and of realigning with nature. Nature has a way of resetting us and relaxing us. This isn't a new observation. In George Beard's 1881 book on nervousness, he wrote about how noises like the moans of the wind and rustlings of leaves are rhythmical, while the sounds of civilization are "unrhythmical, unmelodious and therefore annoying, if not injurious."[33] Studies show that kids feel and perform better after they've been immersed in nature—or even after they've looked at nature posters.[34] The Japanese have a term for this: *shinrin-yoku,* or "forest bathing." Walking in nature "cleans" the prefrontal cortex of its clutter, calming us, centering us, and allowing us to perform better on tasks or tests that demand working memory. Another study showed that after five days in tech-free summer camps, kids demonstrated improvement in empathy.[35] We've personally known dozens of technology-sick kids who went to summer camp and said that after the first week, they didn't even miss their phones or games.

If you're not the backpacking or hiking type, still make an effort to plan excursions where you and your child are surrounded by natural beauty—even if it's in a city park. It may not feel like it's making a difference, but trust us, it is. Chances are, the longer you stay at that park or river or beach, the more you'll notice it.

Inform rather than lecture.

Your job is not to admonish or lecture your kids about their technology use. One of the best things you can do is express confidence in your child's ability to regulate her own technology use and offer to help. As a consultant, you don't need to pass judgment; you get to inform and make recommendations. It's stunning how effective this is.

Ned had a student who was scheduled to take the ACT at her school, but the test was not offered on the weekend. She had to take the exam after a long day at school. Fortunately, she had a free last period so she would have a bit over an hour before she needed to take the test. Ned worried that her brain would be frazzled after a whole day of school, and he knew she was a tech-addicted kid who would likely spend that hour staring at her phone. So he told her about what would be going on in her brain during that hour if she didn't unplug. Then he said, "Do you want my suggestion?" She did. "In a perfect world," he said, "you'd be able to have a good night's sleep, get up, warm up, have a good breakfast, and go take your test. You wouldn't have had all your classes, interactions with teachers and friends, and all the decisions of school before sitting to take the ACT. So here's what I'd recommend you do. After your last class, turn off your cell phone. Put it in your locker. Then, because I know you have those woods behind your school, go for a walk. Maybe for fifteen or twenty minutes. Walking in the woods will allow your brain to space out and forget all the things you've been trying 'to keep in mind.' By clearing your head, you'll have more headspace and will be able to think a bit more clearly and do better on the test." She ended up feeling great about her test performance that day, as her score exceeded her expectations.

Collaborate on a solution.

A few years ago, Janell Burley Hofmann wrote a letter to her thirteen-year-old son on the occasion of giving him his first phone, and it went viral after it was published on the *Huffington Post*. It was filled with warmth, humor, and some excellent advice: "Do not text, e-mail, or say anything through this device you would not say in person." In total, eighteen points were included in what was ultimately a contract for him to accept and sign on to. The letter's popularity spoke to just how familiar this scenario was for so many parents. Without taking anything away from Ms. Hofmann, we suggest that you take the contract idea a step further and create one with your children. If they are a part of the decision making around technology use, they will gain practice thinking critically about the need to self-regulate, and will be much more apt to stick to the agreement.

If you unilaterally clamp down, your child is apt to rebel. Bill saw a kid years ago who would constantly circumvent his parents' efforts to limit his television use. They locked the TV in a cabinet, so he called a locksmith. They cut off cable, so he called the cable provider, skipped school, and had it reinstated. The point is, he was always one step ahead of his parents—and this was twenty years ago, when you could actually physically lock up technology in a way that's near impossible today.

Don't try to work toward a solution in the midst of an argument, or when you're asking your child to shut their technology down. As with any such conversation, find a time when no one's back is up and no action is required immediately.

As the parent, you should not agree to anything that makes you uncomfortable. But hear your child out and don't be afraid to relent if his or her argument seems reasonable, even if you might like to do things differently.

I recently evaluated a thirteen-year-old boy named Ian who has a great talent for graphic design. He's had major companies (who don't know his age) contact him about using his designs for their catalogues and video productions. In many ways, Ian is one of the most successful young adolescents I've ever met. At the same time, he is impulsive, has ADHD, and is somewhat obsessive, which places him at greater risk than most children of having trouble regulating his technology use. The same intensive drive that allows him to hyperfocus on his design-related work for hours at a time makes it very difficult for him to "shift" his attention and transition to less stimulating activities such as homework, chores, or getting ready for bed. Although he has to use his computer for homework and the design work he loves, the more he uses his computer or his cell phone, the more stressed and irritable he becomes. His parents say that trying to get him not to use his laptop or cell phone in bed has provoked such terrible fights that they have had to give in—and just let him be sleep deprived. They point out that the times when they have been able to limit his screen time by simply taking away his computer and phone he has been a much happier and more agreeable boy.

When Ian's parents asked for my advice about how to help him manage his technology use, I asked them the familiar question: "Whose problem is it?" The answer, in this case, turned out to be that it was Ian's problem, as it affected his mood and his schoolwork, but also theirs, as his technology-induced irritability made him hard to live with. I suggested that Ian's parents think of helping him learn to regulate his use of technology in a healthy way as an important long-term goal, rather than as something that has to happen immediately. I have seen many "technology-sick" kids who got so tired of feeling out of control that they limited their own use. I told them to engage in some collaborative problem solving with Ian, underscoring their understanding of how important technology was to him (and how imperative it was for his graphic design work) and emphasizing their desire to be supportive in setting appropriate limits. I suggested that they brainstorm about strategies for keeping his computer and phone use within healthy limits, seeking a mutually agreeable solution (which is usually what comes out of this kind of discussion when it is done respectfully but assertively). I also suggested that they honestly ask Ian's opinion about what should be done if he could not limit his technology use and appeared to have a "technology addiction." Finally, I recommended that if either Ian or his parents felt that technology was controlling him (rather than vice versa), they should meet with a professional who works with kids on managing their use of technology. Ian was relieved. He'd worried I would insist he stop using technology, period, and he liked the idea of working with his parents to figure out a solution.

—Bill

Understand your leverage.

When children are young, you can easily limit their technology use by not giving them access to devices—or turning on parental restrictions so that they can only access approved sites. This gets trickier as kids get older, and with teenagers, you simply can't monitor their tech habits all the time.

But here's what you can do. Always know their password, and let them know that you will always know it. If you are paying for their data plan, you can make that contingent on their respectful use of technology. If they won't put away the phone at night, you don't pay the bill. As we said in Chapter Seven, if your child claims she needs the phone in her bedroom to set the alarm, buy an alarm clock. Most important, let your high schoolers know that although you're looking forward to their getting an excellent education, you won't be sending them off to an expensive college until they can demonstrate that they can regulate their technology use well enough to be successful. Otherwise it will be a waste of their time and your money.

A Few Common Questions

"How much screen time is reasonable?"

This is a simple question with a complicated answer. It used to be that when parents asked us about video-game time, we suggested no more than an hour a day. But then we heard that kids would get frustrated because it took an hour and a half to get to the next level of their favorite game. There is no one right answer here, but we do have some guidelines. For starters, encourage everyone in the family to make a technology-use plan. It is helpful for you to do this together with your children, so that they will see you monitoring your own use. Suggest that they start by mapping out the number of hours they need to sleep, how much time they want to spend on sports or other nontech leisure activities, and how much time they need to spend on schoolwork, dinner, chores, and getting ready for school and for bed. This will make it easier to think about how much tech time will fit comfortably in the daily or weekly schedule. What we can do is plan for the things we know are important and work backward.

The answer is easier for young kids. We believe that preschoolers develop best by interacting with people and, where possible, with nature, by engaging in dramatic play, by singing, building, and making art. There is no evidence that young children need technology to develop optimally or that kids who are exposed to technology early are better for it.

"How do I get my kid who loves electronics to be interested in something else?"

The child who loves video games more than anything is likely to have a different conception of "reasonable use" than you. For school-aged kids, we recommend framing the discussion by recognizing that you want them to be able to use technology, and that you know how important it is to them. If your kid seems technically inclined, say "You may grow up to be a techie." Then you can tell them about some of the other things you don't want them to miss out on—family time, reading, socializing with friends, or sleep. Say something like, "I know how much fun these games are, and I'm not going to say you can't do it, but as your parent, I'm concerned that there are other important things you're missing out on. So it would help me a lot if we could have a conversation about how much time a week you really need to enjoy games you want to play, and come up with other things you'll do each week so I'm not worried about you. If we can both agree on a plan and you can stick to it, I'll leave you alone."

"I want to limit screen time, but my child's school requires him to do his homework onscreen—sometimes hours of it. What can I do?"

Though screen time is a complicated issue, we believe adults should work together to tell our kids that we don't want all their waking hours spent in front of a screen, and we support parents in talking with schools and administrators about the issue. Tell them you are putting your child's health first, and come armed with a study that shows that the amount of time your child is spending in front of a screen is harmful. Offer solutions for a way your child might still complete the homework, but not on a screen. Start a conversation going with other parents and the principal on the subject. Work with other parents who seem to share your concern so that your child doesn't feel singled out and babied.[36]

"My daughter's only in fifth grade, and she desperately wants a smartphone. She says everyone in her class has one and that she feels left out. But I think fifth grade is too young to have a phone. What should I do?"

The bottom line is that you should not do what you don't feel comfortable doing. When Bill's kids were in high school, they often complained about being the only kids in their grade who didn't have a car. Bill was proud of that fact, and feels that in the long run it helped his kids more than it hurt them. The point is, it's okay to say no even if other parents say yes.

At the same time, be open to the fact that there's a problem that requires solving. If your child feels left out, explore where that's coming from. Show empathy, and explain that you don't want her to feel bad. Consider introducing a phone in steps. A lot of kids use their phone to text, so perhaps the first phone is one that allows calls and texts, but has no Internet capability.

We also recommend that you talk to your child's teachers to see if what your child says is actually true. Is your child in fact being left out because she doesn't have a phone?

Also talk to other parents. What are their kids doing? Is it causing problems? Talk about forming some sort of coalition to set similar parameters and limits.

Parents getting together on technology is powerful. Parents and kids getting together on technology is even more powerful.

"I don't want my kid to be left out of a tech-savvy workforce because I've limited her tech use. I've heard a lot about how technology is improving kids' ability to multitask. Doesn't my child need to learn how to do this, too, to keep up?"

Let's put this fear to rest. At the no-tech Waldorf School in Silicon Valley, 75 percent of the students are children of tech executives. When asked if they're concerned their young kids will fall behind in their technical competence, these techies say that they make it so easy to learn, kids can catch up quickly.[37]

And while playing video games for hours on end does seem to make you a better multitasker, you still perform much more poorly than if you were to do one task at a time. You can't do two things at once if they require conscious thought, so multitasking is really a misnomer. If you try to focus on two or more things at once, what you're actually doing is rapidly shifting between tasks. Multitasking compromises the quality of learning and performance. It's highly inefficient, as people make many more errors and in the end perform much more slowly.[38] Multitasking also limits opportunities for deep thought and abstraction and for creativity and invention.[39] This may be why adolescents in what has been called the "app generation" shy away from questions that don't have direct, simple, and quick solutions.[40] Most concerning, multitasking has been shown to elevate cortisol levels, meaning that it puts more stress on the nervous system. One of the main reasons that meditation and mindfulness are so popular is that they are a strong antidote to multitasking: being in the present as opposed to doing three things at once.

"How can I tell if my child is addicted to technology? At what point do I need to get professional help?"

The data vary according to the type of technology, but a UK study showed that kids who spent three hours or more on social media were more than twice as likely to have poor mental health.[41] Researchers such as Douglas Gentile who study video-game addiction use criteria such as:

1. Lying about how much time is spent playing
2. Spending increasing amounts of time and money to feel excited
3. Irritability or restlessness when that time is cut back
4. Escaping problems through game play
5. Skipping chores or homework to play
6. Stealing games or stealing money to buy games.[42]

Kids who are at most risk for developing addictive relationships with games, social media, or the Internet commonly have certain characteristics, such as impulsivity, low social competence, low stress tolerance, cognitive inflexibility, and social anxiety. Boys are more vulnerable than girls, and genetics also plays a role, particularly when it comes to the genes that regulate the dopamine system and the seratonin receptors involved in emotional regulation.[43] Kids with inflexible, obsessive minds and sensitive dopamine systems will have a really hard time setting their own limits and are particularly vulnerable to excessive use or addiction. Bill has evaluated many kids like this, who have said, "I can stop playing, but I can't stop thinking about it."

If you recognize your child is vulnerable to excessive use of technology, it's important that you negotiate firm limits with him. He must comply with the limits you've agreed upon in order to continue his use of technology. In extreme cases, such as when a kid will threaten his parents for taking away his console, parents should seek professional help. We also recommend helping your child to develop social skills, as so many turn to technology because it is the only setting in which they feel comfortable and can connect with other kids.

Another Cultural Shift

We feel optimistic about the way that many teens are talking about the impact of technology and the need to counteract its negative side. There is a countermovement at work, one that we hope will make it easier for parents to place limits on technology. In a study of younger millennials, 80 percent reported needing to unplug and enjoy simple things.[44]

There's been a resurgence in the popularity of quieter, hands-on activities like baking, sewing, and crafting among millennials. Even retail is getting into the low-tech movement, with more and more shops and restaurants branding themselves as tech-free. We know of several restaurants that unapologetically ban cell phones, and a board game store in Seattle (started by Microsofties, ironically) uses the marketing line "Unplug and Reconnect."

Perhaps our favorite example of the low-tech movement comes from the University of Maryland women's basketball team, who created a media stir a few years ago when they voluntarily gave up their phones during tournament time. "To give up our phones is probably one of the best things we decided to do as a team," guard Lexie Brown told the *Washington Post*. "I mean, I like my phone. But this has taught me I don't need it." Instead, the teammates played card games and talked more to one another than they would have otherwise. Another player said, "When we got our phones back, it was like we wanted to give them right back."[45]

What to Do Tonight

- Have a family meeting in which you talk about setting up technology-free times or zones. At the very least there should be no cell phones during meals or in the bedroom, but you may also want to carve out more cell-phone-free zones for the family. A friend's wife says, "No cell phones on the couch. If you are on the couch, talk to me."

- Model healthy use of technology. For example, *never* text while driving. If you need to send a text while you're in the car, be sure to pull over. If you are on your phone when your child walks into the room, stop and greet him or her. If you need to check your phone for a text, e-mail, or alert, ask permission. "Is it okay if I check this? It might be Dad/I told so-and-so I would look for her message."

- Try to have at least thirty minutes of unplugged "private time" every day with your kids during the week and at least an hour a day on weekends when you don't take calls or check your phone. Consider identifying a certain period during the weekend (e.g., Sundays 9:00 A.M. to noon) as tech free—"It's pancake, read the *Times*, and play a game time." Negotiate with your kids if necessary about the best time for digital downtime. If your child has difficulty letting go of her phone, let her set a timer and tell her she can check her texts every ten or fifteen minutes. Ten to fifteen minutes seems obsessive—and it is, in our view—but kids who have a harder time with tech-free time will resent it less if you're not rigid. Be respectful and know that even short periods of tech-free time may be hard for her.

- When out and about, point out social situations in which one person is ignoring the other through their use of a phone (bad dates, parents ignoring soccer games, concerts, Starbucks where every single person is on a phone). Ask them, "What do you think the other person is feeling?"

- If you're ready to give a younger child a phone or Internet access, study resources such as Adam Pletter's iParent101.com and the American Pediatrics Association's Media and Children Communication Toolkit to educate yourself about the games and apps your kid uses. The Entertainment Software Rating Board (esrb.org) offers useful information about setting parental controls on games. Other sources we recommend are OnGuardOnline, which offers tips for protecting your computers; Common Sense Media, which rates programs and apps; and iKeepSafe.org, a fount of information about keeping kids safe online. Above all, talk to your children and let them know that it's your job to help them learn to use technology well. Say, "There's a whole world available on this gadget. If you get into something that's scary for you, I want you to let me know."

- Let kids know you'll check their texts and Twitter page randomly until you feel they are not using it in a way that's hurtful to others or that makes them vulnerable to being hurt—and then do it.

- Make video game use contingent on not freaking out when it's time to quit.

- If your kid is using technology excessively, consider consulting with a psychologist or counselor.

CHAPTER TEN

Exercising the Brain and Body

ELITE ATHLETES WILL DO SOMETHING that at first glance may seem surprising. They'll grab not the weight bar but the yoga ball, and condition their small muscles before working on the big, showy ones. When these small muscles are toned it's not noticeable to the untrained eye, but it makes them much less vulnerable to injury. The boxer who throws out his back while lifting his toddler out of the bathtub has not been paying attention to those small muscles. Neither has the runner who turns an ankle crossing the street. Though they may be in great shape, they've probably neglected the modest fundamentals without which they cannot support the work the rest of their body is doing.

In this chapter we will explore several ways of exercising those small muscles that make a big difference. What we ultimately want is resilient, brain-healthy kids who will be on a strong footing when it comes to life's many obstacles, both big (like not getting into the school of their dreams) and small (like coping with a rejection at a school dance). We want to help our kids develop a brain that's capable of thinking skillfully and of taking hits from all directions. Though we wish them the best at every turn, we don't want our kids to be afraid of taking risks or to unravel when things don't turn out as they'd hoped.

Most kids aren't taught empowering mental strategies, like

planning ahead and visualizing goals, talking back to negative thoughts, or thinking of what you will do if what you want doesn't come through. This chapter lays out some of the strategies for success that we psychologists and educators rely on most in our work with children and in our own lives. We've drawn on the work of influential writers on the psychology of success such as Stephen Covey and Brian Tracy, as well as neuroscientists like Adele Diamond and Daniel Siegel. You may have heard of and may even use some of these techniques yourself. What you probably don't know is that they are just as effective for kids. It's not easy to sit your kids down—particularly when they're in their teens—and say, "Honey, let's talk about how you can exercise your brain, okay?" They are likely to resist you, and that's fair. But knowing these strategies will help, and there are ways to make them a part of your family life without being overly prescriptive.

Exercise #1: Set clear goals.

Virtually everyone who has written about the psychology of success agrees that setting goals is fundamental. Both of us have used goal-setting and visualization strategies to develop our businesses, and we urge you to teach your kids to do this from a young age. For some, writing a simple list of goals works well. For others, it is much more effective to have a visual picture of their goal to refer to. For instance, a disorganized kid who wants to keep a clean desk might take a picture of his desk when it's straightened up. He labels the picture, noting where the pens, pencils, paper, and homework go. When he next needs to clean his desk, he can look at the picture and match it. The same thing goes for getting ready for school. If he agrees that he wants to make getting ready for school a less painful process, he can refer to a picture of himself fully ready for the day with his coat on, hair brushed, holding his backpack and his lunchbox. If he can see what he's after, he is more likely to make it happen. This technique can also be useful for teens who don't organize themselves well because matching a picture places fewer demands on working memory than reading from a checklist.[1]

There is a vast literature on the power of visualizing the accomplishment of goals. The idea is that the brain can't really differentiate between an actual experience and an experience that is vividly imagined (that's why we get scared watching scary movies, even though we know they aren't true). In a fascinating study conducted by the renowned neuroscientist Alvaro Pascual-Leone, a group of people was asked to play piano scales every day for a set period of time. Another group was asked to *think* about playing those scales without actually playing them. Researchers found that the participants in both groups showed growth in the area of the brain that corresponds with finger movements.[2] The implications of this, and similar research, for athletes and rehab patients are enormous.

Once kids get a bit older, an effective method of goal setting is called mental contrasting. Developed by NYU's Gabriele Oettingen, mental contrasting is designed to help students set realistic goals.[3] It's a way of protecting overreachers from disappointments by charting a path to what can actually be accomplished. And it's a way of shoring up Debbie Downers whose first response to any goal is to come up with a dozen reasons why it will never happen.

The first step of mental contrasting is to ask your child to set her own goal. It should not be a group goal, and it should not be influenced by you. The goal has to be something that is both feasible and challenging.

Step two is to encourage your child to write down several words about the hoped-for outcome. They should not edit themselves during this process, but rather should feel free to write whatever comes to mind.

Step three is to ask your child to consider inner obstacles to that goal. Note that you are not asking them to think about external barriers. Again, ask them to take pen to paper and to write down those obstacles, considering how they will be affected and what they can do when they surface.

Sometimes Ned's students set their ACT or SAT scores as their goal. The words they write down for step two might be "calm," "confident," or "focused." When they consider inner obstacles, they write "rushed," "stressed," and "confused." They are mentally preparing themselves for the test, and imagining how that stress or confusion will feel. Then they imagine themselves tackling these obstacles, or at least enduring them. What self-talk will they use? How will they flip to a test-taking shortcut to remind themselves that, unlike in school, unanswered questions may be better than allocating time for every question? What is their plan for coping when they face an obstacle? The knowledge that they have anticipated potential setbacks and allowed for contingencies will help them cope more effectively.

A student of Ned's who struggled socially and was diagnosed with an anxiety disorder after switching schools worked on role playing with a counselor and practiced what she would do or say in social situations that made her uncomfortable. She did this over and over again. Though she rarely used the lines she practiced, knowing that she knew what to say made her less anxious. Social encounters no longer felt quite so unpredictable.

We are also big believers in setting "personal best" goals in the classroom, the music room, on the playing field—or in the backyard. It's not that competition is bad per se—your kid needs to learn how to go for it when she really wants to win—but it is far more effective when the person she is competing with is herself. She may not have control over how much someone else practices or how good they are, but she has total control over how much she practices to beat her prior time or score. Seeing yourself get better at something is enormously rewarding. The truth is, you're never too young to set a personal best goal, or too old.

Ned frequently tells the story of his father-in-law, an expert skier, who decided in later life that he wanted to take up snowboarding. Ned decided to try it, too. As anyone who has spent a day as a novice snowboarder knows, it's deeply discouraging. You fall a lot. You get wet and pretty bruised up, especially if you're over twenty. But then after day one, you start to spend more time upright than on your duff. On day two, you are nearly mediocre. By the end of the week, you may make it off the beginner slopes and start to get the sense that this may really work out. That feeling of learning a new skill and getting better at it fuels your inner drive.

The world of testing is fertile ground for personal best goals. One of Ned's students, Allison, came to see him to prepare for the ACT. Her parents said they wanted her to get a 34 (out of 36). He asked what she was aiming for, and she said she wanted to get a 31 or a 32. Then Ned learned her current score was a 24. It didn't make sense to set her goal at 34; that was her parents' goal, not hers. But it also didn't make sense to set her goal at 32, which was an unrealistic leap from where she was. They talked about it and determined that a reasonable goal for Allison was to get a 28. It was realistic but also challenging. Then, if she could get to 28, she could "lock in," the way rock climbers do. (Most climb a stretch, lock in to the next clip, climb, lock in, and so on. If they fall, it's 10 feet, not 200.) From the comfortable place of a 28, Allison could feel proud of the progress she'd made. Then she could look ahead and aim to hit that 31 or 32, a perfectly appropriate goal.

Whether it's in the testing room, on the slopes, or in the backyard where your child is trying to learn to do a cartwheel, these methods of setting goals for her from A to B fuel her internal motivation and her sense of control.

Exercise #2: Pay attention to what your brain is telling you.

In our experience, when a child understands what is going on in his mind, he has more control of himself and will tend to behave and perform better. Knowing even a little bit about the brain—and about what may be unique about his particular brain—can restore his sense of control.

Even kindergartners are capable of understanding the basic functions of the brain. Dan Siegel, child psychiatrist and author of *The Whole-Brain Child*, uses a visual of four fingers closed over the thumb to teach kids what happens inside their brains when they get stressed. The thumb represents big emotions—things like fear, worry, and anger (this is the amygdala, though that's a big word for kindergartners). The fingers over it represent the parts of their brain that help them to think clearly and solve problems (the prefrontal cortex). When their worry or anger gets too big, the fingers lose their grip on the thumb, which Siegel describes as "flipping your lid." When kids feel themselves beginning to flip their lid, he encourages them to consider what they need to do to calm down—like going to a designated cool-down spot—so that their fist is closed again.

One of the more challenging kids Bill tested was a nine-year-old boy, Ben, whose parents were concerned about his distractibility, his anxiety and perfectionism, and his very low frustration tolerance. They were desperate to find out how they could help Ben be less reactive and difficult at home and in school.

Within the first few minutes of testing, Bill saw what they meant. While Ben was bright and articulate, he peppered his answers with sentences like, "I'm not going to be very good at this," "I can't do anything fast," and "You're gonna give me a bad grade, aren't you?" When he got to the first hard item, he slammed his fist on the desk and said, "I can't do this." If Bill pressed him, Ben became so anxious and upset that he seemed to be on the verge of either crying or exploding.

This conversation followed:

BILL: I can see that this is really stressful for you. Can I tell you what I think is happening?

BEN: Okay.

BILL: I think if a good idea doesn't pop into your head right away you start to feel stupid.

BEN: I do. It's so frustrating.

BILL: I bet you know that you aren't stupid. I mean, you can probably tell that your vocabulary is a lot better than most kids'.

BEN: I do have a good vocabulary. I know words that none of the kids in my grade know.

BILL: The challenge for you is that there's a part of your brain, it's called the amygdala, that's working too hard to keep you safe. The amygdala is a "threat detector." It's on the lookout for anything that could hurt you or make you feel bad. It can't think, it just senses possible danger, and when it picks up something it makes you feel stressed so that you will avoid the danger. I know some kids whose amygdala doesn't seem to find anything threatening, but I also know a lot of kids whose amygdala is sensitive and finds almost everything threatening. I think you're one of the kids who has a *really* sensitive amygdala.

BEN: I must be. I get freaked out and frustrated by everything. You should see me at school.

BILL: That must be really tough for you. For us to work together, we should remember that your amygdala is really sensitive and that it makes a much bigger deal about stuff than it needs to. So if you aren't able to think of an answer right away, we can remind your amygdala that it's overreacting—that you're safe with me and that you really aren't stupid. If you start to get nervous or frustrated or stuck, we'll know that it means your amygdala is trying to shut you down in order to protect you from feeling stupid, which it doesn't need to do because you aren't stupid.

BEN: Okay.

When they went back to testing, it was remarkable how easy it was. For the rest of the morning Ben's intense perfectionism and low frustration tolerance were things Bill and he could joke about, as they reflected on the misguided functions of his primitive brain, rather than a flaw in his character. When Bill asked Ben about his social and emotional life later in the evaluation, he used imagery that would connect with Ben (he was fascinated by explosives):

BILL: Does the frustration that I saw this morning happen a lot at school?

BEN: Yeah. I get mad so easily about everything.

BILL: Would you like to have a longer fuse?

BEN: What do you mean?

BILL: Well, you know how a stick of dynamite can have a long fuse, meaning that it will be slow to go off, or a short fuse, meaning that it will explode really quickly? My guess is that you've got a pretty short fuse because your amygdala is so sensitive.

BEN: [*Motioning two inches*] It's this long.

BILL: Would you like to have a longer fuse?

BEN: A lot longer.

BILL: We'll be talking more about that, and let's talk with your parents, too, about how they can help you. I'll also help find someone who can coach you to be less explosive.

Using simple language and vivid imagery and explaining the science of emotions can be remarkably effective, as is taking the problem out of the realm of the personal and into the scientific. It's not that Ben was less anxious in school right away—it took a lot of work to lengthen his fuse. But giving him the framework to understand what was going on was an important first step. Bill recently reevaluated Ben, who is now fourteen and is dramatically better regulated emotionally. He is still intense and easily frustrated, but he is a highly motivated and very successful student who is managing his life independently. Significantly, testing, once such a source of stress for him, is now comfortable and easy.

Bill feels that one of the most important parts of his job is telling kids what he learned about them from their neuropsychological evaluations. When they understand what they can do better than most people and what does not come easily, it increases their sense of confidence that there will be a place for them in the world as adults.

Exercise #3: Practice Plan B thinking.

Many of the kids we see are anxious and obsessively driven, but Carly, an extremely bright, creative, and spirited seventeen-year-old, was arguably the most anxious adolescent we've ever been around. She was obsessed with going to Columbia and the pressure didn't seem to be coming from her parents. After working with Carly on vocabulary and math problems and testing strategies, it became clear to Ned that her acute anxiety and obsessive focus on one college (out of more than three thousand) were interfering with her ability to think clearly.

Bill had tested her a few years earlier, and Carly and her parents agreed that it would be a good idea to go back to see if he could help. She told him that she was too busy to see her therapist, that she was already taking what her psychiatrist felt to be the highest safe level of antianxiety medication, and that she had too much work to go to bed any earlier. Bill and Carly concluded that every tutoring session with Ned should focus, in part, on what's known as Plan B thinking. Carly needed to think about what she would do if she didn't get into Columbia and, over time, to allow herself to feel okay and even positive about other options. Only by letting go of the fear that she might blow her entire life if she didn't get into Columbia could she calm her stress response sufficiently to focus on answering test questions that she knew the answers to.

Plan B thinking ("What are some other things you could do if it doesn't work out as you hope?") is key to maintaining a healthy approach to potential setbacks. Though Carly was initially resistant, she eventually warmed up to the idea. She started to imagine her life at the University of Michigan, which she had chosen as her backup school. She thought Michigan, with its great campus spirit, would be fun, and she was drawn to the more relaxed atmosphere of Ann Arbor. She spoke to recent graduates and heard about some of the amazing opportunities they had enjoyed. And she was delighted to learn that her dream of grad school might be better nurtured at Michigan, as her grades were likely to be higher. Carly's level of anxiety decreased as she began to visualize an alternative future.

Plan B thinking helps you put things into perspective. By envisioning alternate futures and creating backup plans, kids (and their parents) learn that if Plan A doesn't work, the world won't come to an end. Plan B thinking strengthens the prefrontal cortex's ability to regulate the amygdala. It's the prefrontal cortex's job to formulate plans and goals—and having a clear sense of what you'll do if your first option doesn't work out makes it easier to stay calm and in control. Few things are more stressful to kids than the feeling that "I have to, but I can't." Plan B allows you to think more constructively.

"If I can't do this, then I could do that. . . ." It also increases flexibility and adaptability. Over time, practicing Plan B thinking will give you confidence that you can handle stress and setbacks.

Ned personally practices Plan B thinking constantly, and often takes himself through scenarios from the mundane (If we're out of my favorite cereal, what will I eat this morning?) to the catastrophic (If a fire breaks out on the back of this plane, what will I do?). As a result, he feels in control, because he's anticipated and determined how to handle a variety of situations.

For some, Plan B thinking may include considering radically different routes to success. Hearing stories about those who have developed meaningful, happy lives by following different paths is one of the greatest sources of perspective-giving solace we can offer, and we'll talk more about that in Chapter Fourteen. But just knowing that alternate happy endings are out there and widening the frame a bit can go a long way toward alleviating stress.

> I tutored a great kid, Roger, who got a disappointing ACT score. In deconstructing the test day, it turned out that Roger got lost on the way to the testing site. Our conversation went like this:
>
> "I think you made one wrong turn and had a bad day," I said. "Not every at-bat is a home run. In baseball, if you strike out or ground out seven times out of ten but get hits the other three, that could put you in the Hall of Fame. You just need a good at-bat."
>
> "Yeah, but I need that good at-bat next time."
>
> "Well, I can see why you'd think that. But here's my take: You can take the ACT again in April. If it doesn't go well in April, you can take it in June. If it doesn't go well in June, there's another ACT in September. If it doesn't go well in September, you can take it in October. And if it doesn't go well in October, you can take it once more in December. Now, if by December of your senior year you haven't moved your score an inch, we may need another plan."

Roger smiled. Having a Plan B (or C, D, or E) is awfully helpful. "Heaven knows, pal," I continued, "you must have better things to do with your Saturday mornings than to take this silly test over and over. But because it matters to you given your goals, it's important to realize you have lots of opportunities to get it right. So yes, we would love to see you knock this next one out of the park, do a victory dance, and be done. But if you don't, you can just dust yourself off and try it again."

—Ned

Exercise #4: Talk to yourself with compassion.

"I'm so stupid." "I'm such an idiot." "How could I be so dumb?!" We routinely hear these comments from kids, and many parents despair when they hear consistent self-deprecating comments. But don't race to talk your child out of it. What you might say if your kid is caught in a circle of "I suck at everything" is something like, "That's one way of seeing it. I see things differently. I'd be happy to share my view with you if you want to hear it." If your child doesn't want to hear it, keep it to yourself and hope for a better moment. Unwanted wisdom may make them grab tighter to their negative view of themselves because now it's become a matter of control.

Another inroad to dialogue is to remind your child that you've been through some tough situations, and say, "When that happens, there's something I do. Do you want to hear what it is?" Again, if she says no, don't share it. But often at this point she'll say yes.

If she's open to dialogue, you might say something like, "Have you noticed how sometimes we talk to ourselves in ways we wouldn't speak to others? Imagine if we were on a softball team together. A routine ground ball is hit right at me, but goes between my legs. What would you say? Probably something like, 'It's all right. You'll get the next one.' Why? It certainly was a bad mistake.

But instinctively you know that vocalizing support and encouragement will make me more likely to get the next one than throwing your glove in the dirt and screaming about how lousy I am."

Teach your kids to be as supportive of themselves as they are of their best friend—to say, "C'mon! You can do this, Heather." Third-person self-talk is much more powerful than first-person self-talk. If your daughter refers to herself by name, she is more likely to take the more distanced, supportive-friend stance than to act as critic in chief.[4]

Let's delve a little more into how we process a mistake like a missed ball. If your child views the error as having no rational explanation, and chastises herself as stupid, she has no sense of being able to fix it next time. There's nothing she can do to get a better outcome, except to not be stupid. Effective self-talk allows her to hold on to the notion that she's capable—definitely not stupid—but simply made a mistake. She can then investigate what went wrong. This gives her agency, by suggesting that there is an explanation for what went wrong and thus something in the process that she can work on and change.[5]

The key here is not to take it personally. If there's an explanation that's not threatening to your child's identity, she can look at the mistake, learn from it, and move on.

Exercise #5: Practice reframing problems.

So much of our work involves helping kids to think more skillfully by questioning their thought process and reframing things. Consider stress itself. Simply labeling stress differently will change performance results. Po Bronson reported that professional musicians and athletes experience anxiety prior to a performance, but they interpret it as energizing, whereas amateurs interpret it as detrimental.[6] For one group, anxiety leads to flow. For the other, it is a threat. Much as it is one's sense of control more than control itself that increases motivation and calms anxiety, it's the subjective perception ("Cool! An audience of fifteen hundred people!") rather than the objective reality that impacts the brain and how it responds.

Language is enormously powerful. "I want to" is preferable to "I have to," just as "I'm choosing to" is better than "I have to." It helps to think, "This is annoying but it's not awful," or "This is a setback but it's not a disaster."

We like to think of life as a game of "Choose Your Point of View." *You* get to decide how to frame events. Imagine that your sixteen-year-old daughter is out at a school dance and you had agreed she would text you at 9:00 P.M. It's 9:15 and she hasn't texted you yet and isn't responding to your texts. Is it useful to think that she's trapped in a ditch somewhere? Not really. Is it useful to think that she has most likely forgotten and is so busy with her friends that she hasn't seen your texts? Obviously, the latter is a less crazy-making option, so let's choose that one. That doesn't mean the facts are any different. But what point of view will best serve you while you wait? (If it's 10:00 and you still haven't heard from her, you are likely to choose to be more concerned.) Brent Toleman, a friend and linguistic psychologist, argues that in any given situation, you can choose the point of view that is most helpful. When you ask yourself what the most likely explanation is, it's usually not disaster. There are certainly times when really bad things happen, but it doesn't make sense to catastrophize every day of your life.

Consider this story from our friend Aaron. He was rear-ended on his way to an important meeting at work. As he got out of his car, he was not feeling particularly generous toward the other driver. Then he noticed that the car that had hit him had a "Marine Corps Dad" license plate. The driver apologized profusely and explained that he and his wife were rushing to the hospital for their daughter's surgery. Poof! Point of view changed. Anger and frustration gave way to concern and offers of help. We have the choice to view another driver as a self-absorbed jerk or as someone rightfully in a hurry. We have the choice to view a mistake as proof of our own inadequacy or as a necessary and perhaps even inadvertently helpful part of our life's course.

Reframing involves looking at our own thoughts with care and actively redirecting them. This is the basis of cognitive behavioral therapy. As we discussed, this is also an idea that's incorporated in mindfulness.

Explain to your child that many body sensations are caused by thoughts. Help them connect the two, and pay attention to signs from their body that they are getting nervous, sad, or mad. Teach them to start "hearing" their thoughts and to distinguish between rational and irrational thoughts.

Just the other day one of Ned's students vividly described what happens to him during tests. "Nothing goes into my head," he said. "Nothing makes sense. Then I get down on myself and start thinking I'll never get good scores, will never get into Penn, will never become an architect."

Ned's response went something like this: "Is it true that if you don't get an answer right, you won't do well on that section? Is it true that if you don't do well on that section, you can't get a good score? Is it true that if you don't get a good score, you will never get a good score? Is it true that if you don't get a good score, you can't go to a good college? Is it true that if you don't go to a 'good' college, you can't become an architect?

"What I know," Ned went on, "is that people as curious as you are can get a fantastic education from even the least selective college, and that you can become a great architect regardless of where you go to college. And, of course, you can take the ACT over and over and over. So really think about those ideas that come into your head at moments when you're stressed. Can you trust them?"

One of the most common mental habits that makes us feel out of control is catastrophizing—otherwise known as making a mountain out of a molehill. A simple way to help kids avoid catastrophizing is to teach them to ask themselves, whenever they're upset, "Is this a big problem or a little problem?" In cognitive behavioral therapy, kids are taught to distinguish between a disaster (like famine) and something that's temporarily frustrating or embarrassing, between "I'll die if this happens" and "I'll be disappointed but I probably won't die." If it's a little problem, the first line of defense is to use self-soothing mechanisms, like a cool-down spot, deep breathing, or Plan B thinking, to calm themselves down. For most problems, these tools will be enough. When problems feel too big, we want kids to seek help.

Exercise #6: Move your body and/or play.

One of Ned's students, a regular runner who was susceptible to anxiety, confided that her parents had told her she shouldn't take time away from studying to exercise. This struck Ned as the worst advice he'd heard in a long time.

The Latin root of the word emotion, *emovere*, means "to move." Our bodies and minds are linked, and the part of the brain that tells the body to move is adjacent to the part that's responsible for clearheaded thinking. There is a close overlap between our motor control functions and our mental control, or executive functions, which is one reason why exercise is so beneficial for developing self-regulation.

Exercise is more generally good for the brain and body. It increases levels of dopamine, serotonin, and norepinephrine, which provide stability, focus, mental alertness, and calmness. Exercise stimulates the production of the protein BDNF (brain-derived neurotrophic factor), which is considered a brain "fertilizer" because it's important for the growth of the brain and for helping cells wire together. Exercise provides more glucose and oxygen to the brain, which promotes neurogenesis, the growing of brain cells. In short, it's often said that exercise does more to help clear thinking than thinking does, in part because it stimulates and strengthens the prefrontal cortex's control functions.

Exercise is also critical to a state of relaxed alertness. As John Ratey showed in his book *Spark,* when students exercised heavily as part of their school curriculum, academic performance dramatically improved.[7] Again, Finland is at the head of the class here: they mandate twenty minutes of outdoor play for every forty minutes of instructional time.

For all these reasons, Ned told his student to keep running and encourages all his students to adopt some sort of habit of exercise. (But it's important that they not feel forced. Forced exercise is boot camp, not a road to low stress.) Aerobic exercise confers greater brain benefits than anaerobic, but a good rule of thumb for the right level of intensity is that you should be able to talk but not sing. Exercise should be strenuous, but shouldn't feel like it's killing you.

Adele Diamond, one of the world's leading neuroscientists, is particularly supportive of physical activities that simultaneously demand the core executive functions, working memory, inhibitory control, and cognitive flexibility. Consider dance. When you learn a dance, you have to use your working memory to learn moves. You also have to inhibit your movements (or know when you are moving your leg too slowly or too quickly), and you have to flexibly adjust your moves to changes in the music or to your partner's steps. Yoga, martial arts, horseback riding, fencing, drumming, and rock climbing all fall in a category of exercise in which you are using your mental and motor skills to develop your executive functions.

It's one thing to get a group of high schoolers rock climbing, but the prospect of getting younger kids to engage in this sort of brain-healthy exercise is more daunting. This is where play comes in. Play is crucial for the development of a healthy brain—including a well-functioning cerebellum.

The cerebellum is located at the base of the brain, just above the spinal cord. For at least a hundred years, we've known that coordinated movement depends on the cerebellum, and that if you injure your cerebellum, you will have a hard time even standing upright. But what we've just begun to learn in the last several years is how the cerebellum affects thinking. Patients with cerebellar damage have problems with things like planning, word selection, judging the shape of objects, and creating proportioned drawings.[8] We now know that the cerebellum plays a role in all aspects of learning. Differences in cerebellum functioning have also been linked to ADHD and are a factor in autism. The cerebellum is one of the least heritable brain structures, which means that experience—not genetics—is key to how well it functions.

Play is how children strengthen their cerebellum and learn to master their world. This is not just true of our species: a graph of playfulness in almost every species looks like an inverted U, with rates of play matching the growth of the cerebellum. This suggests that the brain needs the whole-body movements of play to achieve maturity, and that there's a sensitive period in which play is needed for brain stimulation.[9]

For the good of the cerebellum, resist the urge to have your kid do something "useful." Resist the worry that tells you he shouldn't be out of your line of sight for more than a minute. Resist the inclination to sign him up for more organized activities where he will be told what to do. Let him be. Let him play.

What to Do Tonight

- Consider the exercises in this chapter and ask your child if he thinks there's one that would help him, you, or the whole family.

- Have a family meeting in which you share your written goals. Ask your kids for their thoughts on your goals or those of their siblings. Validate their suggestions.

- Encourage your kids to set their own goals—and to visualize achieving them. Ask, "What would you like to do or accomplish for the next week/ month/ semester/ by the end of summer?" Help them make SMART goals (Specific, Measurable, Attainable, Realistic, Time-Bound). When you break a goal down into discrete, actionable steps, you increase the dopamine released when they see progress.

- Build on your child's SMART goals to add in mental contrasting. Are there inner obstacles? How will your child handle it if he is thwarted? How will he feel, and how will he recuperate and move on?

- Make Plan B thinking a family practice. Ask your kids if they want to hear your thoughts about their Plan As and Bs. If they don't, back off.

- Model positive self-talk and self-compassion. You might say something like, "I realized yesterday that I was being really hard on myself about something I screwed up at work, harder than I would have been on anyone else. Everyone messes things up sometimes and getting down on myself won't help me avoid mistakes."

- Make physical fitness a family value. Don't force your child to play a sport and don't choose an activity for him, but explain that it is important that everyone in the family make physical activity a part of their life, and help them to decide what they would like to do.

CHAPTER ELEVEN

Navigating Learning Disabilities, ADHD, and Autism Spectrum Disorders

A SENSE OF CONTROL is good for all kids—at all ages—but parents of kids with learning disabilities, attention deficit hyperactivity disorder (ADHD), or autism spectrum disorder (ASD) face an extra set of challenges. Sometimes the interventions these kids receive will actually lower their sense of autonomy, when they need as much as anyone to feel that they are in control.

Studies have shown that structure and external motivators are often the most effective ways to help kids with autism or ADHD to focus on a task, finish their work, and behave well in class and at home. As a result, many parents and professionals resist giving these children much of a say in the decisions governing their lives. But we take issue with the notion that structure and autonomy are mutually exclusive. Our view is that a high level of structure and organizational support should be provided to these kids, so long as they don't fight it constantly. Kids with learning disabilities and other special needs will learn and perform better when they feel that help is not being done *to them*. Rewards and other external motivators tend to undermine internal motivation for these kids, too, and should be used with care.

Many parents feel that kids with developmental difficulties

can't make appropriate life decisions for themselves. It might be fine for Typical Tom to choose his coursework or decide whether to participate in an after-school enrichment program, but Hyperactive Harry couldn't possibly do that. Again, we disagree. Throughout our decades of work we have seen that when children with ADHD, dyslexia, or other learning difficulties are given all the information necessary to make a decision and don't feel forced, they are extremely capable of choosing thoughtfully. They are still the experts on them. They want their lives to work, and they will often welcome the help that is offered to them and the accommodations that will enable them to learn and perform better.

A few studies have confirmed the benefits of giving kids with special needs autonomy. One showed that when elementary and junior high students with learning disabilities felt a sense of autonomy at home, they tended to do better in the classroom and to navigate personal setbacks more smoothly.[1] A second study found that high-functioning students with ASD who rated their teachers as higher in autonomy reported greater self-determination in school, which in turn correlated with higher academic competence.[2] A new approach to therapy with ADHD adolescents and their parents that places a strong emphasis on the promotion of teen autonomy (the STAND program—Supporting Teens' Autonomy Daily) has recently been developed by Margaret Sibley of Florida International University.[3] But the research in this area is sparse. Our experience, however, is not. We have both seen for years, Bill especially, that when kids with special needs have a sense of control over their lives, they thrive. If you consider the way the brain works, you will quickly see why that is. Brains develop as they're used, and we don't want any child to develop a brain that's accustomed to chronically fighting attempts to be controlled. We know it's stressful to struggle at school or have problems with impulse control. We know that a sense of control combats stress and encourages healthy brain growth. If we want kids *without* special needs to have these advantages, then it's all the more important that kids *with* special needs have them, too.

This chapter won't be relevant to everyone, but it will be relevant to more people than you might think. Six and a half million American kids and teens received special education services in 2013–2014.[4] As many as 20 percent of students have at least one learning disability, 11 percent of children are diagnosed with ADHD, and one in sixty-eight kids has an autism disorder.[5] These statistics are almost certainly low estimates of the actual incidence of learning, attentional, and social difficulties, in part because they do not include students with disorders who have not yet been diagnosed. On a more anecdotal level, we're hard pressed to think of a family with three kids in which at least one does not have a learning disability, ADHD, or an autism spectrum disorder.

This chapter is not intended to be a comprehensive discussion of all special needs and what you should do if your child has one. Each category could be a book in itself. Rather, what we hope to do is to show you what gets in the way of giving these kids a sense of control, and to assure you that you can do it, even if you need to think about it with more care.

Learning Disabilities

Bill tested an eleven-year-old named Michael, a very bright and sweet-natured boy who struggled with math and had significant difficulty regulating his emotions. Although Michael worked very well with Bill during the morning portion of the testing, he became extremely stressed and started to lose control when one of Bill's associates asked him to solve math problems after lunch. He began chanting "no, no, no," and at one point he even hissed and made clawing motions at the associate, clearly indicating that he'd had enough of math. After letting Michael cool down for a few minutes in the waiting room, Bill spoke to his mother about whether to try to finish testing that day or to have him come back for another visit. Michael overheard them and shouted that he had to finish that day so he could go to Toys"R"Us as a reward for working hard during the testing. Bill wanted him to finish, too, but he clearly would not be able to complete the math assessment with a brain that was in panic mode.

Bill took Michael aside and asked him why he freaked out doing math. Michael explained that he felt panicked and frustrated. Bill listened to Michael's answer and then told him that his amygdala had gone into overdrive and alerted the rest of his brain to look out for potential danger. He knew he could be embarrassed, frustrated, or humiliated because math was hard for him. Michael did what he needed to do to escape the threat. This seemed to make sense to Michael. Bill then explained to him that if they could figure out a way for him to feel safe and in control when he was working on math, even though it was hard, they could finish the testing that afternoon. Throughout the conversation, Michael made it clear that he felt safe with Bill and also with Ernie, a small dog who "worked" in Bill's office. They agreed that Michael would return to Bill's office and do the math with Ernie sitting next to him, and that if he started to get stressed he would stop and play with Ernie for a couple of minutes. After two or three minutes Michael was solving math problems, petting Ernie, and humming to himself. This was a dramatic illustration of how increasing a child's sense of control can make it possible for him to work hard, even on tasks that are inherently difficult and frustrating.

Many kids with learning disabilities are like Michael. Jerome Schultz, whose book *Nowhere to Hide* highlights the stressors facing students with learning disabilities, emphasizes that in the classroom, these kids are often unable to mask their deficits from their teachers and classmates. He points out that kids with learning disabilities not only worry about what *all* kids worry about—like whether or not their friend is still mad at them for sitting at a different table at lunch—they also worry about being teased and called stupid or being judged for getting special help or accommodations.

Kids with learning disabilities do need those accommodations. They also need the reading specialist or the math specialist, ideally working with them one-on-one, as intensity of intervention is one of the variables that best predicts good outcomes for students with learning disabilities. The problem is that children commonly experience interventions as being forced upon them. Children of all ages can feel coerced and resentful when they're pulled out of class for special help, and they often perceive that they're being "made to go" for tutoring, speech and language therapy, or occupational therapy after school. When they feel forced, kids resist even things that are helpful to them in order to gain a sense of control.

Rather than being grateful for help, many kids with learning disabilities are angry and resentful and perceive that the problem is with their parents, their teachers, or the tutor who is making them do this extra work. This tension harms the sense of relatedness that's important for all kids, but particularly those with special needs. In the end, help that is forced on kids usually doesn't do much good. What makes this situation particularly stressful for parents is that if they pull the help, they know their kid is likely to fall further behind. Parents often feel, "He's already so discouraged, I'm afraid that if we pull out the supports he's fighting he'll fail completely and get depressed." Parents and teachers have to walk a tightrope between providing enough support to address academic needs, while encouraging kids' autonomy and trying not to force help down their throats.

So what can you do? How do you walk this tightrope? We recommend that you start with three simple steps:

1. **Fight homework that isn't necessary.** Homework for kids with learning disabilities can be extremely stressful for the whole family. If reading is hard for a kid, the requirement to read, orally or silently, for thirty minutes a night when he's tired can feel like cruel and unusual punishment (and tends to be equally stressful for his parents). Similarly, tackling an assignment of twenty math problems when ten would do can feel like running a hundred yards on hot pavement. This is where your advocacy efforts can pay off. It isn't to say that you shouldn't encourage reading, writing, or math at home. Quite the opposite: if your child is alert and up to putting in time to practice something that's hard for him, go for it. But if your child has reading difficulties and hates reading at night, read to him or let him listen to a recorded book. The same brain systems are involved in language comprehension, whether the language is written or spoken, which means that being read to or listening to a recorded book develops the same parts of the brain that will eventually engage in reading comprehension.

2. **Encourage self-understanding.** Help your child understand his learning challenges as well as his strengths. If you do not feel qualified, ask the professional who identified the learning disability or a teacher or tutor who works with your child to talk to him about his strengths and weaknesses. Also help your child understand that having this challenge is "normal." Tell them that one in three kids has some sort of an issue. This should help to alleviate the stress he may feel about being "different." Also, because learning disabilities are rooted, in part, in genetics, tell your child about other family members who have had similar challenges, particularly those who have been able to do well in life. Tell your child about the dozens of famous people who

have acknowledged that, as children, they had dyslexia or another learning disability, like problems with math, writing, or reading comprehension. (A quick Google search will provide you plenty of examples.) In addition, explain that many students with learning disabilities are often late bloomers, as it can take a while for them to develop their weaker skill areas and find their strengths. They *will* develop those areas—they just need to be patient.

3. **Offer but don't force help.** Talk through the pros and cons of resource services, tutoring, or working with a speech/language pathologist or occupational therapist, but unless it's crazy, let your child make the final call. It's far better for him to choose one day a week of tutoring that he is committed to than to force him to do two days of tutoring that he's resisting with all his might. The latter is just a waste of time, money, and goodwill. That doesn't mean you can't negotiate, especially if you think he needs more help than he thinks he does. If the extra tutoring means he's working more than most of his friends have to, offer an incentive to him if he *tries*. But emphasize that he can quit if it doesn't seem to be helping.

If younger school-aged kids resist special help, Bill recommends saying something like, "As a parent, it's my job to make sure that you get the right kind of help because all the experts who really know about learning say that's what you need. However, I want to provide help that is actually going to help you, and I won't know without your input. So if you hate seeing the resource teacher in school, we can opt for more private tutoring, or if you feel that seeing a tutor isn't working, we'll find another way to help you." In Bill's experience, even children who protest initially frequently come to like their tutor or their resource teacher or learning specialist in school and appreciate the benefit that they gain from working with somebody who "gets them." Because children want to do well, we are confident that they will eventually come around as long as they don't feel forced.

When I talk to children about the findings from testing, I start by emphasizing their strengths. When I transition to their challenges, I try to tell them something they already know about themselves, which minimizes the likelihood that they will "fight" me and helps to get their buy-in for treatment. For example, if a child has dyslexia, I will say, "I can tell that sounding out words is not easy for you and that reading is slow and really hard work." If I find they have ADHD, I will say something like, "What I've learned is that it's harder for you than it is for most kids to make yourself pay attention to stuff that's boring, and that it's hard to do something fast without making mistakes." After explaining to kids the things that are hard for them, I usually ask, "Would you like this to be easier for you?" to which the child almost invariably says yes. With school-age children, I then say, "I'm going to work with your school to see how they can help, and I'll help your parents find someone who's great at teaching kids like you whom you could see outside of school." Because these kids generally do want help, they rarely put up a fight. With older children and adolescents, I usually say, "If you want, I can help find a tutor for you, or I could work on getting you accommodations (like extra time for tests) in school. Do you want me to work on this?" I then explain to kids of all ages that if they focus and try hard, the intervention will help them make new connections in their brain that will, over time, make reading, writing, or math a lot easier.

—Bill

ADHD

Bill's clinical practice evaluates hundreds of children, adolescents, and adults with ADHD every year. For some, the condition is a source of extreme embarrassment and even shame, whereas others are accepting and, in fact, have a sense of humor about it. Within the last year, Bill's seen teenagers come in with T-shirts reading:

"My parents say I don't listen—or something like that."

"Organized people are just too lazy to look for things."

We think this is a great trend. If kids can have a sense of humor about their challenges, they can use that self-knowledge to manage their ADHD and strengthen their sense of control.

By definition, kids with ADHD have trouble controlling their attention. This is the case for kids who are diagnosed with the "predominantly inattentive" presentation of ADHD, who tend to be unfocused and disorganized, and those with the "combined presentation," who are impulsive and/or hyperactive as well as unfocused and disorganized. It's hard for kids with ADHD to get themselves to do what's asked of them and, for many, even to stick with things they want to do and that are important to them. Kids with ADHD tend to have low baseline levels of dopamine, and their brains use dopamine less efficiently than most kids. (Stimulant medications like Ritalin work by improving the processing of dopamine.) As a result, they tend to prefer small, immediate rewards to larger, long-term ones. As we explained in Chapter Five, although dopamine used to be linked primarily to pleasure, recent studies have found that it's strongly connected with motivation, drive, and effort.

John Salamone, a researcher at the University of Connecticut, has helped to clarify the link between dopamine, motivation, and effort. He conducted a study in which rats were given a choice between two piles of food—one that was close to them but small, and the other that was twice the size but behind a small fence. The rats with lower levels of dopamine almost always took the easy way out, choosing the small pile instead of jumping the fence for greater reward. Salamone explains, "Low levels of dopamine make people and other animals less likely to work for things, so it has more to do with motivation and cost/benefit analysis than pleasure itself." Research with depressed patients has corroborated the impact of dopamine on motivation.[6] The lower your dopamine, the less inclined you are to jump that fence for a greater treat—or even to get out of bed.

Further complicating things for kids with ADHD is the fact that those with immature impulse control frequently act in ways they regret and, as a result, lack confidence that they'll handle things well. Things get worse if they're corrected or told to stop repeatedly, as if they could simply "behave" through their own willpower. Try as they might, they can't make themselves "be good." They also tend to be very inconsistent in their thinking and behavior, which leads to a sense of unpredictability. They're often told to "try harder," but as some brain-scan studies have shown, the harder they try to focus, the less their brains activate. Remember, stress compromises attention. So if your son is struggling to get dressed in the morning, the last thing you want to do is to stress him out by insistently nagging him.

Many of the interventions that are prescribed to help kids with ADHD involve trying to protect them from themselves. This can be helpful in the short term but problematic down the road. Many kids with ADHD benefit from organizational help throughout their academic career. But if the system is forced on them or managed by Mom, it will lower their sense of control and academic motivation and reinforce the idea that someone other than the child is responsible for his learning, his work, and his behavior. It only postpones the day of reckoning, or the moment when the kid will embrace the idea that he's responsible for his own life.

Margaret Sibley points out that because they have difficulty getting started on things independently and sustaining attention and effort, teens with ADHD can miss opportunities to develop independent skills. This can be triggered by their own task avoidance or by a tendency for adults to provide continual assistance. Sibley estimates that 40 percent of parents who have children with ADHD feel helpless and hopeless by the time their kids are teens, leading to an uninvolved parenting profile, while another 40 percent tighten the reins and are overinvolved in the adolescent's daily life.[7] Bill sees the latter all the time. He often asks kids with ADHD who have trouble turning in their homework, "Who's the most upset if you don't turn in an assignment?" Occasionally a kid will say, "Me. It's so frustrating. I do well on tests, but I get Cs because I can't remember to turn in my work." For the vast majority, however, the answer is almost always "My mom." When Bill asks "Who's next most upset?" they commonly answer, "My dad, then my teacher, then my tutor, then my therapist, then my sister . . ." The kid himself is rarely even on the list.

The adults supporting these kids have the best intentions. They just want to make sure nothing slips through the cracks. But trying to protect a kid from himself year after year will weaken him. If *he* wants to turn in his assignments more consistently, offer him the option of sending in his work electronically to avoid the challenge of remembering to turn them in in class. Or encourage him to ask his teacher to remind him at the beginning or end of every class period. Or brainstorm with the child about a home-school communication system that can help ensure he's getting his assignments done, bringing home the necessary materials, and getting his work turned in. Remember that ultimately his schoolwork is his problem, and that if you work harder to help him than he does, you are doing him no favors.

Offer help, but don't force it. (Remember that opposition and defiance are some kids' way of maintaining a sense of control, and of fighting stress.) Make sure your child knows what's going on in his brain and how he can ask for the help he needs. If it's necessary to motivate a child to do schoolwork or to get ready for school in the morning, you can offer rewards. These can be effective motivators in the short term, as a way of making the child's brain work more optimally (by increasing dopamine), but in most cases don't think of them as a means to get him to do what *you* want him to do. Remind him that as he matures, things will get better and easier for him. Some kids largely outgrow their ADHD symptoms in their teenage years, and others learn effective techniques to mitigate the problem. If your child works hard, things will improve. However, it's important for parents and kids with ADHD to understand that the maturation of the prefrontal cortex in adolescents with ADHD tends to lag years behind that of other children their age.[8] This is why kids with ADHD are so often late bloomers, as they simply have to "wait" until their prefrontal cortex matures and comes fully online to find ways of doing things that they could not do successfully before. We recommend that parents of kids with ADHD voice their understanding that the child is doing the best he can and encourage him to be patient with himself. That is a good message of hope and confidence and one likely to foster a growth mindset.

Issues regarding agency often come up in relation to medication, as children with ADHD are usually encouraged to take stimulant medication such as Adderall, CONCERTA®, or Ritalin to help them focus. Many kids, especially teenagers, tell their parents that they focus better but don't like the way they feel on the medication. When their parents ask Bill for his advice, he usually suggests they tell their child that no one is going to make him take medication—and no one wants him to take medicine that makes him feel bad. We only want him to take medicine if it significantly improves his life with minimal side effects. Parents can tell their kids that different medicines have different side effects and they can try other medications. There may be things he can do (exercise vigorously, get more calories during the day by drinking a protein shake) that could help him tolerate the medication better.

If your child is motivated to seek other ways to improve his ADHD symptoms, there are some options. For instance, we've already spoken about the benefits of cognitive behavioral therapy and the collaborative problem-solving approach in this book, and again we encourage you to study the work of Ross Greene and J. Stuart Ablon, who developed the technique. Also, tell your child that exercise will help boost his natural dopamine production. Some evidence shows that meditation is also helpful in reducing ADHD symptoms, lowering anxiety, and improving brain functioning. In 2009, Bill and his colleague Sarina Grosswald collaborated on a pilot study of the effects of TM on middle school students with ADHD. They found that young teenagers with ADHD could actually sit and meditate for fifteen minutes, and after three months of twice-daily meditation, the students reported a 43 percent reduction in symptoms of stress and anxiety. The study also found better behavioral regulation and emotional control. A second well-controlled study, led by Fred Travis, an expert in the assessment of brain waves, looked at the effects of TM on the brain-wave activity of middle school students with ADHD. This brain-wave activity was of interest because theta waves are usually too powerful in relation to beta waves in kids with ADHD. The subjects were randomly assigned to the TM group or a delayed-start group, the latter of which served as controls for the first three months before learning TM themselves. Three months into the study, the theta/beta ratios increased in the delayed-start group, which is the opposite of the desired effect, while the TM subjects moved closer to normal values. At the six-month mark, after both groups were practicing the TM technique, theta/beta ratios decreased in both groups.[9]

Several researchers are also looking at whether mindfulness practices can improve ADHD symptoms in kids. While there are few well-controlled studies, there's promising evidence that mindfulness practices can be of help.[10] In Bill's experience, although nothing comes close to the power of stimulant medication when it works well (and it doesn't always), anything that lowers stress levels will make the brains of kids with ADHD work more efficiently.

Bill recently evaluated Adam, a six-year-old with ADHD and behavioral problems. His teachers told his mother that although he is a very kind boy, he is one of the most difficult and disruptive children the teachers have ever tried to teach. At home, Adam's oppositional tendencies make him very hard to manage, and his resistance to his mother's direction commonly leads to painful and unproductive fights. A few days after his neuropsychological evaluation, Bill met with Adam's mother to discuss the test results and to talk about ways of promoting his sense of autonomy. Bill talked through the collaborative problem-solving approach we discussed in Chapter Three and told her she was unlikely to see progress if she simply tried to force Adam to comply. A couple of days later, his mother sent Bill this e-mail:

"I tried dealing with Adam's defiance through collaboration, and not by forcing or using authoritarian measures. It worked like a charm. When I said, 'We're going to bed in five minutes,' Adam immediately screamed, 'No, we're not!' He even stood up in a fighting pose, ready to bring me down. Normally I'd scream back, saying, 'Oh yes, you are!' But this time, I didn't fight him. I just looked at him, and then I walked over and hugged him and kissed him on the head, telling him that he didn't have to scream like that. He relaxed and almost melted, and he then decided on his own to turn off the TV and go upstairs. Although he bargained with me about listening to music on my phone before he fell asleep, we averted a major blowup and had a peaceful night."

Margaret Sibley's STAND program takes the same angle, as it recommends a respectful, noncoercive approach to helping adolescents and their parents clarify their own personal goals and assess their need and desire to change. Research on the STAND approach has shown improvement in things like organizational skills, homework behavior, parent-teen contracting, and parenting stress. Not surprisingly, studies have also found that parents enrolled in the STAND program are more likely than parents participating in more traditional therapies to adopt an autonomy-supportive parenting style by the end of treatment.[11]

Ned recently met with a kid with moderate learning disabilities and ADHD. He also had an incredible sense of himself and what he needed to thrive. After going through which classes he liked and didn't, Ned asked him what he liked to do outside of school and learned he was a big fan of video games.

"How much do you play?" Ned asked.

"Lots."

"Does it interfere with school or do you get all that done okay?"

"I get my homework done at school during the day," he said. "By five o'clock, my meds are wearing off and it takes me twice as long to do things, so I push to get it done while I'm focused."

"I love that," Ned said. "I'm amazed how often people put stuff off and spend twice as much time because they're doing it later in the day when they're less efficient."

"I know," he said. "I have my homework done and I can just play video games."

"Are you able to manage how much you play?" Ned asked. "Or do you find yourself up all night?"

"Oh no," he said. "I don't like being tired. I can't focus as well. So no, I'm not up all night."

What this story emphasizes is that ADHD does not prohibit self-knowledge, discipline, and self-control. It's not easy being a kid with a short attention span, limited ability to focus on anything that's not highly interesting, or trouble sitting still and behaving appropriately. And it's not easy to raise kids like this. But it's easier for everyone if we remember that, like all kids, children with ADHD need a sense of autonomy to be happy and to function optimally. Although they sometimes need to be tweaked, the strategies we've talked about in this book can help these kids as much as they help kids with laser focus.

There are some cases in which proactive behavior management strategies such as spending private time with your child, engaging in positive attention, using natural and logical consequences, and collaborative problem solving are not enough. If your child's behavior cannot be brought under control, if he repeatedly makes bad decisions and cannot engage in the kind of dialogue required to make informed decisions, or if he simply cannot motivate himself, we support the use of structured behavioral programs involving rewards and consequences—at least for short periods. (We recommend our friend Dr. Dan Shapiro's book *Parent Child Journey: An Individualized Approach to Raising Your Challenging Child* for in-depth instruction in the use of behavioral strategies.)

Autism Spectrum Disorders (ASD)

In addition to the social difficulty and rigidity that define autism spectrum disorders, kids with autism struggle with stress tolerance and self-motivation.

Children and teens on the spectrum appear to be wired in a way that makes them very easily stressed. Many scientists believe that this is due to abnormalities in the functioning of the amygdala, and in the connection between the amygdala and the circuits in the prefrontal cortex that process emotions and social interactions.[12] Kids on the spectrum find all but the most familiar environments and interactions stressful and unpredictable. It can take them six months to feel safe in a new classroom or with a new therapist. Assemblies and field trips aren't special treats but obstacles that reduce the predictability of the school day. Many kids on the spectrum experience the sensory world more intensely and as more of a threat than most kids. They commonly feel a low sense of control because of their trouble understanding the logic of the social world and their difficulty directing their behavior. According to one theory of autism, many kids on the spectrum will adopt rigid behaviors like flapping, rocking, spinning, pacing, or saying the same thing over and over to help them maintain a sense of order in what feels like a chaotic world. That rigidity places limits on their adaptability. Not surprisingly, anxiety disorders and sleep disturbances are extremely common in kids with ASDs.

Kids on the spectrum benefit greatly from strategies that reduce novelty and unpredictability, and that increase their sense of control. (Remember the N.U.T.S. acronym for stress-causing events.) These strategies include visual schedules (pictorial representations of the activities scheduled in a school day, presented in a sequence), minimizing the number of transitions children have to make, telling them stories to make the world more understandable, teaching them how to understand other people and social relationships, and making sure they have a safe place to go in school if they're too stressed. All these widely used and successful interventions help kids on the spectrum feel safe. Kids with ASD also benefit from learning how to take control of their own thinking. An excellent new program uses Plan B thinking and encourages kids to ask themselves, when they start to get upset, "Is it a big deal or a little deal?"[13] Studies show that other stress-reduction practices like cognitive behavioral therapy, yoga, mindfulness training, and

Transcendental Meditation also hold great promise for kids with ASD.[14] Because these strategies reduce stress, they enable kids to focus their minds on academic learning and allow them to activate their brains' social engagement system more effectively.[15]

In Bill's pilot study on the effect of TM on ADHD kids, one of the students who benefited most dramatically, Bill later learned, had also been diagnosed with autism. Before he started TM, he didn't make eye contact, was socially isolated, and didn't have any friends at school. After three months of meditation, his teachers said that he was starting to joke around with the other kids, and he had asked another kid to come over to his house and play video games. He even set up a meeting to talk with the headmaster about starting a new social club for kids who love video games. By lowering his stress response, he was able to activate the parts of his brain he needed to engage with other kids.

In Bill's second study, a girl who was on the spectrum agreed to meditate if her parents would let her taper her multiple psychiatric medications and eventually let her be drug free. With the support of her psychiatrist, they did, and her teachers told Bill at the end of the study that she was doing better than she'd ever done. This doesn't mean that if kids meditate they will not need medication, but it does suggest that kids on the spectrum can meditate regularly and benefit quite dramatically from it.

Bill recently evaluated a high school student with ASD who, along with his parents, practiced a yoga-based relaxation technique called yoga nidra (presented on a CD). The parents reported that when they did this technique together, the student's day went dramatically better. When Bill asked how often they did it, he was surprised to hear that they did it only once a week. He asked why they didn't do it every day if it made such a big difference, and they simply answered, "We've never thought about it." We are big fans of building in practices for destressing on a regular basis.

All that said, the best documented intervention for autism,

applied behavior analysis (ABA), uses predetermined goals and a specific set of behavioral strategies (including rewards and negative consequences) to reach young children on the spectrum, and places minimal emphasis on promoting a sense of autonomy. This would seem on the surface to contradict our argument, but it is important to remember that the brain's motivation system works differently in children with ASDs. They are less responsive to the kinds of social rewards (like a smiling parent or enthusiastic praise) which motivate most kids. By working on precise goals and using specific rewards to enforce target behaviors, ABA is often very effective at enabling children to engage with others, develop language skills, and behave in a socially acceptable way. Therapeutic approaches that involve controlling the behavior of children with ASD through rewards, pressures, or constraints can be useful for building the basic skills that are necessary if a child is to develop autonomy.[16]

At the same time, many experts on autism believe that behavioral methods should be married with a focus on autonomy. There has been very little actual research in the area, but as noted above, at least one study has shown that when parents and teachers support autonomy, kids with ASD improve both socially and academically.[17] Bill has found wide consensus in his conversations with autism specialists that if children with autism are eventually to become self-motivated and independent, they *have* to experience autonomy. They have to be able to perceive themselves as initiators of their own activities and to feel that they have a choice about how to direct their own lives. He thus supports interventions that place a strong emphasis on supporting autonomy in children on the spectrum.[18] Given that a high percentage of adults with ASD have trouble holding a job, due, in part, to difficulty with self-motivation and low stress tolerance, placing an emphasis on the promotion of autonomy and self-determination as early as possible would appear to be very important.

Parents should, as much as possible, be responsive to their

children's passions and allow kids with ASD to channel the energy that goes into their intense interests so that they may experience flow. Strong interests (like in Pokémon, anime, dinosaurs, or Dora the Explorer) can also be a means through which kids with ASD are able to connect with other kids. Birds of a feather flock together socially, which means that kids with ASD are most likely to befriend other kids with social challenges, especially those who have similar interests.

Owen Suskind, a young adult with ASD, is the subject of a beautiful book written by his Pulitzer Prize–winning father, Ron Suskind, called *Life, Animated* (which was also made into an Academy Award–nominated documentary by the same name). As the book indicates, Bill followed Owen from age three through his graduation from high school and had numerous conversations with him and his parents about his remarkable passion for Walt Disney movies. As a young child, Owen watched the movies over and over, and in these fictional worlds he felt safe and had a deep sense of control. Privately, he began to draw characters from the movies. Over time, Owen's immersion in these films led to the development of great artistic talent (see his work on the Web site lifeanimated .net). It also led to a deep and even profound understanding of life and the responsibilities we have to each other in this world. When Owen was fourteen or so, he bravely spent time with his dying grandfather, reassuring him that, based on themes and moral lessons he'd absorbed from his beloved films, he had led a great life. While other members of the family anxiously avoided going upstairs to be with Owen's grandfather for fear of not knowing what to say or do, Owen knew the right thing to do and did it with confidence and courage. Although the intense interests of children and teens with ASD used to be discouraged, children like Owen have helped to reshape our thinking, and conferences are now being held on "affinities therapies"—using the deep interests and passions of kids with ASD to help them manage the larger world.

Professionals who work with children on the spectrum often say, "If you've met one child with ASD, you've met one child with ASD." Because the spectrum is so broad, parents should feel emboldened to tailor their approach based on *their* kid. Kathleen Atmore is an award-winning autism specialist at Children's National Medical Center and the mother of a child with ASD. She points out that some kids with ASD want more than anything to make friends and to be part of the crowd, while others are perfectly happy being by themselves in their own world. It doesn't make sense to prescribe the same intervention for these very different kinds of kids. "If kids really want to do well socially," she said, "I'll recommend up to thirty hours a week of intervention that focuses on helping to develop their social understanding and their social skill. I know that these kids will be motivated to use the intervention and that it will probably help them a lot. For the kids with low social motivation, a really strong emphasis on social interaction would not only be exceedingly stressful for them, it would be completely ineffective, because they'd continually fight every attempt to help them do better socially. So we have to be thinking of who these kids are as people and what's important to them—rather than thinking that we always know best and laying our treatments on them no matter what they think."

None of what we recommend in this chapter is simple. If you're the parent of a child with special needs, your job is hard. Parenting a child with special needs is stressful. Moms and dads have fears about their kids' futures and about the impact of their negative behaviors on their siblings, and often feel guilty ("He got it from me"). Added to those concerns are the daily hassles of managing appointments and schlepping kids across town to see specialists, and, in many cases, the challenge of managing difficult behavior. Studies have found that the mothers of older adolescents and young adults with autism spectrum disorders have levels of the stress hormone cortisol that are, on average, comparable to those of soldiers in combat.[19]

As we know, kids pick up on their parents' stress. And yet focusing on your own stress reduction and happiness feels harder when your child has challenges. It's tempting for the whole family to adapt around the child's problems—"I can't possibly go out to dinner when Johnny has a homework assignment due"—but all that does is sacrifice your well-being, which Johnny will pick up on. When our kids are struggling, most of our work as parents is really on ourselves. That's why our most fundamental message is to focus on being a nonanxious presence.

You may be fighting your own fears for your child, fighting your daily stressors, and maybe even fighting your child. Breathe. Make sure your own brain isn't flooded before you act. In one family Ned works with, one of the kids has ASD and another is highly anxious. The one with ASD began to meditate, and the mom started to do so, too. She is remarkably tranquil in the midst of what must be a very challenging situation. Her calmness might not fix everything for her kids, but it's hard to think of any situation where being less stressed isn't better. If meditation isn't for you, that's fine. But just as you are providing support for your child, make sure you're doing something that provides support for you.

What to Do Tonight

- Do everything you can to minimize homework-related stress. Even if your kids have significant learning difficulties, play a consultant role. It's far more effective than that of a teacher or taskmaster.

- Offer your child as much choice as possible about the kinds of interventions he receives and when he receives them. Accept that it's okay for him to say no—or to participate in fewer of them.

- If possible, find a school that will accommodate your child, so that he doesn't feel stressed or unable to keep up.

- Encourage your child to try different ways of working and learning to figure out what works best for him. Students with special needs are often slow to develop an understanding of their strengths and weaknesses and can be reluctant to use strategies that "everyone else" isn't using. Therefore, consider this a long-term goal, and keep working at it. Remind your child that "you're the expert on you" and encourage him to pay attention to what helps and what doesn't.

- Use rewards if necessary, but as much as possible provide a rationale that respects your child's autonomy. "I know that when you look at your math work sheet it's incredibly hard for you to get yourself focused enough to work on it. This is because there's not enough dopamine in the front part of your brain to make it interesting enough to focus on. I'll offer you an incentive, because it will make it easier to get your brain going." Some kids dislike homework so much that they'll turn down the incentives. If that is the case you may be able to negotiate with the school about alternatives to homework, like watching educational videos or listening to recorded books.

- If your child is in middle school or high school, advocate for a resource period or an extra study period during the day so that your child can get most of his homework done at school.

- Give your kids opportunities to serve, such as helping younger children or working with animals. This is a wonderful way for children with challenges to develop a healthy sense of control.

- Teach your children how their brains work and tell them that learning how to do something means that more and more brain cells are firing together as one unit. This is why we practice things over and over, so that we get more players on the neuron teams that do reading, math, writing, sports, and many other things.

- Talk out loud to yourself about managing situations that are hard for your kid. For instance: "When I was trying to figure out how to get everything done last night, it probably would have been better if I had written down everything I needed to do, prioritized things, and started with the most important thing. I guess I'll do that next time."

- Because kids with ADHD and ASD are at such high risk for sleep problems, pay careful attention to their ability to fall asleep, the ease with which they wake up, and the extent to which they seem tired during the day. If your child appears to have sleep problems, consult with your pediatrician and, if necessary, with a sleep specialist. Also consult an excellent book by V. Mark Durand, a psychologist and father of a child with autism, called *Sleep Better! A Guide to Improving Sleep for Kids with Special Needs*.

CHAPTER TWELVE

The SAT, ACT,
and Other Four-Letter Words

S TANDARDIZED TESTS LOOM large in the lives of adolescents and their parents. The date is circled on the calendar along with other teenage rites of passage like the driver's test, prom, and graduation. Many see the SAT as the pivotal occurrence of high school, the hours that will determine their fate, the score that will determine Harvard or College U.

While we would love it if parents and kids read this whole book together, we recognize that for the past eleven chapters, we've been addressing parents. This chapter is different. We encourage parents to read it, of course, but we really want high schoolers themselves to have a look. After all, at the end of the day, they're the ones sitting in the exam room. For that reason, this chapter speaks to them directly.

Testing Stinks . . . Usually

There's a lot to be said against standardized tests. Among the many criticisms is the valid point that they allow for only one right answer. Diversity of thought, creativity, divergent thinking: none of these are rewarded by standardized tests. Plus, there's no process of appeal: you cannot question the questioners. In a world where critical-thinking skills are necessary for tackling difficult questions with no clear right answer, you're assessed with tests that insist there are. No partial credit is given, no context considered. Ned's students routinely ask him, "Who are the people who make these tests and who put them in charge?" The short answer is that really nobody put them in charge. Among the very first standardized tests was the Binet-Simon Scale, created by the French educator Alfred Binet. He designed his test not to assess intelligence but as a way to identify children who needed more help. The way the test was used to separate people into categories worried him.

In his book *The Mismeasure of Man*, evolutionary biologist Stephen Jay Gould pointed out that simply assigning a number to something doesn't mean we've measured it. Or, to borrow the old adage, "Not everything that can be measured matters, and not everything that matters can be measured." Our obsession with metrics has led to the testing-industrial complex—a multibillion-dollar business that's only getting bigger.[1]

It isn't the tests themselves but what's done with them and how they're viewed by kids and their parents that's a problem. There is some value to standardized tests. The SAT and ACT often reveal reading problems that have gone undetected. When kids with straight As from academically rigorous schools have mediocre test scores, it can be a sign. Average grades and average scores? No biggie. Killer grades and weak scores? Worth exploring. Ned has directed maybe a hundred kids to get neuropsychological evaluations or to meet with a psychologist or psychiatrist because, based on the discrepancy between grades and scores, he has sniffed out anxiety, attention issues, or learning disabilities. While he doesn't have the tools to diagnose the issue himself, the blunt results of standardized tests can help him see that there is a problem worth investigating.

One of his recent students was very bright but frustrated by school and even more so by standardized tests. While Ned didn't know what the issue was, he noted that the boy was a strong reader but uncommonly slow. A neuropsychological evaluation confirmed it: 98th percentile verbal reasoning ability. Reading speed? Fifth percentile. No wonder he was frustrated. Because he was sharp, not one of his teachers in twelve years of schooling had suspected the problem of a very slow processing speed.

Another student at an elite private girls school had a B+ average and PSAT scores in the 400s, which was unusual. Ned asked her, "Do you underperform on tests in school and do less well than you think you should do? Do you ever run short on time?"

The girl's mom looked at Ned quizzically. "Surely if there were an issue," she asked, "wouldn't one of her teachers have said something by now?"

The straight answer to that is no. Even very good schools will often fail to catch a learning disability if a child is particularly smart or diligent. These kids will develop compensating strategies that make it possible for them to get by. As it turned out, the girl had a massive attention-related problem, which professional evaluation determined was ADHD. But because she was not disruptive, her issues had not drawn the attention of any of her teachers. It's really common for kids (especially girls) who are hardworking and eager to fly under the radar. They don't perform so poorly that anyone is alarmed. Sometimes standardized tests provide the first sign of an issue.

Where tests become problematic is when they are seen as Binet feared they would be—as a marker of intelligence. It's true that you cannot do well on the SAT or ACT unless you know certain things (we'll leave it to others to debate the merits of those things), but one can be smart and know plenty and still not do well. So folks who believe these tests confirm how smart they are and folks who believe the tests do not reflect just how smart they are *are both right*. The bottom line is that it helps to do well on those tests for the purpose of applying to college. But if you're stressed by the notion that the test is judging your intelligence, there is abundant evidence that it is not qualified to do that.

It's worth remembering that the SAT and AP tests don't impact your future nearly as much as you think. Although it isn't easy, we try to talk kids and their parents out of the idea that "one score determines your whole life." Do the numbers: 75 percent of people score below the 75th percentile. That's a lot of people, many of whom have very successful lives.

So standardized testing mostly stinks, but it is a necessary hurdle if you want to go to college. There are almost a thousand colleges that are test-score optional (see fairtest.org for more on this), but that leaves many more that require the SAT or ACT, so you might as well take the darn test. And as long as you're taking it, you might as well learn a thing or two. We're not as interested as you might think in your learning algebraic equations (though that's important, of course). We think the real promise of the test lies in the techniques you can learn to manage stress. As the political philosopher Edmund Burke observed, "No passion so effectually robs the mind of all its powers of acting and reasoning as fear." Put another way, it doesn't matter what you know if you lose your mind when it matters.

N.U.T.S.

We covered this earlier in the book, but if you're just picking up this chapter, we'll fill you in. One of our favorite neuroscientists, Sonia Lupien, uses an acronym to explain the things that make life stressful:

Novelty

Unpredictability

Threat to the ego

Sense of control (or lack thereof)

All of these can apply to the SAT or ACT, but they don't have to. So let's look at the world of testing through the lens of N.U.T.S.

Novelty

Ned once prepped a former army officer for the GMAT who was twenty-six, a West Point grad, and a wounded warrior. It had been years since Mike had taken high school math, and looking at the test material stressed him out. Geometry, which he'd hardly thought of since ninth grade, made him freeze. Ned encouraged Mike by telling him he just needed to revisit the fundamentals of geometry, and by processing it over and over, he'd know just what to do when he came across a geometry question on the GMAT. "Oh," Mike said, "it's just like airborne school." As this was a comparison Ned hadn't heard before, he asked him to explain. "Well, in theory," the soldier said, "you could be taught how to jump out of a plane in the morning and then actually do it that afternoon. But that's not how it works in the U.S. armed services. You spend days perfecting how to use your gear, how to engage the chute, how to jump off platforms, how to land and roll. For two weeks, you just do the same thing over and over so it's ingrained. Then near the end of the second week, you don your gear, go up in the plane, and walk right out of the plane like it's nothing, because you know the process so well."

Like the parachuter, you want to take all the novelty out of test day. You want to know exactly where you're going, how to get there, and what the seats feel like. You want to know what you're likely to see on the test and how you'll handle it. You want to practice the details until they're rote, so that actually taking the test is no big deal.

You may think standardized tests are lousy, but at least they are consistently lousy. Yes, the questions themselves change, but lots of people up at the College Board and ACT headquarters spend all day making sure the difficulty level remains the same. That doesn't mean they feel the same. Students regularly tell Ned that the tests are getting much harder. But Ned has taken the SAT and the ACT himself dozens of times, and he can assure them that this isn't the case. Take practice tests, he reminds them, and the novelty goes away. If something in the test feels novel, it's because something has changed in your process, something you can completely control. For instance, you might be rushing through the reading and so the questions seem harder. Slow down, and you'll see they're not.

Those sample tests that you hate taking are serving an important function. They improve your process and ingrain a focus on the process itself so that nothing on test day is new. As the aphorism goes, "Practice like you'll play so you can play like you've practiced."

One of the first kids I ever tutored, Naomi, cratered on her test in a way I didn't see coming. Her mom called me up distraught, wondering why after all the time and money spent on test prep her daughter's scores had not gone up. I wanted to say, "Beats me. She was doing fine when she left my office. What happened between here and the test?" But wisely I didn't, and waited until I met with Naomi herself.

At first Naomi couldn't really explain what had happened, she just said that the questions were harder than they had been in practice. I asked about disruptions at the test site, like whispering proctors or kids tapping toes. She volunteered that she and her mom had gotten into a fight right before the test. In fact, while driving to the test. Her mom had told her that she hadn't worked hard enough and probably wouldn't do well because of her lack of effort. "So I was in tears and really upset," Naomi said, "but I think I calmed down enough by the time I got to the test room."

"Oh, good," I said. "It's important to be calm for the test, so I'm glad you were."

"Well, yes and no," said Naomi. "There was this other thing." It turned out that Naomi and her boyfriend of seven months had just broken up the week before. And he was in her testing room.

"Okaaaay," I said. "That's pretty stressful. Anything else?"

"Well, there was one other thing. See, I went out with my friends after my boyfriend and I broke up, and I was upset, and there was this other guy I met . . . well, anyway, he was in the testing room, too."

In a nutshell, much about this day for Naomi was new and stressful. Tiger Woods allegedly brought his furniture from home on the road with him so that he could replicate his home, reducing his stress by controlling the details.[2] Now Naomi couldn't control much of her experience, but the likelihood of another day like this was remote. The next time, I suggested that she drive herself to the test (and practice doing so beforehand). Chances are her love life wouldn't be quite so tumultuous at the same time.

—Ned

Unpredictability

We're often asked about the difference between novelty and unpredictability. The simple answer is something that's novel will be unpredictable, but something can be unpredictable that's not novel. For example, if you have a friend who is usually nice but gets mean when he is stressed or under pressure, after a while his snarky comments aren't novel anymore. But they are unpredictable. As a result, you may feel like you have to walk on eggshells when you're around him.

You may feel that the test is unpredictable. After all, you can't predict what questions will be on it. But that's not completely true.

Do enough test prep and you begin to see that while the specific questions change, the types of questions are remarkably similar. By focusing on process, you will minimize unpredictability.

The other way to counter the stress of unpredictability is through Plan B thinking. When you're planning a party or wedding, you don't know what the weather will be like on the big day. So what do you do? The helpful wedding planner suggests that in the event of rain, there's a $5,000 tent you can rent to ensure your guests won't be soaked. This is called Plan B. (It's also called extortion, because there's no way a tent costs that much for any event other than your wedding.)

Psychometricians (a geeky word for people who make tests like the ACT and SAT) rely on the fact that students will respond in predictable ways to certain content. They design questions based not only on what students have been taught but on how they have been taught. It helps the test makers get the right balance of right and wrong responses. Under stress, students will sometimes experience a perceptual narrowing. This means that they default to answering questions in the way they've been taught. It is what's most deeply ingrained, but it is also, not coincidentally, often the hardest way. Ned's colleague Aaron offers this advice: "Don't ask yourself how should I do this problem, which is likely to run you straight into a wall that you cannot surmount. Instead, ask yourself: What can I do? It broadens your vision, opens your mind, and frees you to use any tool you have in your toolbox. Can you eyeball it? Can you plug in numbers? Can you guess and check? These are all methods your math teacher would hate. But since she's not here, use whatever method is best for you right now." If you're doing calculus and you can use the first derivative, knock yourself out. But if counting on your fingers is easier, go for it. Sometimes a bread knife is better than a chainsaw. For any question, it's great to have more than one method (Plans C, D, and E). Then choose the one that's better for you. Simply believing there's more than one way will reduce your stress and help you think more clearly.

In addition to Plan B thinking, we suggest that you do some disaster preparedness planning. It's pretty much like mental contrasting. Ned learned this lesson in a trial by fire. He's always been really good at standardized tests, so when he took the SAT as a professional tutor, he was surprised to see that he had five questions left when the proctor called time. That hadn't happened to him before; he knew his pacing pretty well, and usually finished well ahead of time. He looked around the room at the other students taking the test, and they were all deer-in-the-headlights frozen. Ned froze, too, for a second. But then he addressed the proctor.

"Excuse me," he said. "I'm so sorry, but are you sure the time's elapsed?"

"Yes."

"Okay," Ned said. "It's just that I've taken the test before and this time seemed really quick. Would you mind checking again?"

The proctor sighed and said, "Fine, the test started at 9:05 A.M. and it's a twenty-five-minute section, and now it's . . ." He glanced at his watch. "Oh." He cleared his throat. "Students, you have ten more minutes to complete the test. Please continue testing."

Ned tells this story to all his students, so that they can practice how to be respectful, calm, and yet proactive if something feels off about the exam conditions. Just knowing that you'll know what to do prevents that deer-in-the-headlights sensation and increases your sense of control.

Threat to the ego

Obviously the SAT, ACT, GRE, GMAT, LSAT, and other standardized tests are not inherently dangerous. They might give you nightmares, but they're unlikely to put you in the ER. What they do represent is a threat to your ego. Many terrific students whose first standardized test scores are lower than they expect are seized by panic that the test has "outed them." Perhaps they aren't as "smart" as they had always imagined.

It's worth saying it again: test scores are not an accurate reflection of intelligence. Knowing the definition of "laconic" or how to find the roots of a quadratic equation does not prove you're smart, only that you know those particular things. And not knowing them doesn't make you dumb. The ACT and SAT are tests of acquired knowledge and skills—some you learn in school and some you don't. But your score is not a label you will be marked with for the rest of your life. And if you find yourself at the age of forty boasting about your SAT score, well, something else is seriously wrong.

One of Ned's students, Anne, was really underperforming on practice tests. Ned suspected that she had a problem with anxiety, and met with Anne and her mom. He ran through his usual questions about the test, Anne's life in general, and what she thought might be throwing her. They were about halfway through the questions when her eyes welled up with tears. Ned stopped and asked, as tenderly as he could, "What are you thinking right now?"

Anne paused and then said, "How stupid I am."

"Well," Ned said, "I have no idea whether you can do calculus or advanced physics—I sure can't—but I can say with great certainty that you are not stupid. I've seen a lot of kids and can see that you are very capable. What just happened to you is stress. No matter how good your brain is, when it's really stressed, it cannot do what it's able to do. Stressed brains simply don't work well. So more than test prep, we need to talk about what we can do to help you with your stress, so that you can do what you are already capable of doing."

One particularly pernicious form of threat to self is called stereotype threat, a phenomenon Josh Aronson has studied extensively. When someone experiences stereotype threat, they are fearful of confirming a negative stereotype about the group they belong to. To explain how it works, Josh tells the story of lunch with his real estate agent.[3] At one point she said, "What is it with you Jews and money?" Which, understandably, caught Josh off guard. When he asked what she meant, she said, "Well, I don't really know any Jewish people, but I've worked with a couple recently and I've noticed they're flashy with money."

Now, because Josh studies this stuff for a living, he had the presence of mind to say, "Okay, let me tell you what's happening. You have heard this stereotype about Jews before, and it's actually pretty anti-Semitic, and you are taking that stereotype and applying it to anyone you meet who might be Jewish. You are subscribing to a stereotype and continuing to spread it." After an awkward moment, they continued with their lunch.

Then the bill came. Josh immediately thought, *The stereotype of Jews is that we throw our money around, so I'm not going to pick up this check and enforce that stereotype. She's my real estate agent, she should pick up the check.* Then he thought, *But wait, there's another Jewish stereotype—that Jews are stingy. So if I don't pick up the check, I'm just reinforcing that stereotype for her.* All of this was running through his mind just about picking up a check.

Now take that scenario and apply it to an African American teenage boy sitting among a group of white kids and taking a standardized test. He comes into that exam room with much more than a #2 pencil. It's likely he also brings a backpack loaded with other people's assumptions about him. It doesn't matter if he knows those stereotypes are baseless—he knows that other people subscribe to them, and that alone is threatening. Under that stress, it is easy for his thoughts to slide from thoughts of success to ones of failure. *Everyone who sees my low test score will know I'm black, which will strengthen their belief that black people don't do well.*

We encourage anyone who has experienced a threat to self around a test to spend some time before the test writing about bigger-picture questions. This will shift your thinking and improve your sense of control. Answer questions like, "What are my core values? What do I really care about? Who am I, regardless of how I do on the test?" Lacrosse player, sister, activist, friend. This exercise helps give you perspective and recognize that you are more than a test score. In one study in which kids were given a writing assignment that affirmed their sense of self, African American students' grades increased significantly and the racial achievement gap was reduced by 40 percent.[4]

Another option is to go into warrior mode. One college tennis player we know listens to aggressive gangster rap before she gets on the court. There's a great Bose commercial in which NFL quarterback Russell Wilson is listening to Macklemore's "Downtown" and envisioning Macklemore giving him a pep talk: "Look at that bad man getting his smoothie on. Look at that bad man getting his feet wet. This is Russell Wilson country. And this? [*Sniff*] Russell Wilson air."

There's great research to back this up. The army did a study on the connection between U.S. soldiers' frame of mind under stress and their ability to detect IEDs—the improvised explosive devices responsible for so many deaths in Iraq and Afghanistan. In short, "researchers found that soldiers who were especially good at spotting bombs in simulations tended to think of themselves as predators, not prey." This isn't surprising, and the study confirmed that "even the most perceptive, observant brain on earth will not pick up subtle clues if it is overwhelmed by stress." The "predator" mentality proved the key to these soldiers' success; by reducing their anxiety, it enabled them to outperform their more fearful peers.[5]

What does a study about IEDs have to do with test preparation? A lot, actually. For years Ned has tried to help students understand how their performance on standardized tests can be influenced by their emotions—especially their anxiety. He has seen a lot of kids who know their stuff—and have proven so on multiple practice tests—suddenly begin to clench up as the real test approaches. Out of fear, they change their approach, with devastating results.

It's perfectly normal to get nervous before a test, but you can work to sidestep this stress by choosing your attitude about the test. Look to conquer, rather than survive. Athletes have all sorts of rituals to help them "get into the zone" on game day. That same music, rituals, and active visualizations of success can help you prepare for a test. Remember, it's your choice whether you enter a test with an attitude of "Gulp! My whole future is on the line!" or "I'm going to show these suckers who's the boss!"

Jeffrey was a great high school football player who was really excited about one of the colleges that recruited him, but he was told that if he wanted to go there he would have to get his test scores up. He wasn't making progress. He had worked with two different tutors before his concerned dad called me. He told me that Jeffrey was a good student. He got As in math, but was stuck in the 500s on his tests. More significantly, he'd had a challenging year. He had switched schools mid-year, it turned out. I probed to find out why this had happened, and his dad reluctantly confided that he'd been bullied at his previous school. His football teammates had engaged in quite a bit of hazing, and the coaches had reportedly turned a blind eye. Jeffrey was likely feeling that every bad practice score validated the voices of those boys telling him he was a loser. What he needed was not more practice tests, but a way to push back on the threat to self he was feeling.

I met with Jeffrey twice. It was all the time we had before the test. I explained how fear works to shut down the strategic Pilot in his brain and told him that we needed his "predator brain," not his "prey brain." Focusing on the process would help him. Jeffrey was a wide receiver, so I told him it was like focusing on running tight routes to tune out the crowds, and thinking of taking it to the defenders rather than fearing their hits. I also encouraged him to listen to music on the way to the exam, something that would help him get a swagger going. He needed to go into that test with the mindset of a hunter. "Spend some time thinking about the test, rehearsing the test in your mind," I said, "just like you do a game. Don't picture a cream-puff test, but imagine running your precise routes through a really good defense. Imagine leaving those punks at your old school—and those awful test makers— weeping. Activate your prefrontal cortex (what's the strategic way to take her out?) rather than your amygdala (run, you fool, run!)." We did not look at a single sample test question.

Jeffrey improved his scores by nearly 180 points. Game changer. What had been standing in his way was his fear, and once we were able to develop an effective strategy to conquer that fear, he was able to show what he could really do all along.

—Ned

A question of control

You know how stressful it is when you're late for something to begin with, and then you're hit with a brick wall of traffic? Your hands start sweating, your heart beats faster, and you likely think whoever is in the car with you is a giant pain in the ass. A huge reason this scenario is stressful is that you're stuck—there's nothing you can do to fix the situation. You have no sense of control. If someone asked you to solve a difficult equation, or answer a comprehension question, you probably wouldn't do very well. At moments like this, you are living in the part of your brain designed to escape from predators, and that part of your brain just wants to run like hell, not calmly consider alternatives.

When you feel that you have control over a situation, you are likely to be calmer, more relaxed, and more able to think. You are also likely to make better decisions. Everything we've covered in this chapter—novelty, unpredictability, and threat to the ego—can take away your sense of control.

But the test has patterns and you can learn those patterns and adapt your approach to them. If you're slow and methodical and need to pick up the pace to get through all the test questions, you can work on that—it's a perfectly clear target, and that's really good news. In short, if you focus on process instead of outcome, whether taking a test or jumping out of an airplane, you will have a much greater sense of control.

There's one problem we haven't addressed. What do you do if your mom or dad is constantly on your case? What if they are the wall of traffic causing you stress? Ned talks to kids about this all the time. Here is what he tells them:

First, know that your parents love you. Sometimes love and fear get mixed together, and when parents become overly controlling, they are probably acting out of the fear part of their brains. They may be feeling stressed because they cannot control what happens in your life. When they feel that way, it's easier to criticize or holler to relieve their stress than it is to listen or let go. That doesn't mean it feels great to be on the receiving end, but at least it explains why it happens.

Second, do listen to them. Do your best to strip out the edge of fear, and see if you can glean solid advice behind their words. It's a sign of maturity to be able to gather as much information as possible and consider all perspectives on a given issue.

Our hope is that you listen, but if what they're saying really seems crazy, consider a Jedi mind trick Ned picked up from his wise friend Chrissellene. If your mom or dad comes to you and says, "Hey, Nicky, I really think you should [insert whatever crazy-making advice your parents offer]," you probably usually respond with "Stop nagging me, Mom." How does that work? Parents will, almost without fail, think you're not listening. Or that you don't understand how important this is. And so they rarely let it go and walk away. Usually they repeat it again. With emphasis. Which only gets you more frustrated. Next thing you know, it's a fight, which makes you really not want to listen, and makes them press the point even harder.

So what if you change the whole dynamic? What if when your mom or dad says they think you should do something, you reply, "Thanks for telling me, Mom." Or, "That's a good point." When your parents feel validated, they are much more likely to pat themselves on the back and say, "You're welcome, dear" and go back to doing whatever it is that adults do when they aren't telling their kids what to do. The point is, blowing them off doesn't work. So try validating them instead. If this is hard to do (because you don't feel or believe it), you can say, "That's a good point," and in your head think, "for a crazy person" or "Thanks for telling me [though I'll never believe you are right]."

Finally, do your best to communicate respectfully about your needs. Sometimes it's helpful to write a letter. You might try saying something like, "I know you want the best for me and are trying to help me get the best score. But this test ultimately has to be mine. I appreciate your help but I need you to take into account what I feel is right for me."

If you can do this, it not only will help you in the run-up to the test, but it will help you reset your relationships with your parents for years to come.

I had a student some years ago who was working hard to break 600 on reading and math. Math was especially vexing. Her tendency was to miss too many easy questions, then struggle with the hardest ones. The plan of attack was for her to take her time and nail 70 percent of the questions, so that the last thirty didn't matter at all. If she saw problems she could do in that 30 percent, she could pick and choose a few. She knew what she was supposed to do, but she couldn't follow the plan of attack, and her early errors crushed the 70 percent goal. The real crux was that, though she understood the strategy, she struggled not to do questions. It felt dangerous. Giving her the choice of what problems to do and what problems to skip gave her responsibility and, along with it, guilt. So I grabbed a sample test and crossed out the last four questions of every single math section.

"But what if I can do them?" she asked.

"Nope," I said. "Don't care. You aren't allowed to. Do not even look at anything with a red X through it."

She took the practice test. "How was it?" I asked.

"Soooooo much easier," she said. She didn't do any of the hardest questions. So, math? 610. Nice! Biggest surprise? Reading: 640. See, not only had she conserved her time and attention to do fewer math questions and thus not make "silly" errors, she also had much more energy when she got to the reading.

—Ned

In the week before the test, think of yourself as a marathoner. Runners don't train too hard the week before a race—rather, they taper. They go to great lengths to take care of themselves. Sleep. Exercise. Do a little review so you feel on top of the material, but don't push it. You're reminding yourself of what you already know. Do some mental contrasting; think about how you'll handle it if something goes wrong. Pick a playlist of songs to get you pumped and in predator mode. Put negative or stressful influences (even if they're your parents) on the sidelines. The night before the test, watch a sitcom or funny movie. Laughter is a great way to relieve stress and open up your thinking. And it's much easier to get a good night's sleep after laughing and relaxing than it is after studying. Now get going. #yougotthis!

Parents: Chill out!

"My parents care more about my grades and my score than they do about me." Ned hears this all the time from his students. And while he knows it's not true, there are obviously some mixed signals going on. So parents, this part is for you.

Parents frequently ask Ned if they should make their kid take a particular test. His advice is always the same: Don't make the decision for them. Give them the information they need and let them decide for themselves. Show them you trust them, advise them, and then let go. There are many reasons to take this approach—it's good for your relationship, it teaches problem solving, it encourages autonomy, and it may actually *harm* their score if you push. What kids believe tends to be self-fulfilling. The more pressure they feel, the less working memory they'll have available and the less motivated they'll be. As Ned's son, Matthew, said so eloquently, "The more you or Mom remind me to do something, the less I want to do it."

There's also always the chance that your kid will use the test as a very expensive "screw you." Ned's colleague had one student who was dead set against taking a practice test. Her parents enrolled her anyway. They dropped her off, they made sure she entered the exam room, and—because she suffered from anxiety—they ensured she had special accommodations, including extra time to take the test. The result of the five-hour test? A bubbled-in sheet filled with lovely patterns and designs, but not many correct answers.

We know this is tough. You want the best for your kid, and sometimes it feels that if he would just focus more, or if you could just inch him a little bit closer to his goal, he'd get there. It hurts you to see him struggle or fail at anything; you want to protect him and make his path forward as easy as possible. Remember, we're parents, too. We get it. But you're in it with your kids for the long haul, and part of being a parent is standing on the sidelines sometimes so that they can return to you for a hug and pep talk before going back out there. That's where it's most important for you to stand. So stand tall, don't forget to cheer, and at the end of the day, remind them that you care much more about them than any stupid test score.

What to Do Tonight

- If your child is anxious about test taking, offer to sit in the room while they take a practice test. Read a book rather than checking e-mails.

- Talk through Plan B scenarios weeks (not the week) before a test, to help your child ward off anxiety. You might say something like, "Do you want to talk for a few minutes about ways to think about this that might make it less stressful? If what you want doesn't happen, it's not going to be a disaster. That's not the way the world works. If you're shooting for a 30 or 33 on the ACT, what would happen if you got a 28? What would happen if the college you want to go to is out of your range? Let's talk about a Plan B and let your brain know that it's not the end of the world if you don't reach your goal."

- Ask your child to think or write a paragraph about the values that are most important to her before she takes the exam. Ideally, do not ask to see it. Tell her, "This is for you alone."

- Drive your child to the testing site the week before so he can check it out. If kids can visualize the test in advance, they will feel more control over the situation when the big day comes.

- Familiarize yourself with the more than 850 test-optional colleges and universities at www.fairtest.org. Knowing that plenty of great colleges don't require standardized tests for admission can afford your son or daughter all sorts of Plan B options for college.

- Plan for your child to take the ACT or SAT more than once. Kids do better if they know they can take a mulligan.

- Know that a little stress actually helps kids perform better. But to keep an optimal amount of stress, make sleep a family priority, and talk with your kid about taking the ACT or SAT during a week when there is less going on at school and with extracurricular activities.

CHAPTER THIRTEEN

Who's Ready for College?

MANY PEOPLE SEE college as the end of the road, and never stop to think of what it will be like when they get there. It reminds us of the way expectant parents (especially those expecting their first child) will fret over every aspect of pregnancy and childbirth. Then the baby comes, and the worrying doesn't stop—in fact, they discover that the real challenges have only just begun.

The college environment is drastically different from most kids' experience in high school, and many teens haven't developed some of the fundamental skills they will need to function in that environment before leaving home. They may have worked their tails off to get good scores on their standardized tests, thrown themselves into their homework and extracurriculars, and finished their school applications on time, but it's all been with their parents watching in the background, making sure the wheels don't come off. For many, it's chaos when their parents are no longer there to nag and remind and set limits.

Bill tested Suzanne for learning disabilities off and on beginning in second grade. Suzanne was diagnosed with ADHD, but with the help of Ritalin, she was able to do well throughout elementary, middle, and high school. She enrolled in an elite private university, and saw Bill for testing during her junior year. She complained that she often had to stay up all night to study for tests—and sometimes two nights in a row. The reason studying took so long was that she was having a harder time concentrating, and more trouble learning and remembering things. "I think," she said, "that the Ritalin I've been taking all these years to treat my ADHD is rotting my brain." She added that her mother felt the problem was alcohol.

"So how much do you drink?" Bill asked.

"About five drinks a night, four nights a week," she said. Bill said that was enough for her to qualify as an alcoholic, to which Suzanne responded, "My best friend drinks twelve drinks a night, six nights a week."

There is much to unpack in this story, but what is perhaps the most stunning is that Suzanne had to be led to connect her toxic behavior—sleep deprivation and binge drinking—to her difficulty focusing and learning. College affects many smart kids in similar ways.

This is because college is often a brain-toxic environment. Let's consider for a moment the daily stressors that most college students experience:

An average bedtime of 2:00 to 3:00 A.M. One high school student Bill evaluated finally got his sleep problem under control with the help of melatonin. By the end of his senior year, he was able to go to sleep by midnight on most nights. Then he went to college and his regimen fell apart because his roommates always stayed up until 4:00. As another freshman client recently told Bill, going to bed at 3:30 is "pretty normal" because in college "everything happens between midnight and 3:00 A.M." Extensive research has indicated that college students as a group are massively sleep deprived. The average student sleeps only six to six and a half hours per night—with some studies suggesting even less.[1]

There are practical obstacles to sleep, of course—when your roommate's got the light on or the noise level is high, it's challenging to go to bed. But college students also commonly have highly dysregulated sleep cycles, which Robert Stickgold calls "sleep bulemia" (binging on weekends and vacations and purging on school nights).[2] Given school-related stress, the lack of regularity in their sleep cycles, and the sleep-impairing effects of binge drinking and technology, college students are at least as likely as older adults to experience sleep disorders. Students who do not sleep enough pay for it with poorer academic performance and increased risk for a wide range of emotional problems.[3]

But for many high school and college students, there's also a strange psychological component at work. How little you sleep becomes a badge of honor, something worthy of bragging about.

Ned once had four back-to-back appointments with girls from an elite girls' high school who had just finished their junior year term paper. The first girl looked pretty beat up. "I was up until, like, 2:00 A.M. finishing my paper," she said. When she walked out and the second one walked in, Ned said, "Wow, Susie was really tired. Was the term paper rough?" "Yeah," said the second girl. "I got two hours of sleep last night." The third girl one-upped the previous girl. She'd pulled an all-nighter. And the last? She was like Daffy Duck having a meltdown about Bugs Bunny. "All-nighter? All-nighter? Ha! I haven't slept in two days!!!" These girls, remember, were in high school. The problems only amplify in college, when parents are nowhere to be seen.

The competition for who's most exhausted is ridiculous, of course, but it helps to understand the reasoning behind it. If two roommates are taking the same chemistry midterm, and one goes to sleep at 10:00 P.M. while the other uses the time between 10:00 P.M. and 2:00 A.M. to study, the one who sleeps may feel she hasn't done enough to prepare (when sleeping is actually the best thing she can do). The one who stays up until 2:00 A.M. may think that the extra hours of study exculpate her from responsibility if the test doesn't go well. Hey, at least she did everything she could, right? And on and on it goes.

Hours of unstructured time. College students aren't required to sit in class, nor are they committed to a forty-hour workweek. One survey study found that they spend fifteen hours a week studying, while a second recent study found that students spent nineteen hours a week on education-related activities, and *twenty-nine hours* on socializing and leisure.[4] That leaves many hours to fill, and for many kids, this is their first chance to decide how to spend their time on their own. It's a great opportunity, but for many it can be dangerous. They will find themselves going from highly structured days where their classes are in sequentially planned forty-five-minute increments to total freedom, where classes are optional, meals are erratic, there's a lot of eating after midnight, a lot of late-night partying, and little to no supervision.

A culture where binge drinking is the norm. A recent Harvard University study found that 44 percent of students at four-year colleges drink at the binge level or higher (a minimum of five drinks in a row for boys and four for girls).[5] That is almost half the class. Full-time students between the ages of eighteen and twenty-two are somewhat more likely to drink and to drink more heavily than their peers who are not attending college, suggesting that college life may actually encourage heavy drinking.[6] Bill recently did a consultation with a student who just finished his freshman year at an elite private university. He told Bill that all the "social kids" in college binge drink on Tuesday night, Thursday night, Friday night, Saturday during the day, and Saturday night. He also said that they smoke weed every single day. In addition to making students more likely to get behind in their classes and engage in a lot of dangerous activities (vandalism, trouble with the police, unplanned and unprotected sex, and drunk driving), evidence is emerging that binge drinking compromises learning and memory, in part by affecting the development of new neurons in the hippocampus.[7]

The drinking habits of teens have changed dramatically over the last few decades. Whereas once they used to drink to have fun, now they drink to obliterate themselves.[8] This is not surprising, given that stress plays an important role in the chemical use of young people. Adolescent monkeys will double their alcohol intake under stress,[9] and a recent survey study reported that smoking, drinking, and drug use increased 100 percent in human adolescents when they were under high stress.[10] As we mentioned in Chapter One, young adults are more anxious than ever before, and when life feels out of control, you either cope or you give up. Binge drinking is the way many cope; it offers a profound sense of escape. When kids are drunk they feel more powerful and more connected. It's a quick fix, but long term it's disastrous.

Food-related issues. Many college students have never shopped or prepared food for themselves and don't know how to eat responsibly. And, when you're tired—as so many are—brain chemicals that regulate eating are out of whack. The inhibitory function of the prefrontal cortex, that voice which tells you to stop eating, is enfeebled. Those who eat in a dining hall may be vulnerable to the Freshman Fifteen, and full-blown eating disorders usually begin in college.[11] In fact, 25 percent of college students try to control their weight through bulimia-associated behaviors.[12] Eating disorders are often the manifestation of a rigid and unhealthy attempt to create an illusion of control when healthy opportunities are lacking.

Stimulant abuse. Adderall and other stimulants are used frequently and in an unregulated way by students who haven't been diagnosed with ADHD but who are self-medicating. They are used most often by struggling students, usually in the mistaken belief that they will improve their academic performance. Stimulant users are more likely than other students to drink heavily and to use illegal drugs. Also, many students use stimulants to heighten their experience at parties when they are under the influence of other chemicals.[13]

Put this all together, and college housing may be the most stressful and dysregulated living environment outside of a war zone. We don't shy away from making this connection when we speak, and recently we got this note from an audience member at one of our lectures: "I am a vet from Afghanistan. You are so right. What I see at college is nearly as bad as that was. At least there, we had commanders telling us lights out." It's no wonder that there's a growing epidemic of mental health problems on college campuses, and that suicide is the second leading cause of death among college-aged students.[14]

Dr. Richard Kadison sounded an alarm about the "mental health crisis" on college campuses in 2004.[15] His concern was based in part on the findings from a study of mental health trends at Kansas State University between 1988 and 2001. This study found a 58 percent increase in anxiety and stress-related problems over a thirteen-year period. The rate of depression nearly doubled, as did the rate of personality disorders, developmental disorders, psychiatric medication use, and suicidality.[16] More recent studies have confirmed this trend. College freshmen now report the highest stress and lowest mental health levels in twenty-five years.[17] In one survey conducted in 2010, 44 percent of students seeking help at a college counseling center were found to have very serious psychiatric problems, in contrast to the 16 percent who demonstrated serious problems a decade earlier. Although depression and anxiety are still the most common referral problems for college counseling centers, growing numbers of students report stress-related eating disorders, substance abuse, and self-injury.[18]

Given the brain-toxic lifestyles that many college students lead, it's not surprising that they often don't have much to show for their four or five years on campus. A recent book called *Academically Adrift* by Richard Arum and Josipa Roksa revealed that more than 45 percent of the 2300 undergraduates at twenty-four colleges who took the College Learning Assessment showed no significant improvement by the end of their sophomore year in critical thinking, writing skills, or complex reasoning. After four years, a full 36 percent failed to demonstrate significant improvement in these areas, despite the tremendous maturation in the prefrontal cortex that occurs during this period. Although Arum and Roksa attribute this striking lack of intellectual development to colleges valuing research over teaching, and students seeking easy courses and failing to study adequately, the fact that students' brains tend to function at such a low level of efficiency is also highly relevant. Something is seriously wrong with this picture, and we think it has a lot to do with the lack of control kids have going into college, and the fact that their brains have not been allowed to mature effectively.[19]

Is your kid ready to manage the alternate universe that is college life in America? This is a question that it takes courage to ask—and one that we wish more parents were asking. In this chapter, we'll help you prepare your kids for college in a way that develops their sense of control, and we'll give you ideas for what to do if they're just not ready. But first, you may need to change your own thinking about college.

College Is Not an Entitlement

For many kids, college is a really expensive party. They are usually excited to go, but they look at us blankly when we speak about the long hours they'll need to spend studying.

Todd was bright, and his high SAT scores got him into an excellent school in the Northeast. But all his accomplishments in high school depended on the structure his parents provided. They hounded him to go to bed at night, dragged him out of bed in the morning, restricted his use of television and electronic games, and tried to police his homework. When he went to college and that structure was removed, it all came crashing down. We weren't surprised when Todd was placed on academic probation after his first semester. That summer he was placed on academic leave and was required to take a semester off. It ultimately took two more false starts—and a lot of emotional and financial resources from his parents—for Todd to finish college.

We see lots of kids every year who, like Todd, go off to college before they can independently get themselves into or out of bed, manage their own academic work, hold a part-time job, or regulate their use of their cell phone, video games, and other electronic entertainment. Many of them have had parents or guidance counselors who have essentially force-marched them down the straight path to college, reinforcing the idea that it's more important to try to make kids do well than to help them truly understand that they are responsible for their own lives.

We need to overhaul the way we think about college. Currently, in many middle-class and upper-middle-class families, it's seen as an entitlement, not something that's earned. Bill frequently hears parents say things like, "I know he's not ready for college, but I can't talk him out of going"—as if it were a God-given right. Parents should consider sending their kid to college just as they'd consider a business investment—because it *is* a huge investment. Youth may be wasted on the young, but that's nothing like the education misspent on students who are not yet ready to learn. Would you invest $50,000 for each of the next four years in a company without a proven track record of sound decision making? Of course not. So don't invest money in an experience a kid isn't ready for. Almost 50 percent of the students who enroll in four-year colleges don't graduate.[20] And when they don't, it's painful to the kids and costly to their parents. Kids who attend a four-year college for two or three years commonly have nothing to show for it beyond their student loans. We've seen way too many parents who have not saved for retirement because they've put that money into their child's educa-tion instead. This is a serious financial decision with real conse-quences for everyone in the family, so we need to be smart about it.

Do They Go or Do They Gap? (How to Tell if They're Ready)

There are many reasons why adolescents might not be ready to go to college right after high school. They may lack the adequate aca-demic skills. They may lack self-awareness or self-regulation skills, or struggle with anxiety or depression. They may not be ready to manage the details of living independently. Or they may be burned out from four years of going pedal to the metal in high school. They may be prone to social isolation. Or their brains simply may not be developed enough. Remember, just as kids develop physically at different rates, the same is true of their brains.

Some questions to ask when determining your child's college readiness include:

Does your child accept responsibility for his own life?

Who initiated the college search? If a student is not able to com-plete his applications and college essay independently, or with some help that he seeks out, he is probably not ready to start college. Some kids are so sheltered that they reach the age of seventeen without much of a sense of how to take care of themselves—or even what it would take to do so. Can you really send your child to live on his own in an unregulated environment if he's never once thought of taking care of his laundry or cooking a meal? Ned once tutored a kid who had no idea what a sieve was. "Oh," Ned said, "it's like a colander." The kid looked at Ned blankly. "You know," Ned said encouragingly, "if you're making spaghetti, after it cooks you put it in the colander to drain the water out. It's that metal thing with the holes in the bottom."

"I don't cook. No one in my family does," the kid said.

"Wow, you must eat out a lot," Ned mused.

"Duh, Ned," the boy replied, "we have a housekeeper."

Having a housekeeper does not disqualify one from attending college, obviously. But in this kid's case, he had been raised to believe that everything should be done for him. When he enrolled at the University of Georgia, it did not go well. Ned ran into him over Thanksgiving break, and he proclaimed that everyone at school was "so stupid. What a bunch of idiots." He flunked out by the end of his first semester. He had no sense of ownership whatsoever. Things happened *to* him, and so his failures were all someone else's fault.

Does your kid have adequate self-understanding?

Does she know what's hard for her and how it affects her? Does she recognize that when she doesn't get eight hours of sleep, she gets emotional? Does she know that when she gets stressed, it really helps her to go for a run? Does she understand when she works best and when she needs to rest? Does she know what she is likely to need help with in college? Now you may say that one could ask these questions of many adults and find them wanting, but a basic level of self-understanding and a willingness to take care of oneself and to moderate or change behavior if necessary for one's well-being is essential for your child to thrive in a college environment.

Does your kid have enough self-regulation to run his life?

Can he get himself in and out of bed and stay adequately rested? If his roommate is up until 4:00 A.M., will he be able to hold to his own routine? Can he regulate his use of technology or gaming? If he uses drugs or drinks, does he know when to stop? If the answer to any one of these questions is no, you may want to consider holding off on college until he can gain a better measure of self-control.

Does your kid have adequate self-motivation for school?

Can she say no to something fun when there's homework to do? Does she ask for support when she needs it? Does she keep up with assignments and appointments? Can she work for several hours on a project?

Years ago, Ned met with Joel twice a week through his junior year in high school. His dad explained that Joel would not do any work outside of the tutoring, so Ned should just try to make good use of the time they spent together.

Joel had his eyes on the Ivy League school his whole family had attended. He was really good at math but struggled with vocabulary. Every week he would ask Ned, "Do you think I can get 700s?" Ned said, "Yeah, I do. You can get there. You just need to put in a few minutes of vocab each day, and bit by bit you'll get there."

"Okay," Joel said, "give me stuff to do." The next lesson, he'd show up (as his dad predicted) having done no work and ask, "Do you think I can get 700s?" It was like *Groundhog Day*. He made incremental progress, mainly because his parents were propping him up with twice-weekly visits to Ned. But when he went to college— he did make it into that Ivy League school—he was on his own, and he didn't finish the first semester. Is it any wonder? So often parents carry their kids 26.1 miles of a marathon, then set them down when they're within sight of the finish line. When they cross over that finish line, everyone hugs and congratulates them. But they haven't really gotten there. They had very little to do with it—and they know it.

You won't get a sense of control over your life by avoiding hard work or receiving unearned trophies. It comes from diligence and commitment. Most folks are proud of their scars. Few runners brag about their marathon times, but they will regale you about blisters, cramps, and how they could barely move by the end . . . but still finished. We gain strength from what we invest in and accomplish.

Can your kid manage day-to-day living independently?

Does he make and keep his own appointments? Pay his own traffic fines? Do his own laundry? Manage his own medications? Make good social choices? Can he keep track of important things like his wallet and keys? Many freshmen have called their parents when locked out of their dorm. What are Mom and Dad supposed to do about it from hundreds if not thousands of miles away? Can he problem solve on his own? Or better yet, not lose his keys in the first place?

Does your kid have healthy ways to manage or relieve stress?

Everyone experiences stress. And everyone will find a way to relieve stress. If your kid doesn't have healthy ways to relieve stress, he will find unhealthy ones. We reckon that there would be much less binge drinking and pot smoking on college campuses if there were more sleep, exercise, and meditation.

Is your kid burned out?

Ned sees a lot of exhausted kids who feel they are on a constant treadmill. His student Elaine told him, "When I think about how all I've done in high school is work to get grades and scores, I feel like I wasted four years of my life. I didn't do anything fun." We worry about kids like Elaine. Many are anxious or depressed, and they're going into a dysregulated environment that will exacerbate their vulnerability. Some will develop eating disorders, others will abuse alcohol to let off steam or engage in self-harm. And no parent is there to see what's going on. Does your burned-out kid have healthy coping mechanisms? Know techniques for stress management? Know to take a break sometimes?

Does your child have the academic skills to do college-level work?

College students need to be able to read, understand, and remember information from college-level texts at a speed that allows them to complete their reading, papers, problem sets, and other assignments. In addition, they need to have the ability to plan, organize, and prioritize their multiple academic tasks and to prepare adequately for exams. Many kids are overwhelmed by the volume of work in college, and by the steep step up in academic expectations.

If your student needs academic support, will he ask for it and use it?

Many high school students with learning disabilities, ADHD, and autism spectrum disorders are reluctant to use the accommodations they've been offered, like extra time for tests, or recorded books. This tendency doesn't magically go away in college. Many students resent or are embarrassed by the implication that they need help or need to work with a tutor to improve their writing, so they blow off the tutoring and drift off course.

Does your child have the social competence to manage a complex social environment?

For students who are socially vulnerable, it can be overwhelming to have to manage the new academic challenges of college and the social and independent living demands of a college dormitory simultaneously. Many kids who are awkward or unskilled socially will falter. Perhaps they're great at independent learning—but do they also have the ability to develop friendships and negotiate conflicts with their dorm mates? Can they handle a social environment of frat parties and binge drinking and the pressure to hook up?

When parents answer these questions honestly, many will determine that their kid isn't ready to go off to college . . . at least not right now. So now what?

What to Do if Your Kid Isn't Ready

More kids than ever are going on to college. In some ways, that's great—we're all for giving opportunities to kids who are ready for them. But as moving straight from high school to college has become the norm in more and more communities, there's an attendant belief that if you do not go straight to college it means you are a failure.

This just doesn't make sense. We understand that kids have growth spurts at different times—we know the pipsqueak who couldn't make the basketball team as a freshman may be a star point guard by his senior year. The sheer force of your will won't make your child ready if he isn't ready. He has to get there by himself.

And yet many parents are desperate for their kids to move on. They are tired of the job of chief overseers. Those who have the means don't care so much if the investment in college is a bad one—they just need a break. College is the socially acceptable path, and a way for parents to get that break. They don't know about other options.

In places like Germany, Denmark, Australia, and the UK, taking a "gap year" (or two) to travel, work, or even serve in the military is highly encouraged. In Israel, students start college after two years of military or national service—and thus with the advantage of life experience and two additional years of prefrontal cortex development. Why not in the United States? We aren't the only ones asking this question. Agencies like the Center for Interim Programs are trying to make gap years more mainstream, and Malia Obama's decision to take a gap year has only intensified interest in the subject.

Jason Sarouhan, vice president of the Center for Interim Programs, says there are five categories of students who benefit from taking a gap year:

The worker, *with high test scores and a high grade point average.* To our minds, this is the student like Elaine who's been on a treadmill for four years and is burned out.

The meaning seeker, *generally with high test scores and a lower GPA.* These are kids who are very smart, but don't apply themselves unless they see a compelling reason to do so; they want meaning behind their actions.

The pragmatist, *who wants to attend college with a clearer focus.* J. D. Vance, the author of *Hillbilly Elegy,* is a good example of this. His childhood was unstructured and full of upheaval, and he just could not see taking out the loans to attend college when he wasn't sure he was ready. He chose to enlist in the military first.

The struggler, *whose high school experience has been clouded by learning differences.* For most kids with ADHD, it makes sense to buy some time for their brains to develop a bit more, to set them up for success when they start college.

The floater, *who isn't fully engaged with life and may be on the immature side.* This is the kid who's been carried 26.1 miles of the marathon. He's just not ready to go over the finish line—he hasn't earned it himself yet.[21]

Most kids who aren't ready for college fall into one of these five categories, and most would benefit from taking a break.

"I was always very aware of the change in my life that was going to occur after I graduated high school," wrote Katherine Engman in a blog post about her gap year. "I viewed it as the second chapter to my life; a chapter where I could take control of my future." Katherine helped monkeys reenter the wild and climbed mountains in Costa Rica, both amazing experiences. But we are struck by how making the decision to take a gap year was in itself of enormous value to Katherine. "Every single day I think to myself, this has been the best decision I have ever made. . . . I have become very confident in my decision-making skills and ability to adapt to different environments. . . . I have for the first time, taken control of my life and have chosen to do what makes me happy."[22]

Taking the time to get off autopilot and to be intentional about decisions is a great growth opportunity. Many students who take gap years spend the time focusing on their interest—be it through a wildlife research study or language immersion school or community service of some kind—and are better suited to study that interest and turn it into a career. Others gain practical, real-world experience or military experience that better prepares them to be the adults they in fact are.

Lest you think that gap years are only for the well-to-do whose families can afford to send them traveling, that's not the case. Many gap year programs are work-studies, and while gappers might not be saving for retirement, they're not going into debt over it, either. In fact, those who take a gap year save money by sharpening their focus so that when they do attend college, they finish more quickly.[23]

It's Your Call, but My Investment

Let's say that your child is dead set on college, but you have misgivings. If he has a full scholarship or is paying his own tuition, it's his call. But if you are providing some financial support for the college years, it's reasonable for you to identify yourself as a stakeholder. You might say, "Go to college if you like. But if you want me to make an investment in your education, I need to see certain criteria met before I feel comfortable." This is a perfectly reasonable position. Kids who aren't ready for college often lack the self-awareness to know it. Many of these kids insist that they will get it together when college starts, but they aren't really making informed decisions. You can help them gather the information by simply asking them to prove to you that they're ready.

Mixed in with fear about kids not going to college immediately is the fear that if they don't go right after high school, they won't go at all. This may have been a valid concern once. In the 1950s and early '60s, many seventeen-year-olds dropped out of school and were able to work at a factory job and make enough money to support a family of four. Many of them never needed to go to college. Generally, that's not possible anymore.

There's no shortage of things to worry about as a parent, and concerns about our kids feeling bad are always near the top. This is why parents frequently tell us, "My kid will feel terrible about himself if he doesn't go to college." We particularly hear this concern from families in which college is the norm for their relatives and their communities.

As a parent, you can't make all your kid's disappointment and pressure go away, but you can start planting ideas early that there are alternate routes, which is the subject of the next chapter.

What to Do Tonight

- Prep early. If your child is not ready for college when she graduates in June, she's probably not going to be ready when fall semester starts. The process of encouraging readiness must begin much earlier. Start suggesting as early as ninth grade that college is something that needs to be earned. Begin to outline together the kinds of skills your child will need to develop over the next four years in order to demonstrate their readiness. Tell him you will want to see that he can basically run his own life for at least six months prior to going off to college.

- If your child wants to go to college and appears to be capable of developing college-level academic skills, but is not yet ready, emphasize that the question is one of *when* she'll go, not *if*.

- Encourage your child to get work experience. Successful job experience is a very good predictor of college success.

- If your teen is going to college soon, talk about what it will be like and what it will take for it to be a good experience. Discuss what he or she feels are the best ways for you to be supportive without being intrusive, to stay connected without hovering.

- Prepare yourself for the transition. Stay connected but keep a strong focus on your own life. Remind your child that your home will always be a base. Talk to your spouse about your changing roles.

CHAPTER FOURTEEN

Alternate Routes

A Stressed Teen Manifesto

Do you know how stressful it is to work so hard in everything
and know that there are always other people who are better,
that you can never be the best? And, when you have parents
who are super smart and super successful, and they went to
Harvard and are successful attorneys and you're wondering
how you will ever be successful and be able to afford a house
and have a family? And you're thinking, "My parents are
smart and I go to a great school, so why can't I do the same
thing they do?" And, "I wonder if I'll be able to get into a
good college, even one that isn't nearly as good as where they
went or as good as what they expect of me."

The teen who wrote this, a student of Ned's, sees the route to a
successful life as precariously narrow, with deep drop-offs on either
side. Straight As and great test scores? Awesome, you're on the
path. Stymied by geometry? Yikes, there's the ledge.

This habit of all-or-nothing thinking can start early and persist
well past college. At a workplace picnic, Ned found himself chat-
ting with the boyfriend of one of his colleagues. The subject of
college came up, and Ned asked if the twentysomething guy
had gone.

"No," he said flatly. "I'm not really very smart. School wasn't
for me."

Ned paused for a moment to take in all the messages this young man had internalized, like:

People who don't go to college aren't smart.

Learning is only for some people.

I'm not as good as other people.

"Well," Ned said, "there are lots of ways people can find success in life or contribute to the world. What are you doing right now?"

"Oh, I'm just an EMT," responded the guy.

Just an EMT. As in an emergency medical technician, someone whose job is to *save lives.*

The conversation sparked a question we love to ask kids: What job do you think has saved the most lives over the last hundreds of years? Though a healthy debate could be had, we think the likely answer is sanitation worker. But EMT would be near the top of that list. Think about it this way: In a crisis, who would you most want to show up to help: A) an investment banker, B) a lawyer, C) a neuropsychologist, D) an SAT tutor, or E) an EMT?

Yeah, that's what we thought.

One of the major challenges keeping young people from developing a healthy sense of control is their narrow and distorted views of the adult world and what it takes to be successful and have a satisfying life, which we've discussed earlier in the book. These views foster fear and competition. They affect high-achieving kids, for whom a rigid view of the path to success creates unnecessary stress, anxiety, and mental health problems, and low-achieving kids, many of whom conclude at a young age that they will never be successful, so why try at all. Many of these young people engage in one of the most debilitating forms of self-talk, telling themselves, "I have to do X, Y, and Z, but I can't," or, "I have to do X, Y, and Z, but I hate it."

These kids have a deeply distorted view of what it takes to be successful. Sometimes it comes from their parents, but it can also come from their schools and their peers. Both the obsessively driven and the undermotivated have it in their heads that if they aren't top students, they're losers and will be working at McDonald's at age fifty.

The reality is that we become successful in this world by working hard at something that comes easily to us and that engages us. We need to tell our kids that the skill set required to be a successful student is, in many ways, very different from the skill set that will lead you to have a successful career and a good life.

Being a straight-A student almost by definition requires a high level of conformity, which is not the route to a high level of success. A 4.0 GPA also points to an attempt to be equally good at everything, which doesn't necessarily translate well in the real world. We need to assure kids that the majority of successful people were not straight-A students. It turns out, in fact, that high school valedictorians are no more successful than other college graduates by their late twenties.[1] Ability is not a simple matter of grades.

Don't misunderstand us: being a good student and getting a degree from an elite college clearly have their benefits, but there are alternate paths. Focusing all our attention on just one path will make a lot of kids feel left out.

The Real Reality

Each time he closed his *Prairie Home Companion* series, radio host Garrison Keillor said the following: "Well, that's the news from Lake Wobegon, where all the women are strong, all the men are good-looking, and all the children are above average." His gentle humor is right on point. We all want to believe that our child is above average, and ignore the simple fact that every parent thinks so and we can't all be right. Since we test kids for a living, we know that a third of the population has math and language skills below the 33rd percentile. And yet many kids with these skill levels are preparing to go to college, unaware of the great difficulty they'll have in handling the conceptual and quantitative work they'll encounter. The idea that you *have* to get a college degree is, for many, a toxic message. Many of these students, no matter how hard they try, simply cannot complete four years of college-level work. Instead of living in this delusion, we should be sharing realities, like:

- The majority of Americans do not graduate from college. Although the statistics vary from year to year, the findings have indicated for decades that only somewhere in the neighborhood of 25 to 32 percent of the adult population holds a degree from a four-year college.

- Many people who finish college or graduate school end up taking a circuitous route to academic success.

- Many adults who were top students and have forged successful careers are miserable.

- Where—or if—you go to college does not set the path for your life. Bill Gates, Steve Jobs, and Mark Zuckerberg are probably the most famous college dropouts. Many others went to "just fine" schools and went on to do extremely well, like Google cofounder Sergey Brin, who went to the University of Maryland. The last two dozen Americans to win the Nobel Prize in Medicine got their undergraduate degrees at places like Harvard and Brown, sure, but also from DePauw, Holy Cross, and Gettysburg College.[2] The recently retired president of Princeton University went to Denison University, a small liberal arts school in Ohio.

- Following your passion is more energizing than doing what you feel you have to do.

- There are currently over 3,500 occupations through which Americans make a living, many of which do not require a college degree.

The Virtues of Diversity

Society thrives on the diverse talents of its people. Biodiversity is a sign of a healthy system. We need dreamers, artists, and creative people. We need entrepreneurs and people who make things happen. We need people who are physically strong or gifted at working with their hands. Albert Einstein said, "If you judge a fish by its ability to climb a tree, it will live its whole life believing that it is stupid." As developmental psychologist Howard Gardner pointed out, there are many different forms of intelligence: it can be musical-rhythmic, visual-spatial, verbal-linguistic, logical-mathematical, bodily-kinesthetic, interpersonal, intrapersonal, and naturalistic.[3] In other words, you can be a poor student and a brilliant dancer (or vice versa). You can be average in most things but exceptional at reading others' emotions. The key is in finding your strength.

The problem we see—in high school in particular—is that kids are led to believe that in order to be successful they need to be superior at everything, from English to science to foreign languages. It's all too easy to look around and find others who are better at most anything. Making it your goal to be "the best" means constantly comparing yourself to others. It could motivate you, but more often it will be demotivating. Part of growing up is knowing when to let go, and choosing what not to pursue.

Bill frequently tells the older children and adolescents he is testing, "I hope I find things you suck at—because successful people are good at some things and not so good at others, but wisely make a living doing something they're good at." (With younger kids he simply says, "I hope I find something you're not very good at.") Put another way, you are unlikely to find the path to success by building on your weakest skills and working to become merely adequate. Many students have trouble accepting this. One of Ned's students, David, balked when Ned suggested that part of his work as an adolescent was to explore not only what he liked but what he was better at than most people and to work hard at that.

"But isn't that wrong?" David asked. "Isn't it cheating to just do what's easy?"

Ned's response: "Look, you're five eight and 180 pounds. You can bench press 380 pounds. That's why you're a running back. But you would be a horrible marathoner. You don't have the build."

Ned wasn't suggesting that David give up on everything he wasn't naturally good at. There's important learning to be done in school and in life, even in subjects that don't come easily. But there's also value in recognizing and nurturing your natural talents.

When kids tell their parents, "I'm not as smart as Eric," or "I'm not as smart as most of the kids in my math class," many parents will try to reassure their kids by saying, "Yes, you are. You're just as smart as they are." Bill takes a different approach. He tells kids that you only have to be smart enough to do something interesting in this world—which they are. He also tells them that he's grateful for all the people in his field who are smarter than he is. They're the ones who make up the theories and tests that allow him to make a living by helping people.

Breaking the Mass Psychosis

Bill once evaluated an eight-year-old boy whose mother told him that she would only pay for college if her son went to Harvard, Yale, Princeton, or Brown. Bill laughed, assuming she was joking, but the mother curtly assured him she was not. Trying to sound as reasonable as he could, Bill said, "You realize that's a little crazy, in the sense that the vast majority of successful people do not go to Harvard, Yale, Princeton, or Brown?" The mother was clearly infuriated and snapped, "That's the way I feel about it. That's the way it's going to be."

Many people hold beliefs that are simply not in touch with reality. We refer to this kind of unfounded belief system that many—especially affluent—adults subscribe to as a "shared delusion." Schools know the odds better than parents—after all, they see hundreds of kids each year—and yet they often support this kind of out-of-touch thinking. When we ask high school principals and independent school heads, "Why don't you just tell kids the truth about college? That where you go makes very little difference in later life and isn't a predictor of success?" they consistently say, "If we did that, we would get angry calls and letters from parents who believe that if their children understood the truth, they would not work hard in school and would fail in life."

We have found that simply telling kids the truth about the world—including the advantages of being a good student—increases their flexibility and drive. It motivates unmotivated kids to shift the emphasis from "Here are the hoops I will have to jump through to be successful" to "Here are some of the many ways I can choose to develop myself in order to make an important contribution to this world." When we talk about alternate routes with friends and colleagues and at talks in schools, everybody has a story. Their car mechanic has a PhD in engineering from MIT but left engineering for a more satisfying career; or perhaps their mechanic did not go to college, but was so outstanding at what he did, and was such a successful businessman that he retired at age thirty-two because he had twelve mechanics working for him. Or, on the flip side, their friend has two PhDs but dropped out of high school.

In the name of undermining the mass psychosis, and because anecdotes are often more powerful than statistics, we will use the rest of this chapter to tell some of our favorite stories of happy, successful people who have gotten there via unconventional means. Bill himself took an alternate route to neuropsychology, so we'll start with him.

Bill

I graduated from high school with a 2.8. I was much more interested in playing rock and roll music (organ, bass, guitar) than in studying, and I flunked English the first quarter of my senior year. My intellectual interest did hit, though, when I was nineteen. I got my college degree from the University of Washington and went on to attend graduate school in English at the University of California, Berkeley. I envisioned getting my PhD and becoming Professor Stixrud at age twenty-six. It did not turn out that way. I suffered from anxiety, a lack of self-confidence, and probably overuse of caffeine, and I was more gifted at avoiding assignments than anything else. I went for twenty weeks without turning in a single paper. (I tell the serious underachievers I see, "Top that!") Not surprisingly, I flunked out of graduate school. I was beyond embarrassed and very worried that I had blown up my whole future. Then I came home to the Seattle area to think over what to do next. (My father had recently passed away, and my mother was supportive and encouraging that I would figure out something else.) I took a job in a typing pool, and was soon fired from that . . . probably because my anxiety made the other workers in the typing pool nervous (I wasn't *that* bad a typist). Then I landed a job doing manual labor, filling orders in a warehouse. All things considered, it wasn't a great time in my life.

I had a lot of free time outside of work, and I found that I greatly enjoyed spending time with my four-year-old niece. I remember taking her on her first bus ride and how much fun it was just listening to the questions she asked and the way she answered my questions. I thought back to the times in my life when my family had vacationed with families who had younger children and how, although I didn't like to admit it, I enjoyed being with younger kids. This gave me the idea to work with children.

I started taking education classes and eventually got a degree and became a teacher. I went on to get a master's degree in special education and taught off and on. The one year I taught full time I had a headache every Monday. In retrospect, I think this is because, while I had some strengths as a teacher (I was nice), I had terrible behavior management skills and found it stressful trying to manage a group of young students with special needs. This made me realize that if I was going to work with children, it would have to be in a different context. At the age of thirty-two, I finished up my doctorate in a school psychology program before going on to do a postdoc in clinical neuropsychology. In forty-three years, I have not looked back, and I have not had a headache since that one year of teaching full time.

I realized within six months of leaving Berkeley that flunking out was the best thing that could have happened to me. So often, when it feels like everything is going wrong, things are just being reorganized in helpful ways that we could never anticipate.

Robin

Robin grew up in a middle-class family in Maryland. Through junior high she was at the top of her class and a leader at her school. As an eighth grader, she successfully petitioned to skip the last half of the coursework and move directly on to ninth grade, which she completed in one semester. She began wandering from the standard path the following summer. She became pregnant, ran away with the father of her child, and lived in and out of group homes and seedy hotels. She got her GED, divorced her teenage husband, and soon remarried. Her second husband was a doctor who was controlling and could be cruel.

Though she was a mother of a young boy and stepmother of two others, she found a way to enroll in college at Keene State

College of New Hampshire, and finished at age twenty-seven with a 4.0 GPA. She had always been interested in spirituality, so she applied to Harvard Divinity School. To her surprise, she was accepted. She attended for one semester but then realized that if she wanted to be on a strong-enough financial footing to leave her husband, she would need to make a better living. So she got an MBA and a corporate job as a training and development specialist. When she was more financially secure, Robin left her husband, and soon after, she met Peter, to whom she has been happily married for twenty-four years.

On the professional front, Robin's life took yet another turn. She didn't love the corporate world, so she studied to teach yoga and dance. She published a book on women's spirituality and taught yoga and meditation to at-risk girls. Within a few years, she started working with active-duty military personnel who suffer from acute PTSD and/or traumatic brain injury. She taught yoga and meditation to soldiers at Walter Reed National Military Medical Center, and cofounded an organization, Warriors at Ease, that trains yoga teachers to teach yoga and meditation to soldiers in a way that is sensitive to the effects of trauma and military culture. Her organization has trained over seven hundred teachers around the world, and Warriors at Ease currently serves approximately ten thousand service members each year.

Brian

Brian was a bright kid from a DC suburb who found the school environment to be punishing. His relationship with his parents as a teenager was filled with conflict. They worked hard to set limits, but Brian always managed to work around them. He was cruel to his sister, stayed up late listening to music—largely to keep his parents awake—and challenged them to come in and do something about it.

When he was sixteen, Brian was doing poorly in school, hated it, and spent no time attempting to learn or develop his academic skills. His parents did not feel comfortable letting him drop out, so they ultimately sent him to boarding school in New England. The staff there wasn't much better at setting limits, and Brian ran away to Florida with his girlfriend. In Florida, he and his girlfriend worked at minimum-wage jobs. Eventually, the appeal of freedom waned. The drudgery of menial work caught up with him, and Brian asked his parents if they would fund classes at a community college in Florida, which they agreed to do. After gaining a number of credits there, Brian applied to Evergreen College in Olympia, Washington, where he graduated with a degree in education. Brian later earned a master's degree in education, and he is currently a master educator in the District of Columbia public schools.

The standard route of doing well academically all through school didn't work for Brian. But he was able to find his way to a happy and satisfying career and personal life. Curiously, after struggling to do well academically himself, he has come full circle and his life's work is supporting kids to do well in school.

Peter

Peter was a mediocre student in the Chicago public school system. After attending five different schools he eventually graduated from a small liberal arts college in the Midwest (now an online college) with a degree in English. Because he could find nothing useful to do with his English degree, and because he always enjoyed cooking, he started working as a short-order cook, and pursued the dream of running his own restaurant. For years, Peter held numerous jobs in the food industry, including waiter, maître d', cook, and chef. At one point, he even opened a hot dog stand. Then Peter started working for a chain of restaurants as a lower-level manager, and got experience purchasing supplies. This job was a good match for Peter, who had a good mind for math, exceptional interpersonal skills, and great capacity for "win-win" negotiating. He was soon approached by a start-up restaurant chain with three locations. Peter's work in purchasing impressed his bosses, who gave him shares of stock in the company. When the company went public, it had over three hundred restaurants around the world. Peter has done extremely well professionally and financially, and he also has a wonderful family.

How many ten-year-olds have a burning desire to grow up and be a purchaser for a major restaurant chain? And yet what a wonderful life and career it's been for Peter.

Ben

Ben struggled in school, and remembers science and math as being particularly hard. He found it difficult to motivate himself to do schoolwork, and he (barely) graduated high school with a GPA below 1.0. He always excelled in his art classes, though, and a course he took in calligraphy as a seventh grader made a big impression on him. His parents, a clinical psychologist and an oncology nurse, supported him in taking an alternate route and exploring an art-focused secondary school. Ben's brother had blazed the trail by studying cinematography in a two-year program, and was killing it in Los Angeles. (He is currently one of the most successful cinematographers in Hollywood.) Though Ben enrolled in a three-year art program, he didn't finish three full semesters. He had developed enough skills, though, to get a series of graphic design jobs, and he found one that particularly appealed to him, with an emphasis on branding. When he was just twenty-nine, Ben started his own company, Brand Army. Ironically, since he never got a college degree, his many clients now include George Mason University and Georgetown.

Ben and his brother both followed their passions and were so successful that they're now making far more money than either of their parents. As their dad says, "What I have learned from this is, if you see a spark in your kids, pour gasoline on it."

Lachlan

From the time he was in kindergarten, Lachlan loved to tinker. He was happy to fix broken classroom objects rather than go to recess. In middle school, he impressed his teachers with his intelligence but not his ability to complete assignments. He also showed a rebellious streak. In eighth grade, he hot-wired the school's bell system, which enabled him to push a button at any time to dismiss class. He also put a bypass on the school's alarm system so that he and his friends could get into school whenever they wanted.

As a sixteen-year-old, Lachlan worked at a Shell station. He started off changing tires and oil but soon he was taking the cars apart and rewiring them as a mechanic. He left home and skipped most of his high school classes, and by the end of eleventh grade he had a 0.9 GPA. He managed to squeak by with a high school degree and started to work as an audio engineer. At twenty-one, he was assigned to a contract at the Kennedy Center, where he designed sound systems for the opera house and the concert hall.

Eventually he transitioned into television engineering work. Although he had little prior experience, he worked hard and figured things out on the fly. Through his interests, talents, and efforts, he met people who opened doors that helped him become successful. He started working in engineering management for a national U.S. television network, where he stayed for over twenty years. After a decade he was promoted to a director of engineering position. Clearly Lachlan has an exceptional talent. But he also knew how to do stuff that people would pay for and focused his efforts on improving his skills to measurable ends.

Melody

From an early age, Melody did not enjoy school. She attended kindergarten and first grade only sporadically and by fifth grade she announced to her parents that she would rather not go back to school. Melody's parents had a lot of faith in their daughter, even at the age of ten, and told her that if she wanted to stay home and do an independent study, that was fine with them.

"You can be anything you want to be," they told her. "If that's a professor somewhere, great. If it's a guitar player, great. Just make sure you're doing something you enjoy and work at it to do it well." It was a liberating message, and Melody benefited enormously from the confidence they had in her.

She went back to school for sixth grade and stayed on for a few more years, but when tenth grade came along, again asked to leave. Her parents let her make the call, and she decided to homeschool.

Melody was independent-minded and curious, which made this course of study work for her. But she was also ambitious and wanted to go on to college. She recognized that if college was her goal, she had better return to school for eleventh and twelfth grade, which she did. She went on to attend Stanford, graduating in just over three years, and then worked for ten years before going to law school. For many years now, she's been a partner in a Seattle law firm.

Melody feels the freedom her parents gave her was invaluable, as was their belief that there was not just one narrow path to a good life. "They let me know, 'These aren't permanent decisions. You can decide not to go to fifth grade, and if halfway through you decide you want to go, you can go. That's fine. You're not putting yourself on a path that can't be reversed. You're not making a decision that's going to make or break your entire life. You can always course correct.'"

Interestingly, though Melody appreciated her parents' approach, she didn't adopt it with her own kids. "When my son was done with high school, he said, 'I don't think I want to go to college, I want to take a year off,' and we didn't let him. The fear we had was that—what is he going to do? That could put him off track, maybe he'll have to apply again, maybe he won't go. I don't think we were listening to him say, 'I don't want to do this, I'm not ready.' I have some regret about that."

"But . . .": Questions About Alternate Routes

Parents will often object to the notion that there are alternate routes to a successful and fulfilling life. Part of the reason is that it is very hard to completely separate your own ego from the question of what your child is doing. Some, once their ego has been divested, still have concerns. Here's what we hear most commonly, and how we respond:

"But people who take more standard routes earn so much more money."

It's true that people who are bright and have the discipline to get them through four years of college are likely to do well. But they would be bright and disciplined whether they graduated from college or not. Who can say whether it was their schooling that made them so?

Actor, TV host, and provocateur Mike Rowe started a foundation committed to challenging the idea that success is only available to those with four-year degrees. On the foundation's Web site, Profoundly Disconnected, he makes the argument in three simple bullets:

- A trillion dollars in student loans.
- Record high unemployment.
- Three million good jobs that no one seems to want.[4]

"Isn't going to college more important now that the middle class is shrinking? Employers won't even look at you if you don't have a college degree."

A few points here. First, nobody can predict what the workplace is going to look like in five or ten years, given the influence of robotics and other forms of technology. We know the new workforce will need to have skills, but we don't know what kind of education those skills will require.

Remember Ben, the graphic designer? He said he's confident that he'll always have work because he knows a trade that's needed by other people. He finds more security in knowing how to do something useful than in having a degree.

That said, there are many advantages to having a college degree (and advanced degrees). We want kids to go to college and graduate if they can. But what we really don't want to do is discourage the many kids who can't make it through college. We don't want them to believe that means they can't have a good life.

On Money, Career, and Happiness

It's not within our area of expertise to wax on about how money and success are not one and the same. However, we do think it helps kids to know that, although income and self-reported happiness are highly correlated, the correlation is much stronger at very low levels of income than at high levels—and that after a fairly low level of financial comfort, there is no correlation between increased income and greater happiness.[5] It's not that we want to discourage kids from making money. It's just that we want kids to make thoughtful decisions about their lives based on what's important to them.

We have offered a modest collection of alternate route stories in this chapter, though we have many, many more. Learning about other people's journeys can be enormously empowering, and we hope these will be just the start of your collection. Toward that end, we also recommend that you check out the following books—all great reminders of the many turns happy lives can take:

Shop Class as Soulcraft: An Inquiry into the Value of Work, by Matthew B. Crawford. A reflection by a motorcycle repair shop owner with a PhD in political philosophy about the value of the trades and working with your hands.

The Dirty Life: A Memoir of Farming, Food, and Love, by Kristin Kimball. Kristin was a Harvard-educated New York journalist who left that world behind to run a farm with her husband. She acknowledges, "I was forced to confront my own prejudice. I had come to the farm with the unarticulated belief that concrete things were for dumb people and abstract things were for smart people."

The Element: How Finding Your Passion Changes Everything, by Ken Robinson. Ken is a visionary education consultant who argues that the place where natural talent and personal passion converge is where the magic of life and work happens.

In the end, the best way you can help your child maintain a sense of control and guide him (as a nonanxious consultant) into a satisfying life is to teach him to ask himself two questions: What do I truly love to do? And what can I do better than most people?

It can be that simple.

What to Do Tonight

- Make a list with your child of all the different jobs you can possibly think of together. Not jobs either one of you would necessarily be interested in—just jobs that *someone* is doing. What might those people like about their jobs? What might they be good at?

- Share the stories of alternate routes from this chapter with your child. Tell him or her others you know of, and ask if he or she knows of any.

- Be open about the surprises or disappointments you encountered on your own path, or that your parents or grandparents did, and how you pivoted. Ned's great-grandfather made and lost a fortune in the stock market, and went from the biggest house in town to a small apartment and back again. Knowing that even successful people have ups and downs helped give Ned perspective, as did understanding that resilience was a family tradition.

- Ask your child, What do you love to do? What do you think you're better at than other people? Do you want my view?

- Ask your child, What contributions do you think you would like to make to the world around you? What steps might you take to get there?

- Encourage your child to find a mentor, someone whose life they admire and who can help guide them. Kids will often be more open to guidance from someone who is not their parent.

Onward

BILL ONCE WORKED with a child whose mother was a humorist. Sitting in Bill's office one day, she remarked, "A lot of what we call raising children should really be referred to as lowering parents." It's a clever way to acknowledge that what we recommend isn't easy. In fact, much is plain *hard*. It takes courage to trust a child to make decisions, to trust in a child's brain development, to ignore the pressures that cause us to protect our kids from themselves, or to be overly involved in their lives. It takes courage to face our fears about the future. It also takes humility to accept that we don't often know what's in our kids' best interest. It takes a change in mindset to focus on ourselves—our own emotions and attitudes—as an extremely important element of our child-rearing.

As hard as all of this is, the harder route by far is trying to control what we really can't. And when you are able to do what we've recommended in this book, the result will be liberating and effective.

Everything we have covered—from the science of the brain to the logic of taking alternate routes—is meant to help you instill in your children the models they will carry into their adult lives, the adult relationship they will have with you, and their sense of themselves. As has often been said, people will forget what you said, people will forget what you did, but people will never forget how you made them feel. Think of how you want to make your child feel. Loved. Trusted. Supported. Capable. And above all else, let that be your guide.

ACKNOWLEDGMENTS

This book came to fruition with the help of many talented people who were remarkably generous with their time and took great care in considering our ideas.

To begin with, we are forever grateful for the encouragement and support of our brilliant agent, Howard Yoon, and his wonderful colleague Dara Kaye. Howard and Dara insightfully challenged our thinking and nudged us through times when we felt stuck. They also connected us to our partner in scribe, Jenna Free. It is hard for us to imagine a more enjoyable process than working with Jenna. Bringing the ideas of even one thinker to the page is not for the faint of heart, and two is surely more than twice the challenge. We remain amazed by—and are deeply grateful for—how cheerfully and nimbly Jenna helped to bring together the ideas and stories you hold in your hands.

We're also grateful to Howard for sending our proposal to Joy de Menil, our enormously talented editor at Viking. In our first meeting, Joy asked questions that caused us to clarify our ideas in a way that none of the several other editors with whom we'd met had. We are in awe of her ability to demand the most of each sentence and of the work in its entirety, and her editing of the manuscript made this a much, much better book. Joy's assistant, Haley Swanson, was invaluable in helping us tackle all the ancillary but equally crucial tasks involved in putting together a book. We're grateful as well to Jane Cavolina for the close-eyed copyediting, one of the critical and unheralded roles in bringing a book to print, and to the highly talented Anne Harris, who made the process of revising the text and compiling the references for our notes infinitely easier.

We also want to thank Emily Warner Eskelsen, with whom we worked in the earliest stages of creating this book, without whose deep thinking and Herculean efforts we wouldn't have made it off the starting line, and Kellie Maxwell Bartlett for her help in shaping some of the ideas in Chapter Eight. A word of thanks goes as well to John Fair, a remarkably talented recent graduate of the Siena School who, by the time this book comes to market, will be a freshman at the Savannah College of Art and Design. John created the brain images in Chapter One.

We are also deeply grateful to the scientists and other professionals who allowed us to interview them for this book. We received invaluable insights from Edward Deci, Joshua Aronson, Bruce Marlowe, Daphne Bavelier, Amy Arnsten, and Adele Diamond, and benefited greatly from Monica Adler Werner's thoughts about motivation in kids with autism. A special thanks to our dear friend and eminent scientist Sheila Ohlsson Walker, whose careful reading of an early draft of the manuscript helped us get the science of stress right. We also greatly appreciate the wonderful folks from the Parent Encouragement Program, particularly Patti Cancellier and Kathy Hedge, whose ideas about the promotion of autonomy and suggestions for handling challenging behavior were invaluable.

Bill would like to thank his wife, Starr, for her 24/7 support, and his children, Jora and Elliott, two wonderful self-driven children who are now terrific adults. He also wants to extend thanks to his dear friend, the psychiatrist, scientist, and author Dr. Norman Rosenthal, for his unwavering encouragement as we worked on this project. Thanks, too, to Bob Roth, the executive director of the David Lynch Foundation (DLF) and to Mario Orgotti of DLF's Center for Leadership Performance, who have been a continual source of support over the years.

Ned wishes to thank his colleagues at PrepMatters, from whom he has learned so much about helping students; his parents for teaching him, in their own very different ways; his twin brother, Steve, for sticking with him through thick and thin; his beloved children, Katie and Matthew, who have taught him so much and been willing to listen to his attempts to do the same; and most of all his wife, Vanessa, for, well, everything. Thanks also to Chrissellene Petropoulos and Brent Toleman, his surrogate parents, for years of wise counsel and support, and to Dr. Kathleen O'Connor for always, always helping him.

Lastly, we extend our enormous thanks to all the children and parents with whom we have worked over the many years. We are grateful to all of you who have trusted us to work with your children, and to you kids, who have taught us so much of what we know. Many people were kind enough to share with us their stories of gap years and alternative routes. There are so many paths to success, and we deeply thank those of you who were willing to share your struggles and breakthroughs, to inspire others to forge their own paths.

NOTES

INTRODUCTION: Why a Sense of Control Is Such a Big Deal

1. The extensive research on the power of a sense of control is summarized well in *Why Zebras Don't Get Ulcers* by the eminent stress researcher Robert Sapolsky (3rd ed.; New York: Holt Paperbacks, 2004). See also an influential review article by Jonathon Haidt and Judith Rodin, "Control and Efficacy as Interdisciplinary Bridges," *Review of General Psychology* 3, no. 4 (December 1999): 317–37.

2. Psychologist Jean Twenge studied changes in the locus of control in college students and found that the average college student in 2002 had a stronger *external* locus of control than 80 percent of those studied in the early 1960s. The cause behind the shift, Twenge suggests, is a culture that has increasingly valued extrinsic and self-centered goals such as money, status, and physical attractiveness and devalued community, affiliation, and finding meaning in life. An external locus of control is correlated with poor academic achievement, a sense of helplessness, ineffective stress management, lower self-control, and vulnerability to depression. See Jean M. Twenge et al., "It's Beyond My Control: A Cross-Temporal Meta-Analysis of Increasing Externality in Locus of Control, 1960–2002," *Personality and Social Psychology Review* 8, no. 3 (August 2004): 308–19. For Twenge's findings regarding the increased mental health problems in contemporary young adults see Jean M. Twenge et al., "Birth Cohort Increases in Psychopathology Among Young Americans, 1938–2007: A Cross-Temporal Meta-Analysis of the MMPI," *Clinical Psychology Review* 30, no. 2 (March 2010): 145–54. Also see Jean M. Twenge, "Generational Differences in Mental Health: Are Children and Adolescents Suffering More, or Less?" *American Journal of Orthopsychiatry* 81, no. 4 (October 2011): 469–72.

3. Christopher Mele, "Pushing That Crosswalk Button May Make You Feel Better, but . . ." *New York Times*, October 27, 2016, accessed May 11, 2017, www.nytimes.com/2016/10/28/us/placebo-buttons-elevators-crosswalks.html?src=twr&_r=1.

4. Judith Rodin and Ellen Langer. "Long-Term Effects of a Control-Relevant Intervention with the Institutionalized Aged," *Journal of Personality and Social Psychology* 35, no. 12 (December 1977): 897–902.

CHAPTER ONE: The Most Stressful Thing in the Universe

1. Evidence for the increased incidence of mental health problems in young people comes from many sources, including the previously mentioned studies

by Jean Twenge. Also, research summarized in a journal published by the Woodrow Wilson School of Public and International Affairs at Princeton University and the Brookings Institution found that, for the first time in fifty years, the top five disabilities affecting U.S. children are mental health problems rather than physical problems. Janet Currie and Robert Kahn, "Children with Disabilities: Introducing the Issue," *Future of Children* 22, no. 1 (Spring 2012): 3–11; Anita Slomski, "Chronic Mental Health Issues in Children Now Loom Larger Than Physical Problems," *Journal of the American Medical Association* 308, no. 3 (July 18, 2012): 223–25.

Additionally, see Christopher Munsey, "The Kids Aren't All Right," *APA Monitor on Psychology*, January 2010, 22. A recent *Time* article sounded a similar theme, reporting that anxiety and depression in high school students have been on the rise since 2012, particularly among adolescent girls; Susanna Schrobsdorff, "Teen Depression and Anxiety: Why the Kids Are Not Alright," *Time*, October 26, 2016, accessed May 12, 2017, time.com/4547322/american-teens-anxious-depressed-overwhelmed/. Recent data from NIMH concludes that about 30 percent of girls and 20 percent of boys will have had an anxiety disorder. These statistics probably underestimate the actual scope, as the large majority of young people with anxiety and depression do not seek help. Kathleen Ries Merikangas et al., "Lifetime Prevalence of Mental Disorders in US Adolescents: Results from the National Comorbidity Study-Adolescent Supplement (NCS-A)," *Journal of the American Academy of Child and Adolescent Psychiatry* 49, no. 10 (October 2010): 980–89. Also, according to a recent survey in Montana, nearly 30 percent of the state's adolescents reported that they felt sad and hopeless almost every day for the last previous two weeks. The article emphasized the role of social media in embroiling students in stressful situations of which their parents are largely unaware. "2015 Montana Youth Risk Behavior Survey," Montana Office of Public Instruction. 2015, accessed May 12, 2017, opi .mt.gov/pdf/YRBS/15/15MT_YRBS_FullReport.pdf.

Moreover, a recent study of depression in adolescents concluded that the prevalence of self-reported symptoms of major depressive disorder in teenagers increased significantly from 2005 to 2014, particularly in young people from 12 to 20 years of age. Overall, there was a 37 percent increase. Ramin Mojtabai et al., "National Trends in the Prevalence and Treatment of Depression in Adolescents and Young Adults," *Pediatrics* (November 14, 2016), accessed May 12, 2017, pediatrics.aappublications.org/content /early/2016/11/10/peds.2016-1878.info. Nonsuicidal self-injury has also increased, particularly in adolescent girls. See Jennifer J. Muehlencamp et al., "Rates of Non-Suicidal Self-Injury in High School Students Across Five Years," *Archives of Suicide Research* 13, no. 4 (October 17, 2009): 317–29.

2. Madeline Levine, *The Price of Privilege* (New York: Harper, 2006). Levine hypothesizes that the higher risk of affluent kids is due, in part, to their experiencing heightened pressure to perform but reduced parental support.

3. The results from the not-yet-published study by Stuart Slavin are discussed in a *New York Times* article by Vicki Abeles, "Is the Drive for Success Making Our Children Sick?," *New York Times*, January 2, 2016, accessed May 16,

2017, www.nytimes.com/2016/01/03/opinion/sunday/is-the-drive-for-suc cess-making-our-children-sick.html.

4. World Health Organization, "WHO Fact Sheet on Depression," February 2017, www.who.int/mediacentre/factsheets/fs369/en/.

5. Centre for Studies on Human Stress (CSHS), "Understand your stress: Recipe for stress," accessed August 11, 2017, www.humanstress.ca/stress/ understand-your-stress/sources-of-stress.html.

6. Steven F. Maier, "Behavioral Control Blunts Reactions to Contemporane- ous and Future Adverse Events: Medial Prefrontal Cortex Plasticity and a Corticostriatal Network," *Neurobiology of Stress* 1 (January 1, 2015): 12–22.

7. David C. Glass and Jerome E. Singer, *Urban Stress: Experiments on Noise and Social Stressors* (New York: Academic Press, 1972).

8. Jonathon Haidt and Judith Rodin, "Control and Efficacy as Interdisciplin- ary Bridges," *Review of General Psychology* 3, no. 4 (December 1999): 317–37. Also, see Joseph Powers et al., "The Far-Reaching Effects of Believing Peo- ple Can Change: Implicit Theories of Personality Shape Stress, Health, and Achievement During Adolescence," *Journal of Personality and Social Psychology* (2014), doi: 10.1037/A0036335.

9. Maier, "Behavioral Control Blunts Reactions."

10. National Scientific Council on the Developing Child, "Excessive Stress Dis- rupts the Architecture of the Developing Brain: Working Paper 3," Harvard University Center on the Developing Child, Reports & Working Papers, 2005, accessed May 16, 2017, developingchild.harvard.edu/resources/ wp3/.

11. Michael J. Meaney et al., "The Effects of Postnatal Handling on the Devel- opment of the Glucocorticoid Receptor Systems and Stress Recovery in the Rat," *Progress in Neuro-Psychopharmacology and Biological Psychiatry* 9, no. 5–6 (1985): 731–34.

12. Maier, "Behavioral Control Blunts Reactions."

13. National Scientific Council on the Developing Child. "Excessive Stress Dis- rupts the Architecture of the Developing Brain."

14. Paul M. Plotsky and Michael J. Meaney, "Early, Postnatal Experience Al- ters Hypothalamic Corticotropin-Releasing Factor (CRF) mRNA, Median Eminence CRF Content and Stress-Induced Release in Adult Rats," *Mo- lecular Brain Research* 18, no. 3 (June 1993): 195–200.

15. Yale School of Medicine, "Keeping the Brain in Balance," *Medicine@Yale* 6, no. 1 (Jan. and Feb. 2010), accessed May 16, 2017, www.medicineatyale .org/janfeb2010/people/peoplearticles/55147/.

16. Amy F. T. Arnsten, "Stress Signalling Pathways That Impair Prefrontal Cortex Structure and Function," *National Review of Neuroscience* 10, no. 6 (June 2009): 410–22. Amy Arnsten et al., "This Is Your Brain in Melt- down," *Scientific American*, April 2012, 48–53.

17. *Dopamine Jackpot! Sapolsky on the Science of Pleasure*, produced by the Califor- nia Academy of Sciences, performed by Robert Sapolsky (February 15, 2011; FORA.tv), accessed May 16, 2017, library.fora.tv/2011/02/15/Robert _Sapolsky_Are_Humans_Just_Another_Primate/Dopamine_Jackpot_ Sapolsky_on_the_Science_of_Pleasure.

18. Marcus E. Raichle, "The Brain's Dark Energy," *Scientific American*, March 2010, 44–49.

19. Mary Helen Immordino-Yang et al., "Rest Is Not Idleness: Implications of the Brain's Default Mode for Human Development and Education," *Perspectives on Psychological Science* 7, no 4 (2012), doi:10.1177/1745691612447308 http://journals.sagepub.com/doi/abs/10.1177/1745691612447308.

20. Robert Sapolsky, *Why Zebras Don't Get Ulcers*, 3rd ed. (New York: Holt Paperbacks, 2004). Linda Mah et al., "Can Anxiety Damage the Brain?," *Current Opinion in Psychiatry* 29, no. 1 (December 2015): 56–63.

21. Bruce McEwen, *The End of Stress As We Know It* (New York: Dana Press, 2002).

22. Sapolsky, *Why Zebras Don't Get Ulcers*. H. M. Van Praag, "Can Stress Cause Depression?" *World Journal of Biological Psychiatry* 28, no. 5 (August 2004): 891–907.

23. For a very readable discussion on the effects of early stress on the developing brain, see the National Scientific Council on the Developing Child. "Excessive Stress Disrupts the Architecture of the Developing Brain."

    Regarding adolescents' particular vulnerability to stress, see research by B. J. Casey et al., "The Storm and Stress of Adolescence: Insights from Human Imaging and Mouse Genetics," *Psychobiology* 52, no. 3 (April 2010): 225–35. Todd A. Hare et al., "Biological Substrates of Emotional Reactivity and Regulation in Adolescents During an Emotional Go-Nogo Task," *Biological Psychiatry* 63, no. 10 (May 15, 2008): 927–34. Additionally, Frances Jensen's book provides a more popular discussion of adolescents' susceptibility to stress. Frances E. Jensen, *The Teenage Brain: A Neuroscientist's Survival Guide to Raising Adolescents and Young Adults* (New York: Harper Paperbacks, 2016). Melanie P. Leussis et al., "Depressive-Like Behavior in Adolescents After Maternal Separation: Sex Differences, Controllability, and GABA," *Developmental Neuroscience* 34, no. 2–3 (2012): 210–17. See, too, Sheryl S. Smith, "The Influence of Stress at Puberty on Mood and Learning: Role of the $\alpha4\beta\delta$ GABA$_A$ receptor," *Neuroscience* 249 (September 26, 2013): 192–213.

24. Jensen, *The Teenage Brain*.

25. Hui Shen et al., "Reversal of Neurosteroid Effects at $\alpha4\beta2\delta$ GABA$_A$ Receptors Triggers Anxiety at Puberty," *Nature Neuroscience* 10, no. 4 (April 2007): 469–77.

26. Bruce Pennington, *The Development of Psychopathology: Nature and Nurture* (New York: Guilford Press, 2002).

27. Regarding the idea that depression "scars" the brain, see Peter M. Lewinsohn et al., "Natural Course of Adolescent Major Depressive Disorder in a Community Sample: Predictors of Recurrence in Young Adults," *American Journal of Psychiatry* 157, no. 10 (October 2000): 1584–91. Also, Kelly Allot et al., "Characterizing Neurocognitive Impairment in Young People with Major Depression: State, Trait, or Scar?," *Brain and Behavior* 6, no. 10 (October 2016), doi:10.1002/brb3.527.

CHAPTER TWO: "I Love You Too Much to Fight with
You About Your Homework": The Parent as Consultant

1. Eckhart Tolle, *A New Earth: Awakening to Your Life's Purpose* (New York: Plume, 2006): 101.

2. Diana Baumrind, a developmental psychologist at the University of California, Berkeley, conducted extensive research on parenting styles beginning in the 1960s. She identified three primary styles of parenting: authoritative parenting, authoritarian parenting, and permissive parenting. Of the three, authoritative parenting has been found to produce the best outcomes in study after study. Authoritative parenting is a child-centered approach in which parents attempt to understand their children's thoughts and emotions and teach them to regulate their feelings. They tend to be forgiving and to allow children to explore and make their own decisions. Authoritative parents also set clear standards for their children, and enforce consistent limits. Extensive research has demonstrated that children of authoritative parents are more likely to be successful, well liked by others, generous, and self-reliant. The power of authoritative parenting is explained in many books written for parents, including Laurence Steinberg's excellent book on adolescence, *Age of Opportunity* (New York: Mariner Books, 2015) and Madeline Levine's important and influential book, *The Price of Privilege* (New York: HarperCollins, 2006).

3. Recall the research of Steven Maier discussed in Chapter One. The rats in Maier's studies who had control over a stressful experience attempted to exert control in subsequent stressful situations, accompanied by strong activation of the prefrontal cortex, even when they had no actual control.

4. This theory was developed at Gordon Training International by its employee Noel Burch in the 1970s, www.gordontraining.com/free-workplace-articles /learning-a-new-skill-is-easier-said-than-done/#.

5. Rudolf Dreikurs, *Children: The Challenge* (1964; New York: Plume/Penguin, 1990).

CHAPTER THREE: "It's Your Call": Kids as Decision Makers

1. Collaborative problem solving is a method of parent-child interaction that grew out of work with oppositional and explosive children. Dr. Ross Greene and J. Stewart Albon developed this technique when it became clear to them that trying to force resistant children to comply (to show them who's boss) was ineffective, as neither threats nor rewards offered for compliance had any meaning to a child once he became stressed and could no longer think straight. Although this technique developed as a way of dealing with extremely difficult children, it's a good model for resolving conflict and for helping all children make good decisions. You can learn more about Ross Greene's work at livesinthebalance.org. Also, collaborative problem solving is discussed extensively in Dr. Greene's recent book, *Raising Human Beings: Creating a Collaborative Partnership with Your Child* (New York: Scribner, 2016). You can learn more about J. Stuart Ablon's work at thinkkids.org.

2. Lori Gottlieb, "How to Land Your Kid in Therapy," *Atlantic* (July/August 2011).

3. Lois A. Weithorn et al., "The Competency of Children and Adolescents to Make Informed Treatment Decisions," *Child Development* 53 (1982): 1589–91.

4. The "adultness inventory" is discussed in detail in Robert Epstein's book, *Teen 2.0: Saving Our Children and Families from the Torment of Adolescence* (Fresno,

CA: Quill Driver Books, 2010). Epstein argues that adolescents are highly creative, intelligent, and capable—and that they are infantilized by contemporary society. He points out that prior to the 1950s, adolescents spent most of their time with adults, wanting to be adults. They listened to the same music and saw the same movies that their parents did, as there was not, as yet, any such thing as a multibillion-dollar teen culture. He champions the competence of teens, who he believes should be able to marry, own property, and play other roles in society currently reserved for adults.

5. P. L. Spear, "The Biology of Adolescence" (paper presented at IOM Committee on the Science of Adolescence Workshop, Washington, DC, 2009). Laurence Steinberg, "Should the Science of Adolescent Brain Development Inform Public Health Policy?," *American Psychologist* 64, no. 8 (2009): 739–50.

6. The important role that emotions play in decision making was initially discovered by Antonio Damasio and reported in his book *Descartes' Error: Emotion, Reason and the Human Brain* (New York: Avon Books, 1994). Damasio's thinking is also presented in an article based on a recent interview with Jason Pontin, "The Importance of Feelings," *MIT Technology Review* (June 17, 2014). In addition, see an excellent discussion of the important role that emotions play in children's learning and thinking in a chapter by Damasio and Mary Helen Immordino-Yang called "We Feel, Therefore We Learn: The Relevance of Affective and Social Neuroscience to Education," *Emotions, Learning, and the Brain: Exploring the Educational Implications of Affective Neuroscience* (New York: W. W. Norton & Company, 2016).

7. Daniel J. Siegel, *Brainstorm: The Power and Purpose of the Teenage Brain* (New York: TarcherPerigee, 2014). Laurence Steinberg, *The Age of Opportunity* (New York: Houghton Mifflin Harcourt, 2014).

CHAPTER FOUR: The Nonanxious Presence: How to Help Your Kids Find a Sense of Control by Finding Your Own

1. Neil Strauss, "Why We're Living in the Age of Fear," *Rolling Stone*, October 6, 2016, 44.

2. Robert Epstein, "What Makes a Good Parent?," *Scientific American Mind*, Special Collectors Edition. Raise Great Kids: How to Help Them Thrive in School and Life. Vol. 25, No. 2, summer 2016. Epstein reports the results of a scientific analysis of parenting practices. The first most effective strategy was showing children love, affection, support, and acceptance through physical affection and spending one-on-one time together, while the second was reducing parental stress and attempting to lower the child's stress level. Parental stress management ranked higher even than maintaining a good relationship with a spouse (#3) and supporting autonomy and independence (#4). It ranked higher than offering children educational opportunities, using effective behavior management strategies, and trying to ensure a child's safety.

3. W. Thomas Boyce and Bruce J. Ellis, Biological Sensitivity to Context: I. An Evolutionary-Developmental Theory of the Origins and Functions of Stress

Reactivity, *Development and Psychopathology* 17, no. 2 (Spring 2005), 271–301. The work of Boyce and Ellis is discussed in an article by Wray Herbert, "On the Trail of the Orchid Child," *Scientific American Mind*, November 1, 2011.

4. Numerous studies have supported the idea that stress is contagious. For example, a study by Eva Oberle found a link between teachers' self-reported levels of burnout and emotional exhaustion and higher cortisol levels in elementary school students; Eva Oberle and Kimberly Schonert-Reichl, "Stress Contagion in the Classroom? The Link Between Classroom Teacher Burnout and Morning Cortisol in Elementary School Students," *Social Science & Medicine* 159 (June 2016): 30–37, doi: 10.1016/j.socscimed.2016.04.031. Also, a study of infants and their mothers found that when mothers participated in a stressful task, the babies' physiological reactions mirrored those of the mother's; Sara F. Waters et al., "Stress Contagion: Physiological Covariation Between Mothers and Infants," *Psychological Science* 25, no. 5 (April 2014): 934–42, doi:10.1177/0956797613518352.

5. Daniel P. Keating, *Born Anxious: The Lifelong Impact of Early Life Adversity— and How to Break the Cycle* (New York: St. Martin's Press, 2017).

6. Marilyn J. Essex, "Epigenetic Vestiges of Early Developmental Diversity: Childhood Stress Exposure and DNA Methylation in Adolescence," *Child Development* (2011), doi:10,1111/j.1467-8264.2011.01641.x. There is also a good summary of this article in a media release from the University of British Columbia, "Parents' Stress Leaves Lasting Marks on Children's Genes," UBC-CFRI Research, August 30, 2011.

7. Erin A. Maloney, "Intergenerational Effects of Parents' Math Anxiety on Children's Math Achievement and Anxiety," *Psychological Science* 26, no. 9 (2015). See also an article about this topic by Jan Hoffman, "Square Root of Kids' Math Anxiety: Their Parents' Help," *New York Times*, May 24, 2015.

8. Malcolm Gladwell, "The Naked Face," *New Yorker*, posted on Gladwell.com on August 5, 2002.

9. Robert Sapolsky, "How to Relieve Stress," *Greater Good*, University of California, Berkeley, March 22, 2012, greatergood.berkeley.edu/article/item/how_to_relieve_stress.

10. Golda S. Ginsberg et al., "Preventing Onset of Anxiety Disorders in Offspring of Anxious Parents: A Randomized Controlled Trial of a Family-Based Intervention," *American Journal of Psychiatry* 172, no. 12 (December 1, 2015): 1207–14.

11. Jeffrey E. Pela et al., "Child Anxiety Prevention Study: Impact on Functional Outcomes" *Child Psychiatry and Human Development* 48, no. 3 (July 8, 2016): 1–11, doi:10.1007/s,10578-016-0667-y.

12. Edwin H. Friedman, *A Failure of Nerve: Leadership in the Age of the Quick Fix* (New York: Seabury Books, 2007).

13. For a scientific review, see Michael J. Meaney, "Maternal Care, Gene Expression, and the Transmission of Individual Differences in Stress Reactivity Across Generations," *Annual Review of Neuroscience* 24, no. 1161–92 (March 2001), doi:10.1146/annurev.neuro.24.1.1161. Another article that discusses the benefits of fostering rats with genetic vulnerability to anxiety to high-nurturing mothers is by Meaney and his colleagues: I. C. Weaver et al.,

"Epigenetic Programming by Maternal Behavior," *Nature Neuroscience* 7 (published online June 27, 2004): 847–54, doi:10.1038/nn1276. Meaney's research is also discussed in an article by Carl Zimmer, "The Brain: The Switches That Can Turn Mental Illness On and Off," *Discover*, June 16, 2010.

14. Ellen Galinsky, *Ask the Children: What America's Children Really Think About Working Parents* (New York: William Morrow, 1999). Galinsky asked a representative national sample of American children, third grade through twelfth grade, whose parents worked what they wished for their parents. Although parents expected that their children would wish for more time with parents, the children's top wish was actually for their parents to be happier and less stressed.

15. Lenore Skenazy, Free-Range Kids.com, "Crime Statistics," www.freerange kids.com/crime-statistics/.

16. Hanna Rosin, "The Overprotected Kid," *Atlantic*, April 2014.

17. Gary Emery and James Campbell, *Rapid Relief from Emotional Distress* (New York: Ballantine Books, 1987).

18. Byron Katie, *Loving What Is: Four Questions That Can Change Your Life* (New York: Crown Archetype, 2002).

CHAPTER FIVE: Inner Drive: How to Help Your Kids
Develop Internal Motivation

1. Alfie Kohn, *Punished by Rewards: The Trouble with Gold Stars, Incentive Plans, A's, Praise, and Other Bribes* (New York: Houghton Mifflin Harcourt, 1999). See also Edward L Deci et al., "Extrinsic Rewards and Intrinsic Motivation in Education: Reconsidered Once Again," *Review of Educational Research* 71, no. 1 (Spring 2001): 1–27. Interestingly, a study conducted in 2010 tracked brain activation when subjects were offered financial incentives. The scientists found that activity in the anterior striatum and the prefrontal cortex correlated with diminished motivation: Kou Murayama et al., "Neural Basis of the Undermining Effect of Monetary Reward on Intrinsic Motivation," *Proceedings of the National Academy of Sciences of the United States of America* 107, no. 49 (2010): 20911–16, doi:10.1073/pnas.1013305107.

2. Joseph Powers et al., "The Far-Reaching Effects of Believing People Can Change: Implicit Theories of Personality Shape Stress, Health, and Achievement During Adolescence," *Journal of Personality and Social Psychology* (2014), doi:10.1037/a0036335. Carol S. Dweck, *Mindset: The New Psychology of Success* (New York: Random House, 2006).

3. Carol Dweck, "The Secret to Raising Smart Kids," *Scientific American*, January 1, 2015. https://www.scientificamerican.com/article/the-secret-to-raising -smart-kids1/.

4. Christopher Niemiec and Richard M. Ryan, "Autonomy, Competence, and Relatedness in the Classroom: Applying Self-Determination Theory to Educational Practice," *Theory and Research in Education* 7, no. 2 (2009): 133–44, doi:10.1177/1477878509104318. We interviewed Edward Deci by telephone for this book.

5. The fact that the brain changes in response to experience was discovered, in part, by Marian Diamond, a neuroscientist at the University of California, Berkeley. Diamond describes the effects of experience on the brain—and the implications for child-rearing—in her book with Janet Hopson, *Magic Trees of the Mind* (New York: Dutton, 1998). The brain's changing response to experience is also discussed in a number of popular books, including Norman Doidge, MD's *The Brain That Changes Itself* (New York: Viking, 2007).

6. Steven Kotler, "Flow States and Creativity," PsychologyToday.com, February 25, 2014.

7. Reed W. Larson and Natalie Rusk, "Intrinsic Motivation and Positive Development," *Advances in Child Development and Behavior* 41, *Positive Youth Development* (2011). Richard M. Learner et al. (eds), *Advances in Child Development and Behavior*, Vol. 1, Burlington: Academic Press (2011): 89–130.

8. Diamond and Hopson, *Magic Trees of the Mind*.

9. Reed W. Larson and Natalie Rusk, "Intrinsic Motivation and Positive Development."

10. Although the differences in the performance of males and females on almost any metric are greater *within* gender than *between* genders, there are generalities that hold up. See Leonard Sax's book, *Why Gender Matters* (New York: Doubleday, 2005). Also, Simon Baron-Cohen, one of the world's experts on autism, theorizes that what characterizes the female brain primarily is a capacity for empathy, whereas what characterizes the typical male brain is a capacity for creating logical systems. See his book *The Essential Difference: The Truth About the Male and Female Brain* (New York: Basic Books, 2003). The eminent neuroscientist Adele Diamond has also told Bill that boys, on average, perform best under mild stress, whereas girls, on average, perform best under no stress at all. Personal communication, October 2010.

11. Studies by Nora Volkow and her colleagues have identified deficits in dopamine processing in adults with ADHD. Volkow refers to ADHD as a motivational deficit disorder, which she links to dysfunction in the dopamine reward pathway. It has also been discovered recently that stimulant medications such as Ritalin improve children's attention and self-control in large part by increasing the availability and uptake of dopamine. Nora D. Volkow et al., "Evaluating Dopamine Reward Pathway in ADHD: Clinical Implications," *Journal of the American Medical Association* 302, no. 10 (September 9, 2009): 1084–91, doi:10.1001/jama.2009.1308. Nora D. Volkow et al., "Motivation Deficit in ADHD Is Associated with Dysfunction of the Dopamine Reward Pathway," *Molecular Psychiatry* 6, no. 11 (November 2011): 1147–54.

12. Many psychologists and motivational specialists have written about different "motivational styles" that are demonstrated by children, adolescents, and adults. See, for example, Richard Lavoie's *The Motivation Breakthrough* (New York: Touchstone, 2007). For understanding older adolescents and young adults, consider investigating TriMetrix, which holds that people tend to be primarily motivated by six different factors: knowledge, utility, surroundings, others, power, and methodologies.

13. Dustin Wax, "Writing and Remembering: Why We Remember What We Write," Lifehack.com, www.lifehack.org/articles/featured/writing -and-remembering-why-we-remember-what-we-write.html.

14. For a review of the benefits of peer tutoring, see Page Kalkowski, "Peer and Cross-Age Tutoring," Northwest Regional Educational Labortory School Improvement Research Series (March 1995), educationnorthwest.org/sites /default/files/peer-and-cross-age-tutoring.pdf. For dopamine spike, see Ian Clark and Guillaume Dumas, "Toward a Neural Basis for Peer-Interaction: What Makes Peer-Learning Tick?," *Frontiers in Psychology* 10 (February 2015), doi:org/10.3389/fpsyg.2015.00028.

15. Andrew P. Allen and Andrew P. Smith, "Chewing Gum: Cognitive Performance, Mood, Well-Being, and Associated Physiology," Biomed Research International (May 17, 2015), doi:10.1155/2015/654806.

16. Ken Robinson with Lou Aronica, *The Element: How Finding Your Passion Changes Everything* (New York: Penguin, 2009), 2–6.

17. Julie Lythcott-Haims, *How to Raise an Adult: Break Free of the Overparenting Trap and Prepare Your Kid for Success* (New York: Henry Holt, 2015).

18. Stacy Berg Dale and Alan B. Krueger, "Estimating the Return to College Selectivity over the Career Using Administrative Earnings Data," National Bureau of Economic Research Working Paper No. w17159 (June 2011), https://ssrn.com/abstract=1871566.

19. Julie Ray and Stephanie Kafka, "Life in College Matters for Life After College," Gallup.com, May 6, 2014, www.gallup.com/poll/168848/life-college -matters-life-college.aspx.

20. Anna Brown, "Public and Private College Grads Rank About Equally in Life Satisfaction," Pew Research Center Fact Tank, May 19, 2014, www .pewresearch.org/fact-tank/2014/05/19/public-and-private-college-grads -rank-about-equally-in-life-satisfaction/.

21. The big-fish-little-pond theory, developed by Herbert Marsh, has been replicated by studies in over thirty countries. See the article Herbert W. Marsh et al., "The Big-Fish-Little-Pond Effect Stands Up to Critical Scrutiny: Implications for Theory, Methodology, and Future Research," *Educational Psychology Review* 20, no. 3 (September 2008), 319–50.

22. Malcolm Gladwell, *David and Goliath* (New York: Little, Brown, 2013), 68.

CHAPTER SIX: Radical Downtime

1. Timothy D. Wilson et al., "Just Think: The Challenges of the Disengaged Mind," *Science* 345, no. 6192 (July 4, 2014): 75–77 doi:10.1126/science.1250830.

2. Marcus E. Raichle et al., "A default mode of brain function," *Proceedings of the National Academy of Sciences* 98, no. 2 (2001): 676–682, doi:10. 1073/pnas.98.2.676. Also see Mary Helen Immordino-Yang et al., "Rest Is Not Idleness: Implications of the Brain's Default Mode for Human Development and Education," *Perspectives on Pyschological Science* 7, no. 4 (2012), doi: 10.1177/1745691612447308, http://journals.sagepub.com/doi/abs/10.1177/ 1745691612447308.

3. Marcus E. Raichle, "The Brain's Dark Energy," *Scientific American,* March 2010, 44–49. Virginia Hughes, "The Brain's Dark Energy," TheLast WordonNothing.com, October 6, 2010, www.lastwordonnothing.com/2010/10/06/brain-default-mode/.

4. Interestingly, recent research has found that substantial activity in the DMN is observed during sleep, although there's a disconnect during sleep between the DMN systems in the front of the brain and the back of the brain. Silvina G. Horovitz et al., "Decoupling of the Brain's Default Mode Network During Deep Sleep," *Proceedings of the National Academy of Sciences* 106, no. 7 (2009): 11376–381, doi:10.1073/pnas.0901435106.

5. Jerome L. Singer, *Daydreaming: An Introduction to the Experimental Study of Innerexperience* (New York: Random House, 1966). An article by Rebecca McMillan, Scott Barry Kaufman, and Jerome Singer called "Ode to Positive and Constructive Daydreaming" provides a detailed summary of research on the benefits of letting the mind wander; *Frontiers in Psychology* 4 (September 2013): 626, doi:10.3389/fpsyg.2013.00626.

6. Daniel J. Levitin, *The Organized Mind: Thinking Straight in the Age of Information Overload* (New York: Dutton (2014). See also: Daniel J. Levitin, "Hit the Reset Button in Your Brain," *New York Times,* August 10, 2014.

7. Carlo Rovelli, *Seven Brief Lessons on Physics* (New York: Riverhead Books, 2016), 3–4.

8. Immordino-Yang et al., "Rest Is Not Idleness."

9. Sherry Turkle, "Reclaiming Conversation" (talk given at Google, Cambridge, MA, October 30, 2105), video, produced by Talks at Google, www.youtube.com/watch?v=awFQtX7tPoI&t=1966s.

10. Adam J. Cox, "The Case for Boredom," *New Atlantis* 27 (Spring 2010): 122–25.

11. Olivia Goldhill, "Psychologists Recommend Children Be Bored in the Summer," Quartz Media (June 11, 2016), qz.com/704723/to-be-more-self-reliant-children-need-boring-summers/.

12. Sarah Zoogman et al., "Mindfulness Interventions with Youth: A Meta-Analysis," *Springer Science and Business Media* (Spring 2014), doi:10.1007/s12671-013-0260-4. This meta-analysis reviewed the results of twenty studies of mindfulness practices with children and teenagers. The authors concluded that mindfulness interventions can be helpful but generally have small to moderate effects. The largest treatment effect size was found in the reduction of psychological symptoms (more than improvement in other areas). A stronger treatment effect was found in clinical samples (e.g., children with anxiety disorders) than nonclinical samples. See also Katherine Weare, "Evidence for the Impact of Mindfulness on Children and Young People," The Mindfulness in Schools Project, University of Exeter Mood Disorders Centre (April 2012), mindfulnessinschools.org/wp-content/uploads/2013/02/MiSP-Research-Summary-2012.pdf.

13. Alberto Chiesa and Alessandro Serretti, "A Systematic Review of Neurobiological and Clinical Features of Mindfulness Meditations," *Psychological Medicine* 40, no 8 (November 2009), 1239–52, doi:10.1017/s0033291709991747. Matthieu Ricard, "Mind of the Meditator," *Scientific American* (November 2014), 38–45.

14. Michael Dillbeck and David Orme-Johnson, "Physiological Differences Between Transcendental Meditation and Rest," *American Psychologist* 42, no. 9 (September 1987): 879–81, doi:10.1037/0003-066x.42.9.879.

15. Michael Dillbeck and Edward Bronson, "Short-Term Longitudinal Efects on EEG Power and Coherence," *International Journal of Neuroscience* 14, no. 3–4 (1981): 147–51.

   There have been over 340 peer-reviewed articles describing the effects of TM. Many of the most important of these are discussed in the best general introduction to TM, a book written by the psychiatrist and scientist Norman Rosenthal, MD, who discovered seasonal affective disorder. Dr. Rosenthal's book, *Transcendence*, offers an excellent discussion of the research and practical benefits of TM from the standpoint of a clinician and scientist. His second book on TM, *Super Mind*, discusses the ways in which meditation changes the mind over time. Norman E. Rosenthal, *Transcendence: Healing and Transformation Through Transcendental Meditation* (New York: Jeremy P. Tarcher/Penguin, 2012). Rosenthal, *Super Mind: How to Boost Performance and Live a Richer and Happier Life Through Transcendental Meditation* (New York: Tarcher/Perigee, 2016).

16. A comprehensive discussion of the documented benefits of TM for children and adolescents appears in a chapter written by Bill. William Stixrud and Sarina Grosswald, "The TM Program and the Treatment of Childhood Disorders," in *Prescribing Health: Transcendental Meditation in Contemporary Medical Care*, ed. David O'Connell and Deborah Bevvino (Lanham, MD: Rowman & Littlefield, 2015).

17. Both of Dr. Rosenthal's books include extensive discussion of the use of Transcendental Meditation in schools. Chapter 8 of *Transcendence*, called "An Island of Safety in a Sea of Trouble," discusses the remarkable effects of the Quiet Time Program, which has been implemented in a number of low-income schools across the country. In *Super Mind*, he discusses recent studies conducted with college-age students at universities and military academies. For another interesting account of the effects of the Quiet Time Program see Jennie Rothenberg Gritz, "Mantras Before Math Class," *Atlantic*, November 10, 2015, www.theatlantic.com/education/archive/2015/11/mantras-before-math-class/412618/.

CHAPTER SEVEN: Sleep: The Most Radical Downtime

1. K. M. Keyes et al., "The Great Sleep Recession: Changes in Sleep Duration Among U.S. Adolescents, 1991–2012," *Pediatrics* 135, no. 3 (March 2015): 460–68, doi:10.1542/peds.2014-2707.

2. Brown University, "Early School Start Times Pit Teens in a Conflict Between Society, Biology," Brown.edu, *News from Brown*, April 12, 2017, news.brown.edu/articles/2017/04/teens.

3. Valerie Strauss, "Teens Waking Up to Unique Sleep Needs," *Washington Post*, January 10, 2006.

4. Craig Lambert, "Deep into Sleep: While Researchers Probe Sleep's Functions, Sleep Itself Is Becoming a Lost Art," *Harvard Magazine*, July–August 2005, 25–33.

5. Bruce McEwen with Elizabeth Norton Lasley, *The End of Stress As We Know It* (Washington, DC: National Academies Press, 2012).

6. A. N. Goldstein and M. P. Walker, "The Role of Sleep in Emotional Brain Function," *Annual Review of Clinical Psychology* 10 (2014): 679–708. See also two articles by Yasmin Anwar about Walker's research: "Sleep Loss Linked to Psychiatric Disorders," Berkeley.edu, *UC Berkeley News*, October 22, 2007 and "Tired and Edgy? Sleep Deprivation Boosts Anticipatory Anxiety," News.Berkeley. edu, *Berkeley News*, June 25, 2013. Additionally, see the report of an interview with Matthew Walker in Jill Suttie, "Why You Should Sleep Your Way to the Top," *Greater Good*, University of California, Berkeley, December 14, 2013.

7. Juliann Garey, "Teens and Sleep: What Happens When Teenagers Don't Get Enough Sleep," *Child Mind Institute*, childmind.org/article/happens -teenagers-dont-get-enough-sleep/.

8. Robert Stickgold, "Beyond Memory: The Benefits of Sleep," *Scientific American*, September 15, 2015.

9. Seung-Schik Yoo et al., "The Human Emotional Brain Without Sleep—A Prefrontal Amygdala Disconnect," *Current Biology* 17, no. 20 (October 23, 2007): 877–78.

10. Goldstein and Walker, "The Role of Sleep in Emotional Brain Function."

11. Po Bronson and Ashley Merryman, *NurtureShock: New Thinking About Children* (New York: Twelve Books, 2009), 41.

12. N. K. Gupta et al., "Is Obesity Associated with Poor Sleep Quality in Adolescents?," *American Journal of Human Biology* 14, no. 6 (November–December 2002), 762–68, doi:10.1002/ajhb.10093.

13. N. F. Watson et al., "Transcriptional Signatures of Sleep Duration Discordance in Monozygotic Twins," *Sleep* 40, no. 1 (January 2017), doi:10.1093/sleep/zsw019.

14. American Cancer Society, "Known and Probable Human Carcinogens," Cancer.org (November 3, 2016), www.cancer.org/cancer/cancer-causes/general-info/known-and-probable-human-carcinogens.html.

15. Avi Sadeh et al., "The Effects of Sleep Restriction and Extension on School-Aged Children: What a Difference an Hour Makes," *Child Development* 74, no. 2 (March/April 2003): 444–55.

16. Indre Viskontas, "9 Reasons You Really Need to Go to Sleep," *Mother Jones* (January 16, 2015), www.motherjones.com/environment/2015/01/inquiring -minds-matt-walker/.

17. Matthew Walker et al., "Practice with Sleep Makes Perfect: Sleep-Dependent Motor Skill Learning," *Neuron* 35, no. 1 (July 3, 2002): 205–11, walkerlab .berkeley.edu/reprints/Walker%20et%20al._Neuron_2002.pdf.

18. Amy R. Wolfson et al., "Understanding Adolescents' Sleep Patterns and School Performance: A Critical Appraisal," *Sleep Medicine Reviews* 7, no. 6 (2003): 491–506, doi:10.1053/smrv.2002.0258.

19. Mark Fischetti, "Sleepy Teens: High School Should Start Later in the Morning," August 26, 2014, blogs.scientificamerican.com/observations/sleepy -teens-high-school-should-start-later-in-the-morning/. Kyla Wahlstrom, "Changing Times: Findings from the First Longitudinal Study of High School Start Times," *NASSP Bulletin* 86, no. 633 (December 1, 2002): 3–21.

20. Suttie, "How Sleep Makes You Smart."

21. National Sleep Foundation, "National Sleep Foundation Recommends New Sleep Times," February 2, 2015, sleepfoundation.org/press-release/national-sleep-foundation-recommends-new-sleep-times.

22. Personal communication with The Stixrud Group, September 8, 2011.

23. One study of children with ADHD found that 50 percent showed signs of sleep-disordered breathing; N. Golin et al., "Sleep Disorders and Daytime Sleepiness in Children with Attention-Deficit/Hyperactivity Disorder," *Sleep* 27, no. 2 (March 15, 2004): 261–66.

24. Kyla Wahlstrom, "Later Start Times for Teens Improve Grades, Mood, Safety" *Phi Delta Kappan*, kappanonline.org.

25. Helene A. Emsellem, *Snooze . . . or Lose!: 10 "No-War" Ways to Improve Your Teen's Sleep Habits* (Washington, DC: Joseph Henry Press, 2006).

26. Ned has, on more than one occasion, paid students to go to bed early the week of their big tests. When Bill lectures about sleep, parents frequently tell him that having a reasonable bedtime is linked to allowance.

27. Jennifer L. Temple, "Caffeine Use in Children: What We Know, What We Have Left to Learn, and Why We Should Worry," *Neuroscience Biobehavioral Reviews* 33, no. 6 (June 2009): 793–806, doi:10.1016/j.neubiorev.2009.01.001.

28. B. E. Statland and T. J. Demas, "Serum Caffeine Half-Lives. Healthy Subjects vs. Patients Having Alcoholic Hepatic Disease," *American Journal of Clinical Pathology* 73, no. 3 (March 1980): 390–93, www.ncbi.nlm.nih.gov/pubmed/7361718?dopt=Abstract.

29. Cheri Mah et al., "The Effects of Sleep Extension on the Athletic Performance of Collegiate Basketball Players," *SLEEP* 34, no. 7 (July 1, 2011): 943–50, doi:10.5665/SLEEP.1132. In the following 2016 interview, Mah, who has been consulting with the world champion Golden State Warriors, recommends that elite athletes get eight to ten hours of sleep a night. Alec Rosenberg, "How to Sleep Like a Pro," University of California, News, www.universityofcalifornia/news/how-sleep-pro-athlete.

CHAPTER EIGHT: Taking a Sense of Control to School

1. Ellen Skinner and Teresa Greene, "Perceived Control: Engagement, Coping, and Development," in *21st Century Education: A Reference Handbook*, vol. 1, ed. Thomas L. Good (Newbury Park, CA: Sage Publications, 2008).

2. Denise Clark Pope makes this same point in her important book, *Doing School*. Pope followed five highly motivated students in an affluent suburban high school in Los Angeles for a year. All five students told her that they were "doing school," as they only committed effort to school-related tasks that would help them get a good grade or build their academic resume. Pope, *Doing School: How We Are Creating a Generation of Stressed-Out, Materialistic, and Miseducated Students* (New Haven, CT: Yale University Press, 2003).

3. Richard M. Ryan and Edward L. Deci, "Promoting Self-Determined School Engagement: Motivation, Learning, and Well-Being," in *Handbook of Motivation at School*, ed. Kathryn R. Wentzel and Allan Wigfield (New York: Routledge, 2009).

4. Dinah Sparks and Matt Malkus, "Public School Teacher Autonomy in the Classroom Across School Years 2003–04, 2007–08, and 2011–12," U.S. Department of Education, National Center for Education Statistics (December 2015), 4.

5. David Diamond, "Cognitive, Endocrine and Mechanistic Perspectives on Non-Linear Relationships Between Arousal and Brain Function," *Nonlinearity in Biology, Toxicology, and Medicine* 3, no. 1 (January 2005): 1–7, doi:10.2201/nonlin.003.01.001.

6. Scientists have concluded that inhibition, working memory, and cognitive flexibility are the three core executive functions, as these are the executive skills that are most evident early in life. We don't generally think to assess infants' organizational or planning skills, but even in the first year of life we see improvements in their ability to inhibit their behavior, to hold an idea or image in mind, and to try different approaches to solving a problem if the first way doesn't work. Adele Diamond and Kathleen Lee, "Interventions Shown to Aid Executive Function Development in Children 4–12 Years Old," *Science* 333, no. 6045 (August 2011): 959–964, doi:10.1126/science.1204529.

7. Tracy and Ross Alloway, *New IQ: Use Your Working Memory to Work Stronger, Smarter, Faster* (New York: Fourth Estate, 2014).

8. A great resource for parents who want to support a healthy academic environment for their kids is Stanford University's Challenge Success Web site: www.challengesuccess.org/parents/parenting-guidelines/.

9. F. Thomas Juster et al., "Changing Times of American Youth: 1981–2003," University of Michigan Institute for Social Research, ns.UMich.edu, *University of Michigan News* (November 2004), ns.umich.edu/Releases/2004/Nov04/teen_time_report.pdf.

10. Robert M. Pressman et al., "Homework and Family Stress: With Consideration of Parents' Self Confidence, Educational Level, and Cultural Background," *American Journal of Family Therapy* 43, no. 4 (July 2015): 297–313.

11. Mollie Galloway et al., "Nonacademic Effects of Homework in Privileged, High-Performing High Schools," *Journal of Experimental Education* 81, no. 4 (2013): 490–510.

12. Harris Cooper et al., "Does Homework Improve Academic Achievement? A Synthesis of Research, 1987–2003," *Review of Educational Research*, 76, no. 1 (2006), doi:10.310/00346543071001001. See also Alfie Kohn, *The Myth of Homework* (Cambridge, MA: Da Capo Press, 2007).

13. A. V. Alpern, "Student Engagement in High Performing Urban High Schools: A Case Study," (PhD diss., University of Southern California, 2008).

14. Pasi Sahlberg, *Finnish Lessons: What Can the World Learn from Educational Change in Finland?* (New York: Teachers College Press, 2011). Ellen Gamerman, "What Makes Finnish Kids So Smart?," *Wall Street Journal* (February 29, 2008), www.wsj.com/articles/SB120425355065601997. Amanda Ripley, *The Smartest Kids in the World* (New York: Simon & Schuster, 2014).

15. Sahlberg cited the Organization for Economic Cooperation and Development (OECD) for this finding.

16. Sahlberg, *Finnish Lessons.*
17. See Maryanne Wolf, *Proust and the Squid* (New York: Harper Perennial, 2008): 94–96.
18. Donna St. George, "Three Out of Four High Schoolers Failed Algebra 1 Final Exams in Md. District," *Washington Post,* July 22, 2015.
19. Jessica Lahey, "Students Should Be Tested More, Not Less," *Atlantic,* January 21, 2014, www.theatlantic.com/education/archive/2014/01/students -should-be-tested-more-not-less/283195/.
20. Bill recently coauthored a chapter in an excellent book on the integration of the arts in instruction: William Stixrud and Bruce A. Marlowe, "School Reform with a Brain: The Neuropsychological Foundation for Arts Integration," in *Arts Integration in Education*, ed. Gail Humphries Mardirosian and Yvonne Pelletier Lewis (Bristol, UK: Intellect Ltd., 2016).
21. Jennie Rothenberg Gritz, "Mantras Before Math Class," *Atlantic*, November 10, 2015, www.theatlantic.com/education/archive/2015/11/mantras -before-math-class/412618/.

CHAPTER NINE: Wired 24/7: Taming the Beast of Technology

1. Amanda Lenhart, "Teens, Social Media & Technology Overview 2015," Pew Research Center, April 9, 2015, www.pewinternet.org/2015/04/ 09/a-majority-of-american-teens-report-access-to-a-computer-game-console -smartphone-and-a-tablet/.
2. Aric Sigman, "Time for a View on Screen Time," *Archives of Disease in Childhood* 97, no. 11 (October 25, 2012), adc.bmj.com/content/97/11/935.
3. Amanda Lenhart, "Teens, Smartphones & Texting," Pew Research Center, March 19, 2012, www.pewinternet.org/2012/03/19/teens-smartphones -texting/.
4. Kaiser Family Foundation, "Daily Media Use Among Children and Teens Up Dramatically from Five Years Ago," KFF.org, January 10, 2010, kff.org /disparities-policy/press-release/daily-media-use-among-children-and-teens- up-dramatically-from-five-years-ago/.
5. In a study from University of Maryland's International Center for Media & the Public Agenda, two hundred students were challenged to forgo media for a day and blog about it. The blogs conveyed their anxiety at feeling cut off; Philip Merrill College of Journalism, "Merrill Study: Students Unable to Disconnect," University of Maryland, Merrill.umd.edu, merrill.umd .edu/2010/04/merrill-study-college-students-unable-to-disconnect/.
6. Adam Alter, *Irresistible: The Rise of Addictive Technology and the Business of Keeping Us Hooked* (New York: Penguin Press, 2017).
7. Nick Bilton, "Steve Jobs Was a Low-Tech Parent," *New York Times*, September 10, 2014, www.nytimes.com/2014/09/11/fashion/steve-jobs-apple-was-a -low-tech-parent.html?_r=0.
8. Larry D. Rosen, *Rewired* (New York: St. Martin's Griffin, 2010).
9. Tracy Hampton, "Can Video Games Help Train Surgeons?," Beth Israel Deaconess Medical Center, bidmc.org, March 2013, www.bidmc.org/YourHealth /Health-Notes/SurgicalInnovations/Advances/VideoGames.aspx.

10. Daphne Bavelier and C. Shawn Green, "Brain Tune-up from Action Video Game Play," *Scientific American*, July 2016.

11. When participants in a study at Michigan State University were interrupted for 2.8 seconds while performing a task, they were twice as likely to make errors as when not interrupted. Harvard Business Review Staff, "The Multitasking Paradox," *Harvard Business Review*, March 2013, hbr.org/2013/03/the-multitasking-paradox; MSU Today, "Brief Interruptions Spawn Errors," msutoday.msu.edu, msutoday.msu.edu/news/2013/brief-interruptions-spawn-errors/.

12. Jane McGonigal, "Gaming Can Make a Better World," TED Talk, February 2010, www.ted.com/talks/jane_mcgonigal_gaming_can_make_a_better_world#t-11825.

13. Michael S. Rosenwald, "Serious Reading Takes a Hit from Online Scanning and Skimming," *Washington Post*, April 6, 2014, www.washingtonpost.com/local/serious-reading-takes-a-hit-from-online-scanning-and-skimming-researchers-say/2014/04/06/088028d2-b5d2-11e3-b899-20667de76985_story.html?utm_term=.63a22afe15f7.

14. Larry Rosen, *Rewired*. Ian Jukes et al., *Understanding the Digital Generation: Teaching and Learning in the New Digital Landscape* (Thousand Oaks, CA: Corwin, 2010).

15. George Beard, *American Nervousness: Its Causes and Consequences—A Supplement to Nervous Exhaustion (Neurasthenia)* (South Yarra, Australia: Leopold Classic Library, 2016).

16. Lisa Eadicicco, "Americans Check Their Phones 8 Billion Times a Day," *Time*, December 15, 2015, time.com/4147614/smartphone-usage-us-2015/.

17. Kelly Wallace, "Half of Teens Think They're Addicted to Their Smartphones," CNN, July 29, 2016, www.cnn.com/2016/05/03/health/teens-cell-phone-addiction-parents/.

18. Larry D. Rosen et al., "Media and Technology Use Predicts Ill-Being Among Children," *Computers in Human Behavior* 35 (June 2014): 364–75, doi: 10.1016/j.chb.2014.01.036. Sigman, "Time for a View on Screen Time."

19. When asked during a 2014 lecture if technology causes these problems, or if kids with attention and behavioral problems are drawn more to technology, Larry Rosen said that his studies and those of others have controlled for so many variables that tech seems to *cause* the problems.

20. Jean M. Twenge, "Have Smartphones Destroyed a Generation?" *The Atlantic*, September 2017.

21. Sigman, "Time for a View on Screen Time."

22. Teddy Wayne, "The Trauma of Violent News on the Internet," *New York Times*, September 10, 2016, www.nytimes.com/2016/09/11/fashion/the-trauma-of-violent-news-on-the-internet.html.

23. H. B. Shakya and N. A. Christakis, "Association of Facebook Use with Compromised Well-Being: A Longitudinal Study," *American Journal of Epidemiology* 185, no. 2 (February 1, 2017): 203–211.

24. Jessica Contrera, "13, Right Now," *Washington Post*, May 25, 2016, www.washingtonpost.com/sf/style/2016/05/25/13-right-now-this-is-what-its-like-to-grow-up-in-the-age-of-likes-lols-and-longing/.

25. Larry Rosen, *iDisorder: Understanding Our Obsession with Technology and Overcoming Its Hold on Us* (New York: St. Martin's Press, 2013).

26. MTV Networks, "MTV's 'The Millennial Edge: Phase 3,'" *Consumer Insights*, Viacom, March/April 2011, www.viacom.com/inspiration/ConsumerInsight/VMN%20Consumer%20Insights%20Newsletter%20MARCHAPRIL%202011.pdf.

27. Amanda Lenhart et al., "Teens and Mobile Phones—Chapter Three: Attitudes Toward Cell Phones," Pew Research Center, April 20, 2010, www.pewinternet.org/2010/04/20/chapter-three-attitudes-towards-cell-phones/. Peter G. Polos et al., "The Impact of Sleep Time-Related Information and Communication Technology (STRICT) on Sleep Patterns and Daytime Functioning in American Adolescents," *Journal of Adolescence* 44 (October 2015): 232–44, www.ncbi.nlm.nih.gov/pubmed/26302334.

28. Douglas Gentile, "Pathological Videogame Use Among Youth 8–18: A National Study," *Psychological Science* 20, no. 5 (May 2009): 594–602. Gentile et al., "Pathological Videogame Use Among Youth: A Two-Year Longitudinal Study," *Pediatrics* 127, no. 2 (February 2011): e319–e329.

29. Ben Carter et al., "Association Between Portable Screen-Based Media Device Access or Use and Sleep Outcomes," *JAMA Pediatrics* 170, no. 12 (December 2016): 1202–8.

30. Nicholas Bakalar, "What Keeps Kids Up at Night? Cellphones and Tablets," *New York Times*, October 31, 2016, www.nytimes.com/2016/10/31/well/mind/what-keeps-kids-up-at-night-it-could-be-their-cellphone.html.

31. Sara Konrath et al., "Changes in Dispositional Empathy in American College Students over Time," *Personality and Social Psychology Review* 15, no. 2 (May 2011): 180–98.

32. John Bingham, "Screen Addict Parents Accused of Hypocrisy by Their Children," *Telegraph*, July 22, 2014, www.telegraph.co.uk/technology/news/10981242/Screen-addict-parents-accused-of-hypocrisy-by-their-children.html.

33. Beard, *American Nervousness*.

34. For kids' exposure to greenery around schools: Olga Khazan, "Green Space Makes Kids Smarter," *Atlantic*, June 16, 2015, www.theatlantic.com/health/archive/2015/06/green-spaces-make-kids-smarter/395924/. For adults: Ruth Ann Atchley et al., "Creativity in the Wild: Improving Creative Reasoning through Immersion in Natural Settings," *PLoS One* 7, no. 12 (December 12, 2012), journals.plos.org/plosone/article?id=10.1371/journal.pone.0051474; C. J. Beukeboom et al., "Stress-Reducing Effects of Real and Artificial Nature," *Journal of Alternative and Complementary Medicine* 18, no. 4 (2012): 329–33; and Byoung-Suk Kweon et al., "Anger and Stress: The Role of Landscape Posters in an Office Setting," *Environment and Behavior* 40, no. 3 (2008): 355.

35. Yalda T. Uhls et al., "Five Days at Outdoor Education Camp Without Screens Improves Preteen Skills with Nonverbal Emotion Cues," *Computers in Human Behavior* 39 (October 2014): 387–92.

36. Rosen, "Media and Technology Use Predicts Ill-Being Among Children."

37. Matt Richtel, "A Silicon Valley School That Doesn't Compute," *New York Times,* October 22, 2011, www.nytimes.com/2011/10/23/technology/at -waldorf-school-in-silicon-valley-technology-can-wait.html?mcubz=0.

38. A frequently cited study by David Meyer and colleagues is J. S. Rubinstein, D. E. Meyer, & J. E. Evans, (2001). "Executive Control of Cognitive Processes in Task Switching," *Journal of Experimental Psychology: Human Perception and Performance,* 27(4), 763–97.

   The work of Meyer and colleagues is also discussed in a number of articles in the popular press. See, for example: "Study: Multitasking Is Counterproductive (Your Boss May Not Like This One)" CNN.com, August 7, 2001; Robin Marantz Heing, "Driving? Maybe You Shouldn't Be Reading This," *New York Times,* July 13, 2004.

39. Christine Rosen, "The Myth of Multitasking," *New Atlantis* 20 (Spring 2008): 105–10.

40. Howard Gardner, *The App Generation* (New Haven, CT: Yale University Press, 2014).

41. Office for National Statistics, "Measuring National Well-Being: Insights into Children's Mental Health and Well-Being," ons.gov.uk, October 20, 2015, www.ons.gov.uk/peoplepopulationandcommunity/wellbeing/articles/ measuringnationalwellbeing/2015-10-20.

42. Gentile, "Pathological Videogame Use among Youth 8–18: A National Study."

43. Aviv M. Weinstein, "New Developments on the Neurobiological and Pharmaco-Genetic Mechanisms Underlying Internet and Videogame Addiction," *Directions in Psychiatry* 33, no. 2 (January 2013): 117–34.

44. Allison Hillhouse, "Consumer Insights: New Millennials Keep Calm & Carry On," *Blog.Viacom,* October 8, 2013, blog.viacom.com/2013/10/mtvs -the-new-millennials-will-keep-calm-and-carry-on/.

45. Dan Steinberg, "College Kids Giving Up Their Cellphones: The Incredible Tale of the Maryland Women's Team," *Washington Post,* April 2, 2015, www .washingtonpost.com/news/dc-sports-bog/wp/2015/04/02/college-kids -giving-up-their- cellphones-the-incredible-tale-of-the-maryland-womens -team/.

CHAPTER TEN: Exercising the Brain and Body

1. Sarah Ward offers an excellent seminar on improving executive functions in students using an approach she developed with her colleagues at Cognitive Connections in Boston. This approach emphasizes beginning with the end in mind.

2. Alvaro Pascual-Leone et al., "Modulation of Muscle Responses Evoked by Transcranial Magnetic Stimulation During the Acquisition of New Fine Motor Skills," *Journal of Neurophysiology* 74, no. 3 (September 1995): 1037–45. This research is also discussed in a fascinating *Time* magazine article on how the brain changes in response to experience: Sharon Begley, "How the Brain Rewires Itself," *Time,* January 19, 2005.

3. Gabriele Oettingen and Peter Gollwitzer, "Strategies of Setting and Implementing Goals," in *Social Psychological Foundations of Clinical Psychology,* ed. James E. Maddux and June Price Tangney (New York: Guilford Press, 2010), 114–35.
4. Pamela Weintraub, "The Voice of Reason," *Psychology Today,* May 4, 2015, www.psychologytoday.com/articles/201505/the-voice-reason.
5. Kristin Neff, "Why Self-Compassion Trumps Self-Esteem," *Greater Good,* University of California, Berkeley, May 27, 2011, greatergood.berkeley.edu/article/item/try_selfcompassion.
6. Po Bronson and Ashley Merryman, "Why Can Some Kids Handle Pressure While Others Fall Apart?," *New York Times Magazine,* February 16, 2013, www .nytimes.com/2013/02/10/magazine/why-can-some-kids-handle-pressure -while-others-fall-apart.html.
7. John J. Ratey, MD, *Spark: The Revolutionary New Science of Exercise and the Brain* (New York: Little, Brown, 2008).
8. John J. Ratey, MD, *A User's Guide to the Brain: Perception, Attention, and the Four Theaters of the Brain* (New York: Vintage Books, 2002).
9. Robin Marantz Henig, "Taking Play Seriously," *New York Times Magazine,* February 17, 2008, www.nytimes.com/2008/02/17/magazine/17play .html.

CHAPTER ELEVEN: Navigating Learning Disabilities,
ADHD, and Autism Spectrum Disorders

1. Edward L. Deci et al., "Autonomy and Competence as the Motivational Factors in Students with Learning Disabilities and Emotional Handicaps," *Journal of Learning Disabilities* 25 (1992): 457–71.
2. N. M. Shea et al., "Perceived Autonomy Support in Children with Autism Spectrum Disorder," *Autism* 3, no. 2 (2013), doi:10.4172/2165-7890. 1000114.
3. Margaret H. Sibley, "Supporting Autonomy Development in Teens with ADHD: How Professionals Can Help," *ADHD Report* 25, no. 1 (February 2017).
4. Institute of Education Sciences, "Children and Youth with Disabilities," U.S. Department of Education, National Center for Education Statistics, updated May 2017, https://nces.ed.gov/programs/coe/indicator_cgg.asp.
5. Centers for Disease Control and Prevention, "Autism Spectrum Disorder ASD)," www.cdc.gov/ncbddd/autism/index.html.
6. John Salamone and Mercè Correa, "The Mysterious Motivational Functions of Mesolimbic Dopamine," *Neuron* 76, no. 3 (November 8, 2012): 470–85, doi:10.1016/j.neuron.2012.10.021.
7. Sibley, "Supporting Autonomy Development in Teens with ADHD: How Professionals Can Help."
8. P. Shaw et al., "Development of Cortical Surface Area and Gyrification in Attention-Deficit/Hyperactivity Disorder," *Biological Psychiatry* 72, no. 3 (2012): 191, doi:10.1016/j.biopsych.2012.01.031. National Institutes of Health, "Brain Matures a Few Years Late in ADHD, but Follows Nor-

mal Pattern," News Release, November 12, 2007, www.nih.gov/news-events/news-releases/brain-matures-few-years-late-adhd-follows-normal-pattern.

9. Sarina J. Grosswald et al., "Use of the Transcendental Meditation Technique to Reduce Symptoms of Attention Deficit/Hyperactivity Disorder (ADHD) by Reducing Stress and Anxiety: An Exploratory Study," *Current Issues in Education* 10, no. 2 (2008). Frederick Travis et al., "ADHD, Brain Functioning and Transcendental Meditation Practice," *Mind and Brain, the Journal of Psychiatry* 2, no. 1 (2011): 73–81.

10. Lisa Flook et al., "Effects of Mindful Awareness Practices on Executive Functions in Elementary School Children," *Journal of Applied School Psychology* 26, no. 1 (February 2010): 70–95, doi:10.1080/15377900903379125. Saskia van der Oord et al., "The Effectiveness of Mindfulness Training for Children with ADHD and Mindful Parenting for their Parents," *Journal of Child and Family Studies* 21, no. 1 (February 2012): 139–47, doi:10.1007/s10826-011-9457-0.

11. Sibley's STAND program is described in the new book: Margaret H. Sibley, *Parent-Teen Therapy for Executive Function Deficits and ADHD: Building Skills and Motivation* (New York: Guilford Press, 2016).

12. Tiziana Zalla, "The Amygdala and the Relevance Detection Theory of Autism," *Frontiers in Human Neuroscience* 30 (December 2013), doi:org/10.3389/fnhum.2013.00894.

13. These strategies are included in the new Unstuck and On Target! program developed by Lauren Kenworthy, an autism specialist at Children's National Medical Center, and special educators from the Ivymount School's Model Asperger Program. These and other approaches are discussed in a book written for teachers and a book written for parents. For teachers: Lynn Cannon et al., *Unstuck & On Target!: An Executive Function Curriculum to Improve Flexibility for Children with Autism Spectrum Disorders*, research edition (Baltimore: Paul H. Brookes Publishing, 2011). For parents: Lauren Kenworthy, *Solving Executive Function Challenges: Simple Ways of Getting Kids with Autism Unstuck & On Target* (Baltimore: Paul H. Brookes Publishing, 2014).

14. The use of yoga as a tool for treating students with autism spectrum disorders was pioneered by Molly Kenny. The application of her Integrated Movement Therapy with students is discussed in Kenny, "Integrated Movement Therapy™: Yoga-Based Therapy as a Viable and Effective Intervention for Autism Spectrum and Related Disorders," *International Journal of Yoga Therapy* 12, no. 1, (2002): 71–79.

    For the use of mindfulness in youth with ASD and their caregivers, see: Rebekah Keenan-Mount et al., "Mindfulness-Based Approaches for Young People with Autism Spectrum Disorder and Their Caregivers: Do These Approaches Hold Benefits for Teachers?," *Australian Journal of Teacher Education* 41, no. 6 (2016), doi:/10.14221/ajte.2016v41n6.5. See also Nirbhay N. Singh et. al., "A Mindfulness-Based Strategy for Self-Management of Aggressive Behaviors in Adolescents with Autism," *Research in Autism Spectrum Disorders* 5, no. 3 (2011): 1153–58, doi:10.1016/j.rasd.2010.12.012.

Regarding TM practice and kids with ADHD, a series of case studies have been published: Yvonne Kurtz, "Adam, Asperger's Syndrome, and the Transcendental Mediation Technique," *Autism Digest* (July/August 2011): 46–47, www.adhd-tm.org/pdf/aspergers-JulAUG2011.pdf; David O. Black et al., "Transcendental Meditation for Autism Spectrum Disorders? A Perspective," *Cogent Psychology* 2, no. 1 (2015), doi:org/10.1080/23311908.2015.1071028. The latter paper, written by David Black, an autism researcher at the National Institute of Mental Health, and psychiatrist and researcher Norman Rosenthal, discussed six adolescents and young adults with ASD who learned to meditate and meditated twice daily with high consistency. All six subjects reported—and their parents confirmed—decreased stress and anxiety, improved behavioral and emotional regulation, increased productivity, and greater flexibility in coping with change and transitions. The parents also reported observing a willingness to take on more responsibility, and faster recovery time following stressful experiences. Improvement in concentration and sleep, decreases in test anxiety and tantrums, and fewer physiological symptoms of stress were also reported.

15. The role of what Stephen Porges calls the social engagement system in ASD is discussed in Dr. Porges's book, *The Polyvagal Theory: Neurophysiological Foundations of Emotions, Attachment, Communication, Self-Regulation* (New York: W. W. Norton, 2011).

16. Nicole M. Shea et al., "Perceived Autonomy Support in Children with Autism Spectrum Disorder," *Autism* 3, no. 114 (2013), doi:10.4172/2165-7890-1000114.

17. Ibid.

18. These interventions include the DIR Floortime model developed by Stanley Greenspan and Pivotal Response Treatment, which developed through ABA and includes an emphasis on child choice and the use of natural, direct reinforcement based on a child's intrinsic interests or desires.

19. Marsha Mailick Seltzer et al., "Maternal Cortisol Levels and Behavior Problems in Adolescents and Adults with ASD," *Journal of Autism and Developmental Disorders* 40, no. 4 (April 2010): 457–69, doi: 10.1007/s10803-009-0887-0.

CHAPTER TWELVE: The SAT, ACT, and Other Four-Letter Words

1. Valerie Strauss, "Five Reasons Standardized Testing Isn't Likely to Let Up," *Washington Post*, March 11, 2015, www.washingtonpost.com/news/answer-sheet/wp/2015/03/11/five-reasons-standardized-testing-isnt-likely-to-let-up/?utm_term=.aad3311ed86d.

2. Rick Reilly, "An Ad Doesn't Take Care of Everything," ESPN.com, March 28, 2013, www.espn.com/espn/story/_/id/9112095/tiger-ad-way-bounds.

3. Joshua Aronson tells this story in an article called "The Threat of Stereotype" in *Educational Leadership* 2, no. 3 (2004): 14–19.

4. Geoffrey Cohen et al., "Reducing the Racial Achievement Gap: A Social-Psychological Intervention," *Science* 313, no. 5791 (September 1, 2006): 1307–10, doi:10.1126/science.1128317.

5. Benedict Carey, "In Battle, Hunches Prove to Be Valuable," *New York Times*, July 27, 2009, www.nytimes.com/2009/07/28/health/research/28brain .html?emc=eta1.

CHAPTER THIRTEEN: Who's Ready for College?

1. Amy R. Wolfson and Mary A. Carskadon, "Sleep Schedules and Daytime Functioning in Adolescents," *Child Development* 69, no. 4 (1998): 875–87. R. Hicks et al., "Self-Reported Sleep Durations of College Students: Normative Data for 1978–79, 1988–89 and 2000–01," *Perceptual and Motor Skills* 91, no. 1 (2001): 139–41.

2. Craig Lambert, "Deep into Sleep: While Researchers Probe Sleep's Functions, Sleep Itself Is Becoming a Lost Art," *Harvard Magazine*, July–August 2005, 25–33.

3. J. F. Gaultney, "The Prevalence of Sleep Disorders in College Students: Impact on Academic Performance," *Journal of American College Health* 59, no. 2 (2010), 91–97.

4. A survey study of over four thousand students conducted by Alexander McCormick and colleagues as part of the National Survey of Student Engagement found that college students currently study fifteen hours a week on average. National Survey of Student Engagement, "Fostering Student Engagement Campuswide: Annual Results 2011," (Bloomington, IN: Indiana University Center for Postsecondary Research, 2011), nsse.indiana.edu/ NSSE_2011_Results/pdf/NSSE_2011_AnnualResults.pdf. A second study by Lindsey Burke and colleagues found that students on average spent nineteen hours a week on education-related activities; Lindsey Burke et al., "Big Debt, Little Study: What Taxpayers Should Know About College Students' Time Use," Heritage Foundation, July 19, 2016, www.heritage.org /education/report/big-debt-little-study-what-taxpayers-should-know-about -college-students-time-use.

5. H. Weschler and T. F. Nelson, "What We Have Learned from the Harvard School of Public Health College Alcohol Study: Focusing Attention on College Student Alcohol Consumption and the Environmental Conditions That Promote It," *Journal of Studies on Alcohol and Drugs* 69 (2008): 481–90.

6. Department of Health and Human Services, "Results from the 2005 National Survey on Drug Use and Health: National Findings" (Rockville, MD: Substance and Abuse and Mental Health Services Administration, 2005).

7. S. A. Morris et al., "Alcohol Inhibition of Neurogenesis: A Mechanism of Hippocampal Neurodegeneration in an Adolescent Alcohol Abuse Model," *Hippocampus* 20, no. 5 (2010): 596–607.

8. Barbara Strauch, *The Primal Teen: What the New Discoveries About the Teenage Brain Tell Us About Our Kids* (New York: Doubleday, 2003).

9. C. S. Barr et al., "The Use of Adolescent Nonhuman Primates to Model Human Alcohol Intake: Neurobiological, Genetic, and Psychological Variables," *Annals of the New York Academy of Sciences* 1021 (2004): 221–23.

10. T. Johnson, R. Shapiro and R. Tourangeau, "National Survey of American Attitudes on Substance Abuse XVI: Teens and Parents," National

Center on Addiction and Substance Abuse at Columbia University, August 2011, www.centeronaddiction.org/addiction-research/reports/national-survey-american-attitudes-substance-abuse-teens-parents-2011.

11. J. I. Hudson et al., "The Prevalence and Correlates of Eating Disorders in the National Comorbidity Survey Replication," *Biological Psychiatry* 61, no. 3 (February 1, 2007): 348–58.

12. The Renfrew Center Foundation for Eating Disorders, "Eating Disorders 101 Guide: A Summary of Issues, Statistics, and Resources," September 2002, revised October 2003, www.renfrew.org.

13. A.A. Arria et al., "Nonmedical Prescription Stimulant Use Among College Students: Why We Need to Do Something and What We Need to Do," *Journal of Addictive Diseases* 29, no. 4 (2010).

14. Morgan Baskin, "Overhauling 'Band-Aid Fixes': Universities Meet Growing Need for Comprehensive Mental Healthcare," *USA Today*, January 30, 2015, college.usatoday.com/2015/01/30/overhauling-band-aid-fixes-universities-meet-growing-need-for-comprehensive-mental-healthcare/.

15. Richard Kadison, MD, and Theresa Foy DiGeronimo, *College of the Overwhelmed: The Campus Mental Health Crisis and What to Do About It* (San Francisco: Jossey-Bass, 2004).

16. S. A. Benton et al., "Changes in Counseling Center Client Problems Across 13 Years," *Professional Psychology: Research and Practice* 34, no. 1 (2003): 66–72.

17. J. H, Pryor et al., *The American Freshman: National Norms for Fall 2010* (Los Angeles: University of California Press Books, 2011).

18. Robert P. Gallagher, "National Survey of Counseling Center Directors 2010," Project Report, International Association of Counseling Services, Alexandria, VA. Also, a recent study of students at Princeton and Cornell found that almost 18 percent reported a history of self-injury (J. Whitlock et al., "Self-Injurious Behaviors in a College Population," *Pediatrics* 117, no. 6 [2006]: 1939–48). Self injury is often seen in students who do not have a psychiatric diagnosis but who have limited stress management and coping skills.

19. Arum and Roksa, *Academically Adrift: Limited Learning on College Campuses* (Chicago: University of Chicago Press, 2011).

20. D. Shapiro et al., "Completing College: A National View of Student Attainment Rates—Fall 2009 Cohort" (Signature Report No. 10), National Student Clearinghouse Research Center, Herndon, VA, November 2015.

21. Center for Interim Programs, "5 Types of Students Who Choose a Gap Year," www.interimprograms.com/2015/10/5-types-of-students-who-choose-gap-year.html.

22. Katherine Engman, "Why I Chose to Take a Gap Year," Center for Interim Programs, November 30, 2105, www.interimprograms.com/2015/11/why-i-chose-to-take-gap-year-by.html.

23. Center for Interim Programs, "Facts and Figures," www.interimprograms.com/p/facts-and-figures.html.

CHAPTER FOURTEEN: Alternate Routes

1. Karen Arnold, *Lives of Promise: What Becomes of High School Valedictorians* (San Francisco: Jossey-Bass, 1995).

2. Malcolm Gladwell, *Outliers: The Story of Success* (New York: Little, Brown, 2008).

3. Howard Gardner, *Frames of Mind: The Theory of Multiple Intelligence* (New York: Basic Books, 1983).

4. Mike Rowe WORKS Foundation, "Are You Profoundly Disconnected?," Profoundlydisconnected.com.

5. Belinda Luscombe, "Do We Need $75,000 a Year to Be Happy?," Time .com, September 6, 2010, content.time.com/time/magazine/article /0,9171,2019628,00.html.

INDEX